Fantasy Authors

Fantasy Authors: A Research Guide

Jen Stevens and Dorothea Salo

Author Research Series

James Bracken and Steven Galbraith, Series Editors

Westport, Connecticut • London

Library of Congress Cataloging-in-Publication Data

Stevens, Jen, 1970–
Fantasy authors : a research guide / Jen Stevens and Dorothea Salo.
p. cm. — (Author research series)
Includes bibliographical references and index.
ISBN 978–1–59158–497–1 (alk. paper)
1. Fantasy fiction, American—Bio–bibliography—Dictionaries. 2. American fiction—20th century—Bio–bibliography—Dictionaries. 3. Novelists, American—20th century—Biography—Dictionaries. 4. Fantasy fiction—Bio–bibliography—Dictionaries. I. Salo, Dorothea, 1972– II. Title.
Z1231.F32S74 2008
[PS374.F27]
016.813′0876608—dc22 2007044970

British Library Cataloguing in Publication Data is available.

Library of Congress Catalog Card Number: 2007044970
ISBN-13: 978–1–59158–497–1

First published in 2008

Libraries Unlimited, 88 Post Road West, Westport, CT 06881
An member of the Greenwood Publishing Group, Inc.
www.lu.com

Printed in the United States of America

The paper used in this book complies with the Permanent Paper Standard issued by the National Information Standards Organization (Z39.48–1984).

10 9 8 7 6 5 4 3 2 1

Contents

Acknowledgments

My thanks to my friends, colleagues, and family for their support with this project. I'd like to especially thank the GMU Libraries for granting me Research Leave release time, and Adina Ochiana and Gretchen Beasley, my graduate research assistants, who checked (and rechecked!) all of the web links for us.

J.S.S.

Introduction

Fantasy Authors: A Research Guide, part of the *Author Research Guide* series, fills a gap between readers' advisory books on fantasy writers and reference works that provide biographical information and/or critical bibliographies. Essentially, this volume is intended for those who already know of a given writer and want to learn more about that writer and/or find other similar authors. However, you may also wish to simply browse through the guide to see who looks interesting. In addition, close examination of specific authors within a genre can lead to a greater understanding of the genre as a whole.

The Authors

We have focused on both contemporary and historical fantasy writers, with an emphasis on diversity and writers with current and/or growing popularity and impact on the genre. However, because the fantasy genre is so broad, we have limited our scope. For the purposes of this volume, we have defined fantasy as works that include magic and/or powers such as telepathy. Thus, we are excluding alternate history and talking animal books such as *The Wind in the Willows* that do not include magic and/or powers beyond anthropomorphism (such as telepathy). In the case of writers that could be considered part of another genre such as science fiction or children's, we have made decisions based on their inclusion in other volumes in the *Author Research Guide* series (e.g., *Children's Authors*), how much of their overall published output falls under fantasy, and their impact on and position in the genre.

We have included authors of fantasy graphic novels since graphic novels as a whole are becoming increasingly important for libraries and researchers. However, we have not included movies, television shows, games, or purely Web-based publications, nor have we included anthologies of short stories that those authors edited. We also focus on writers who have novels in print rather than only short stories.

Organization of Entries

Author entries are arranged in order of the author's last name. Author teams are listed as joint entries (i.e., David and Leigh Eddings) or separately (i.e., Margaret Weis and Tracy Hickman) depending on how they have published individually. Each author entry includes a short biographical sketch and information about key books that the author has published as well biographical and critical material published about them. The latter could include interviews, scholarly articles, books, biographies, Web sites, and so forth. We've included both print and online sources and evaluated all sources for inclusion according to criteria such as accuracy, depth, currency, and bias.

The following abbreviations are used for general encyclopedias and handbooks that contain information on fantasy authors:

EF—*Encylopedia of Science Fiction*, edited by Clute and Grant.
HDF—Harris-Fain and Darren's *Fantasy and Science Fiction Writers*
SJGF—*St. James Guide to Fantasy Writers*, edited by Pringle

For complete bibliographic information and an annotation on these titles, please refer to the General Bibliography.

Some entries also have sections that suggest similar books and authors to try (i.e., "if you like J.R.R. Tolkien, then you might like. . . . "). Each entry also has subject tags assigned to it that you can use to find other similar authors (i.e., woman writers, writers who work with non-European-influenced settings, and so forth). We've also provided tips on doing research on fantasy authors as well as a bibliography for general research.

Writers by Type

We have identified various "types" of writers and included the type categories in lists included later in the volume. In addition to getting a quick sense of the sort of books that a given writer publishes, you can also use these type "tags" to find other writers that you might enjoy (i.e., if you enjoy Terry Pratchett's satire, then you might also enjoy Esther Friesner's novels).

Early Writers. Highly influential on later writers, these early writers are considered key to the development of the fantasy genre.

Fairy Tales/Myth. These writers make use of myths and fairy tales in their works, some from a traditional perspective, and others from a more revisionist angle.

Feminist. These writers, both male and female, have written works with feminist ideas and ideals.

High Fantasy/Sword & Sorcery. These writers write works in the "classic" high fantasy style, often involving magic and various heroics.

Humorous/Satirical. These writers are known for their use of humor and/or satire, much of it quirky and offbeat.

Non-European Themes and Motifs. These writers make use of non-European themes, motifs, and mythologies.

Shared Worlds. These writers created worlds and/or story arcs that they then invited other writers to contribute to.

Urban Fantasy. These writers set much of their fiction in an urban, often "modern" setting, often with an edge.

Young Adult/Children's. These writers have written a number of works intended for young adults and children. However, many adults enjoy these works as well.

Fantasy As a Genre

In a very real sense, fantasy could be considered one of the oldest, if not the oldest genre. There are numerous legends and myths in most human cultures, about fantastic beings and magic. Many fantasy writers, past and present, have continued to draw on mythic material in their work. For instance, Marion Zimmer Bradley used the King Arthur mythos. Still other writers, such as J.R.R. Tolkien, have developed their own mythologies. So-called fairy tales are also important. Although contemporary writers continue to draw on Western fairy tales such as those collected by the Brothers Grimm, there is growing interest in fairy tales from non-Western cultures. Still other writers, such as Angela Carter, have used fairy tales, but in such a fashion as to critique the cultures that created them.

Many of the writers that are now regarded as "fantasy" writers in a more modern "genre" sense first started publishing during the nineteenth century. These include writers such as Lord Dunsany, George MacDonald, and E. Nesbit. During the 1930s and 1940s, the so-called pulp magazines published numerous fantasy short stories along with stories from other speculative genres such as science fiction and horror. Many writers published both science fiction and fantasy. Some have even argued that science fiction is really just a subset of fantasy (of course, there is also the corresponding argument that fantasy is really just a subset of science fiction!).

At the same time that the pulp magazines were emerging, Oxford don J.R.R. Tolkien was laboring over the *Lord of the Rings*. First published in England in the 1950s, his trilogy enjoyed first quiet success, then explosive ongoing popularity starting in the late 1960s. Tolkien continues to be influential on fantasy writers and readers.

There are presently a number of publishing trends and movements within the genre of fantasy. Young adult fantasy, which has existed at least since E. Nesbit, has gotten a recent boost from the world wide popularity of the Harry Potter books. Still other writers, such as Charles de Lint, write urban fantasy, that is, fantasy that is set in the "real," otherwise realistic world, while others create their own secondary worlds. Others, such as Michael Moorcock, blend their fantasy with a bit of science fiction "steam punk." And still others continue to write in the so-called high fantasy tradition with medieval settings. As mentioned earlier, fantasy can mean a great many things to writers and readers, and although we have chosen to focus on fantasy that uses "magic" for the purposes of this volume, there are a great number of other related genres and strands to be enjoyed.

Fantasy Timeline

Precursors, 1858–1929

Authors: L. Frank Baum, James Branch Cabell, Lord Dunsany, E.R. Eddison, Charlotte Perkins Gilman, H. Rider Haggard, George MacDonald, E. Nesbit

Literary Events

- 1858—*Phantastes*
- 1885—*King Solomon's Mines*
- 1900—*The Wonderful Wizard of Oz*
- 1902—*Five Children and It*
- 1905—*The Gods of Peganá*
- 1915—*Herland*
- 1919—*Jurgen, a Comedy of Justice*
- 1922—*The Worm Ouroboros*

World Events

- 1878—Anglo-Zulu War
- 1899–1902—Boer War
- 1903—Wright brothers' first flight
- 1912—Sinking of the *Titanic*
- 1914–1918—First World War
- 1919—League of Nations established
- 1925—Scopes trial
- 1927—Lindbergh flies across the Atlantic

The Pulp Age, 1930–1945

Authors: L. Sprague de Camp, Robert E. Howard, Fritz Leiber, C.L. Moore, Evangeline Walton

Literary Events

- 1934—*Black God's Kiss*
- 1935—*The Hour of the Dragon*
- 1936—*Two Sought Adventure, The Island of the Mighty*
- 1941—*The Incomplete Enchanter*

World Events

- 1929—Wall Street stock crash
- 1929–1939—Great Depression
- 1933—Hitler in power in Germany
- 1939–1945—Second World War
- 1941—Attack on Pearl Harbor
- 1945—Germany and Japan surrender

The Postwar Era, 1946–1962

Authors: Poul Anderson, Ray Bradbury, Marion Zimmer Bradley, Mervyn Peake, J.R.R. Tolkien, Jack Vance

Literary Events

- 1946—*Titus Groan*
- 1950—*The Dying Earth*
- 1953—*Three Hearts and Three Lions*
- 1954—*The Fellowship of the Ring*
- 1958—*The Planet Savers*
- 1962—*Something Wicked This Way Comes*

World Events

- 1945—Foundation of United Nations Organization
- 1947–1960—Independence of British colonial territories
- 1950–1953—Korean War Lions
- Early 1950s—Rock & roll becomes popular
- 1954—Brown vs. Board of Education
- 1957—Sputnik in orbit
- 1962—Cuban Missile Crisis

The New Wave, 1963–1974

Authors: Lloyd Alexander, Peter S. Beagle, Angela Carter, Susan Cooper, Ursula K. Le Guin, Anne McCaffrey, Michael Moorcock, Andre Norton, Fred Saberhagen, Mary Steward, Jane Yolen, Roger Zelazny

Literary Events

- 1963—*Witch World, The Stealer of Souls*
- 1964—*The Book of Three*
- 1965—*Over Sea, Under Stone*
- 1968—*A Wizard of Earthsea, Dragonflight, The Broken Lands, The Last Unicorn, Several Perceptions*
- 1969—*The Wizard of Washington Square*
- 1970—*Nine Princes in Amber*

World Events

- 1963—Betty Friedan's *The Feminine Mystique*
- 1964—Civil Rights Act, British rock & roll comes to United States
- 1964–1970—Vietnam War protests
- 1969—Stonewall riots, Moon landing, Woodstock
- 1972—U.S. Equal Rights Amendment proposed
- 1973—United States leaves Vietnam
- 1974—Watergate scandal

Pop Fantasy, 1975–1985

Authors: Piers Anthony, Robert Lynn Asprin, James P. Blaylock, Terry Brooks, Steven K. Brust, C.J. Cherryh, Charles de Lint, Gordon R. Dickson, Stephen R.

Donaldson, David and Leigh Eddings, Raymond E. Feist, John M. Ford, Alan Dean Foster, Esther Friesner, Randall Garrett, Mary Gentle, Lisa Goldstein, Barbara Hambly, Vicki Ann Heydron, Tracy Hickman, Robert Holdstock, Diana Wynne Jones, Guy Gavriel Kay, Tanith Lee, Patricia McKillip, Robin McKinley, Pat Murphy, Diana L. Paxson, Richard and Wendy Pini, Tim Powers, Terry Pratchett, Elizabeth Ann Scarborough, Robert Silverberg, Nancy Springer, Judith Tarr, Sheri S. Tepper, Margaret Weis, Gene Wolfe, Patricia Wrede

Literary Events

- 1976—*The Dragon and the George*
- 1977—*A Spell for Chameleon*
- 1978—*Elfquest, Night's Master*
- 1979—*The Oak King's Daughter*
- 1980—*Web of Angels*
- 1981—*The Steel of Raithskar*
- 1982—*The Time of the Dark*
- 1983—*The Colour of Magic*
- 1984—*Dragons of Autumn Twilight*

World Events

- 1975–1979—East-West *détente*
- 1979—Iranian revolution, oil crisis, Soviet invasion of Afghanistan
- 1979–1980—Conservatives in power in United States and United Kingdom
- 1980–1981—Iranian hostage crisis
- 1982—Falklands War

Social Fantasy 1986–1996

Authors: Francesca Lia Block, Kate Elliott, Carol Emshwiller, Neil Gaiman, Terry Goodkind, Robert Jordan, Katharine Kerr, J. Gregory Keyes, Rosemary Kirstein, Ellen Kushner, Mercedes Lackey, Stephen Lawhead, Gregory Maguire, George R.R. Martin, Linda Medley, Elizabeth Moon, Garth Nix, Philip Pullman, R.A. Salvatore, Susan Shwartz, Jeff Smith, Midori Snyder, Caroline Stevermer, Martha Wells

Literary Events

- 1987—*Sandman, Swordspoint*
- 1988—*Sheepfarmer's Daughter*
- 1989—*The Steerswoman*
- 1991—*Bone*
- 1995—*Northern Lights*
- 1996—*Castle Waiting*

World Events

- 1989—Revolutions in Eastern Europe, Soviets leave Afghanistan
- 1991—Gulf War, August coup and disintegration of Soviet Union
- 1991–1995—Yugoslav War

Recent Fantasy, 1997–2007

Authors: Lois McMaster Bujold, Jacqueline Carey, Susanna Clarke, Nalo Hopkinson, Kij Johnson, China Miéville, J.K. Rowling

Literary Events

- 1997—*Harry Potter and the Philosopher's Stone*
- 1998—*Brown Girl in the Ring, King Rat*
- 1999—*The Fox Woman*
- 2001—*Kushiel's Dart, The Curse of Chalion*
- 2004—*Jonathan Strange and Mr. Norrell*

World Events

- 1997—Labor Party win United Kingdom elections
- 1998–1999—Clinton impeachment
- 2000—Republicans win U.S. elections
- 2001—Terrorist attack on World Trade Center; war in Afghanistan
- 2003—War in Iraq

How to Use This Book

We've written this book for a variety of audiences and needs.

Fans (and other Readers): You can browse through to scope out potentially interesting authors and books to read. If you'd like to find out more about an author, check the "Biographies and Interviews." Interviews can be an especially fascinating way to get to know your favorite authors. You might want to also check the "Web Sites" section since many authors have their own Web sites and blogs.

For a more in depth look at a particular novel or story, consult the "Criticism and Readers' Guides." And finally, if you'd like to get a larger perspective on the fantasy genre, check the "General Bibliography"–we've included the names of major fan and writer organizations as well as general encyclopedias on fantasy. You may also want to consult the "Awards" section at the back of the book.

Students: You can browse through the book to get ideas for authors to use for your projects and papers. The "Major Works" section will give you a quick idea of what they've published and when.

To find out more about an author's life, check the "Biographies and Interviews." They might include interviews with the author, books and articles about the author's life, or collected letters to or by the author. Some authors have even written autobiographies. We've listed a number of author Web sites and blogs under "Web Sites"; these can give you even more information about an author (and their opinions!).

To get information about the books that the authors wrote, consult the "Criticism and Readers' Guides" section. There, you'll find discussions and interpretations of the novels and stories. Some of these articles will be formal academic essays while others may be more popular articles and "reader's guides." You can also find brief articles on authors in the "Encyclopedias and Handbooks" section. Incidentally, literary criticism is often referred to as "secondary," as opposed the "primary" novels, short stories, letters, and other things that were written by the authors themselves.

Teachers: You can browse through the book to find potential authors to use in your curriculum and syllabi planning. More specifically, the "Major Works" will help you select specific novels and short stories for class or to recommend to students for free reading. The "Biographical" and "Criticism and Readers' Guides" sections provide essays and books that you can use in planning lectures and lessons, or directing student research. For shorter articles on authors, you can also check the "Encyclopedias and Handbooks"–we've indicated major fantasy literature encyclopedias that have short author articles. Although many of the Web sites listed under "Web Sites" may be less academic, they can provide additional perspectives. Students may especially enjoy the immediacy of reading authors' blogs.

We've also provided a "General Bibliography" that you can consult for broader sources for the fantasy genre as a whole.

Librarians: The "Major Works" lists provide quick lists of books by authors to consult in reader's advisory questions. Some entries even include a "Read Alike" section that you can use to find books for the patron who has read all of their favorite author's books and needs more. These lists may also be helpful for collection development.

In turn, the "Biographical" sections and "Criticism and Readers' Guides" will prove useful for reference questions concerning writers and their works. You can use them, as well as the "General Bibliography," for collection development. The "Web Sites" can also be helpful for answering reference questions, or for posting on online pathfinders.

Book Club Leaders: You can browse through the book to find authors and books that your book club might be interested in. The "Biographical" sections may be especially helpful to you for background information as you prepare for book club discussions. We've listed a number of author Web sites that you can use to see what your authors are working on now (they can also be a lot of fun to read!).

Going Beyond This Book

Authors keep writing books, and researchers keep writing books and articles about them. Although the sources we've listed will remain useful, you may want to look for more current ones. Here are some tips:

Check the Bibliography. We've listed a number of reference books, indexes, and Web portals that you can use to find additional sources.

One Good Source Deserves Another. If you find a book or Web site that you like (or even halfway like), look in the index, foot notes, bibliography, or "Links" for more sources.

Talk to Your Local Reference Librarian. They may have ideas for further searching, or know about new sources and updates.

Of course, you can also search the Web, which leads us to . . .

Going Beyond Google (or Wikipedia)

One of the reasons that we wrote this book is that doing author research online can be really hard. The first few (or several) pages of Google results are often full of hits from online book vendors, genealogy charts, or, sad to say, Web sites that tend to all say the same thing. And while some Wikipedia articles can be really informative, others can be really sketchy or biased. We used a variety of techniques to search for more in depth articles:

Think about your search terms. Try combining various terms such as "interview" or "article" along with the author name (i.e., "Peter Beagle" AND "interview"). Putting the author's name in quotation marks will also tell the search engine to keep the names together (so you don't end up with hits for every "Piers" when all you wanted was "Piers Anthony").

Look for links on Web sites. Even so-so Web sites or Wikipedia entries can provide links to really great ones. Fantasy association and journal Web sites are often especially helpful for this (i.e., *Locus*). Author web sites can also be a great source.

Check reference books for recommended links (this also works for finding books and articles!)

Check an index. Many indexes are starting to include Web sites (i.e., the Modern Language Bibliography (MLA) and Annual Biography of English Language and Literature (ABELL)).

Evaluating What You Find

Anyone can post a Web site, and (almost) anyone can edit a Wikipedia entry. Even books aren't always trustworthy. As you do research, consider these factors:

Currency: How old is the information? Does it matter? Currency tends to be more important for authors who are still alive (and publishing).

Authority: Who wrote the book, or created the Web site? What makes them qualified to do so? Do they list credentials? When in doubt check to see if you can find the same information in at least two other sources (this is also known as "triangulation").

Point of View: A publisher's Web site and a *Locus* article may have very different points of view. Publisher sites are generally focused on selling books, while Web sites, books, and articles produced by third parties are more likely to be neutral or even critical. Look for sources from a variety of viewpoints.

Audience: Who is the article written for? Who is the Web site produced for? Web sites and articles directed to fans often differ from those directed toward scholars and critics. In general, *scholarly* Web sites and publications tend to be more focused and specialized. They may also assume prior knowledge of the author and their books.

What to Do If the Web Site Links Don't Work

We've made every effort to make sure that the Web site links that we included are current, but Web site URLs do often change over time. If you should come across a URL that doesn't work, try the following:

- First, try a different Web browser. Some pages won't work in particular browsers.
- Next, try looking up the title of the page on an Internet search engine such as www.google.com. Google also caches sites, so try the cache link if the current link doesn't work.
- If it's a page from a publisher Web site, try doing an internal search in the Web site (many publishers have a habit of rearranging their sites every so often).
- Finally, try looking up the nonworking URL in the Internet Archive (www.archive.org. Last visited January 30, 2008), an online archive for both active and obsolete Web sites. The archive doesn't have every page that's ever been online, but it has a large number of them.

Alphabetical List of Authors

Alexander, Lloyd
Anderson, Poul and Anderson, Karen
Anthony, Piers
Asprin, Robert Lynn
Baum, Lyman Frank (L. Frank Baum)
Beagle, Peter S.
Blaylock, James P.
Block, Francesca Lia
Bradbury, Ray
Bradley, Marion Zimmer
Brooks, Terry
Brust, Steven K.
Bujold, Lois McMaster
Cabell, James Branch
Carey, Jacqueline
Carter, Angela
Cherryh, Carolyn Janice (C.J. Cherryh)
Clarke, Susanna
Cooper, Susan
de Camp, Lyon Sprague (L. Sprague de Camp) and Crook, Catherine
de Lint, Charles
Dickson, Gordon R.
Donaldson, Stephen R.
Dunsany, Lord
Eddings, David and Eddings, Leigh
Eddison, Eric Rucker (E.R. Eddison)
Elliott, Kate
Emshwiller, Carol
Feist, Raymond E.
Ford, John M.
Foster, Alan Dean
Friesner, Esther
Gaiman, Neil
Garrett, Randall and Heydron, Vicki Ann
Gentle, Mary
Gilman, Charlotte Perkins
Goldstein, Lisa
Goodkind, Terry
Haggard, Henry Rider (H. Rider Haggard)
Hambly, Barbara
Hickman, Tracy
Holdstock, Robert
Hopkinson, Nalo
Howard, Robert E.
Johnson, Kij
Jones, Diana Wynne
Jordan, Robert

Kay, Guy Gavriel
Kerr, Katharine
Keyes, Gregory
Kirstein, Rosemary
Kushner, Ellen
Lackey, Mercedes
Lawhead, Stephen R.
Lee, Tanith
Le Guin, Ursula K.
Leiber, Fritz
MacDonald, George
Maguire, Gregory
Martin, George R.R.
McCaffrey, Anne
McKillip, Patricia
McKinley, Robin
Medley, Linda
Miéville, China
Moon, Elizabeth
Moorcock, Michael
Moore, Catherine Lucille (C.L. Moore)
Murphy, Pat
Nesbit, Edith (E. Nesbit)
Nix, Garth
Norton, Andre
Paxson, Diana L.
Peake, Mervyn
Pini, Wendy and Pini, Richard
Powers, Tim
Pratchett, Terry
Pullman, Philip
Rowling, Joanne Kathleen (J.K. Rowling)
Saberhagen, Fred
Salvatore, Robert Anthony (R.A. Salvatore)
Scarborough, Elizabeth Ann
Shwartz, Susan
Silverberg, Robert
Smith, Jeff
Snyder, Midori
Springer, Nancy
Stevermer, Caroline
Stewart, Mary
Tarr, Judith
Tepper, Sheri S.
Tolkien, John Ronald Reuel (J.R.R. Tolkien)
Vance, Jack
Walton, Evangeline
Weis, Margaret
Wells, Martha
Wolfe, Gene
Wrede, Patricia
Yolen, Jane
Zelazny, Roger

Lloyd Alexander (1924–2007)

Biographical Sketch

Lloyd Alexander was born in Philadelphia, Pennsylvania, in 1924; he resided near Philadelphia in Drexel Hill at the time of his death. During World War II he served in the U.S. Army, eventually serving in counterintelligence. He met his wife while attending the University of Paris just after the war; nearly a decade after their marriage in 1946 and after seven years of trying, he published his first book.

Though Alexander's work is usually shelved with young adult fiction, its themes of responsibility, honesty, and friendship across lines of class and gender appeal also to adults. His Prydain series, still his best-known work, captured a Newbery Honor mention in 1966, and the Newbery Medal itself in 1969. Later works explore non-European settings and myths.

> Most of my books have been written in the form of fantasy. Using the device of an imaginary world allows me in some strange way to go to the central issues—it's one of many ways to express feelings about real people, about real human relationships. My concern is how we learn to be genuine human beings.—(Lloyd Alexander, http://content.schoLastic.com/browse/contributor.jsp?id=1217. Last visited January 25, 2008)

Major Works

Novels

The Westmark trilogy: *Westmark* (1981), *The Kestrel* (1982), *The Beggar Queen* (1984)

Children's/Young Adult Fiction

The Prydain series: *The Book of Three* (1964), *The Black Cauldron* (1965), *Coll and His White Pig* (1965), *The Castle of Llyr* (1966), *The Truthful Harp* (1967), *Taran Wanderer* (1967), *The High King* (1968), *The Foundling and Other Tales from Prydain* (1970)

The Remarkable Journey of Prince Jen (1991)

The Fortune-Tellers (1992)

Research Sources

Encyclopedias and Handbooks: EF, HDF, SJGF

Biographies and Interviews

Alexander, Lloyd. "A Manner of Speaking." In Charlotte F. Otten and Gary D. Schmidt, eds., *The Voice of the Narrator in Children's Literature: Insight from Writers and Critics*. New York: Greenwood, 1989, pp. 123–131.

Wolfe, Gregory. "A Conversation with Lloyd Alexander." *Image* 30 (Spring 2001), pp. 41–50.

Criticism and Readers' Guides

Bagnall, Norma. "An American Hero in Welsh Fantasy: The Mabinogion, Alan Garner and Lloyd Alexander." *The New Welsh Review* 2(4) (Spring 1990), pp. 26–29.

Kuznets, Lois R. "'High Fantasy' in America: A Study of Lloyd Alexander, Ursula Le Guin, and Susan Cooper." *The Lion and the Unicorn* 9 (1985), pp. 19–35.

Mitchell, Judith N. "The Boy Who Would Be King." *Journal of Popular Culture* 17(4) (Spring 1984), pp. 134–137.

Stotts, Jon C. "Alexander's Chronicles of Prydain: The Nature of Beginnings." In Perry Nodelman and Jill P. May, eds., *Touchstones: Reflections on the Best in Children's Literature,* Volume 1. West Lafayette, IN: Children's Literature Association, 1985, pp. 21–29.

Zahorski, Kenneth J. and Robert H. Boyer. *Lloyd Alexander, Evangeline Walton Ensley, Kenneth Morris: A Primary and Secondary Bibliography*. Boston, MA: Hall, 1981.

Web Sites

"Lloyd Alexander's Biography" (*Author and Illustrator Index*). Includes an interview with Alexander, and a brief autobiography http://www.scholastic.com/librarians/ab/biolist.htm. Last visited January 30, 2008.

Lloyd Alexander: On Fantasy. http://www.cbcbooks.org/cbcmagazine/meet/lloydalexander.html. Last visited January 25, 2008.

If you like Lloyd Alexander

Based on Welsh mythology, Alexander's Prydain series tells the story of Taran, an assistant pig keeper who is anxious to prove himself as a hero. *The Kestrel* and its sequels tell of Mickle, the beggar-girl who learned to be a queen. Alexander wrote a number of other fantasy books for young adults, including *The Cat Who Wished to Be a Man* and *The Wizard in the Tree.*

Then you might like

Susan Cooper

Cooper's The Dark Is Rising series is a grand saga of the efforts of the Light to defeat the Dark. Like Alexander's work, it draws heavily on Celtic and other western European legends. Other Cooper fantasies include *Seaward* and *The Boggart.*

Diana Wynne Jones

Like Alexander's, Jones' books are full of magic and humor. She is probably best known for the so-called Chrestomanci books, including *Charmed Life* and *The Lives of Christopher Chant*, but has written numerous other books such as *The Merlin Conspiracy* and *Howl's Moving Castle*, which was recently adapted as a motion picture.

Linda Medley

Medley's *Castle Waiting* graphic-novel series shares Alexander's themes of self-exploration and self-acceptance. Its characters pop off the page, ranging from Sleeping Beauty's ladies-in-waiting to a stork-headed chamberlain to a bearded-lady nun, brim-full of personality and humor.

Edith Nesbit (E. Nesbit)

One of the first children's fantasy writers, Nesbit wrote several magically humorous books, including *Five Children and It*, *The Phoenix and the Carpet*, and *The Enchanted Castle*. Like Alexander, Nesbit portrayed children as less than angelic and possessed of their own personalities. Nesbit also wrote less magical (but still humorous) books such as *The Wouldbegoods.*

Nnedi Okorafor-Mbachu

Like Alexander, Okorafor-Mbachu mines myth and legend for her young adult books, *The Shadow Speaker* and *Zahrah the Windseeker*. Her chosen legends, however, are those of West Africa, and her work will appeal to anyone wishing to expand horizons beyond standard European settings.

Poul Anderson (1926–2001) and Karen Anderson (1932–)

Biographical Sketch

Trained physicist, literary agent, editor, and historical reenactor as well as fantasy and science-fiction author, Poul Anderson's busy and varied life informed his enormous written output. He lived most of his adult life in southern California with his wife and writing partner Karen Kruse Anderson.

Poul Anderson's seven Hugos, three Nebulas, and various other awards reward above all his accuracy and attention to detail; his fantasy worlds reveal just as deep an awareness of political organization and ethnography as his science-fictional worlds do physics. Indeed, Anderson enjoyed poking fun at poorly imagined heroic-fantasy worlds via satire and essay. Karen Kruse Anderson's keen awareness of the genre fan community is exemplified by her pioneering use in a 1953 article of the phrase "filk music" for genre-inspired rewrites of popular song lyrics.

> Beneath the magic, derring-do, and other glamour, an imaginary world has to *work* right. In particular, a pre-industrial society, which is what virtually all h[igh] f[antasy] uses for a setting, differs from ours today in countless ways.—(Poul Anderson, "Of Thud and Blunder")

Major Works

Novels

King of Ys series: *Roma Mater* (1986), *Gallicenae* (1987), *Dahut* (1987), *The Dog and the Wolf* (1988)
Three Hearts and Three Lions (1953)
The Broken Sword (1954)

Short Story Collections

The Unicorn Trade (1984)
Fantasy (1991)
The Armies of Elfland (1992)

Research Sources

Encyclopedias and Handbooks: EF, HDF, SJGF

Biographies and Interviews

Locus 47(3) (September 2001). Contains several obituary essays including one by Karen Anderson.
"Poul Anderson: Fifty Years of Science Fiction." *Locus* #435 (April 1997).
Reyes, Raul S. "An Interview with Poul Anderson." *Bradley's* #31 (Spring 1996).

Criticism and Readers' Guides

Miesel, Sarah. *Against Time's Arrow: The High Crusade of Poul Anderson.* San Bernardino, CA: Borgo Press, 1978.

Milosh, Joseph E., Jr. "Reason and Mysticism in Fantasy and Science Fiction." In Milicent Lenz and Ramona M. Mahood, eds., *Young Adult Literature: Background and Criticism.* Chicago, IL: American Library Association, 1980, pp. 433–440.

Tiedemann, Mark W. "Hybrids." *New York Review of Science Fiction* 12(10) (June 2000), pp. 15–17.

Web Sites

McDavid, Glenn T. "Religion in the Fiction of Poul Anderson." 1989. http://home.comcast.net/~gmcdavid/html_dir/anderson.html. Last visited January 25, 2008.

Piers Anthony (1934–)

Biographical Sketch

Piers Anthony Dillingham Jacob came to the United States from Britain as a child. He lives with his wife in Florida and has two daughters. Although his dislike for travel keeps him from attending conventions, he pours his heart out in the author's notes to his books, is active in electronic publishing, and is well-known for maintaining active correspondences with (sometimes troubled) fans.

His Xanth books are generally lighthearted romps through the pun-heavy, character-driven, almost cartoonish peninsular realm of Xanth. The nebbishy heroes and straightforward quest plots of the first few books gave way to large-ensemble casts and byzantine plots as various bit players caught on among fans. His later ChroMagic series, though it shares Xanth's central motif of a single magic talent born in each person, is noticeably more adult in topic and tone than Xanth, and may be a reaction to the gradual evolution of the Xanth series into a young adult rather than adult niche.

> Collaborator Cliff Pickover, author of numerous nonfiction books, asked me for my ten favorite words . . . I sent him these: Honor, Empathy, Realism, Imagination, Sex, Pantheism, Magic, Chocolate, Idealism, Verisimilitude.—(Piers Anthony, http://www.hipiers.com/04feb.html. Last visited January 25, 2008)

Major Works

Novels

Xanth series: *A Spell for Chameleon* (1977), *The Source of Magic* (1979), *Castle Roogna* (1979), 26 others.

ChroMagic series: *Key to Havoc* (2002), *Key to Chroma* (2003), *Key to Destiny* (2004)

Research Sources

Encyclopedias and Handbooks: EF, HDF, SJGF

Biographies and Interviews

Anthony, Piers. *Bio of an Ogre: the Autobiography of Piers Anthony to Age 50.* New York: Ace Books, 1988.

Anthony, Piers. *How Precious Was That While: an Autobiography.* New York: Tor, 2001.

Swaim, Don. "Audio Interview with Piers Anthony." 1987. *Don Swaim Interviews.* http://wiredforbooks.org/piersanthony/. Last visited January 25, 2008.

Web Sites

Hi Piers: The OfficialHome Page of Piers Anthony and Xanth. Author's Web site. Includes Web log-like newsletter dating back to 1997. http://www.hipiers.com/. Last visited January 25, 2008.

Piers Anthony Thread Homepage. Fan site. Includes interviews with Anthony and his collaborators. http://www.piersthread.com/. Last visited January 25, 2008.

Reitz, Daniel J., Sr. *The Compleat Piers Anthony.* Last updated in 2005. Includes bibliography, book-blurb collection, convention reports. http://www.piers-anthony.com/. Last visited January 25, 2008.

Robert Lynn Asprin (1946–)

Biographical Sketch

After a short stint in the U.S. military and a longer one as a corporate accountant, Robert L. Asprin turned to writing with the encouragement of well-known author Gordon Dickson. He partnered with then wife Lynn Abbey to edit the Thieves' World series, which attracted several name authors (notably Marion Zimmer Bradley) during its dozen-collection run and was also adapted into a graphic-novel series. Troubles with finances and writers' block caused Asprin's output to drop precipitously in the late 1990s; he has co-authored all his published books since returning to the scene in 2001.

Thieves' World, one of the first shared-world publications ever, tracks an odd variety of characters through a dangerous faux-medieval city called Sanctuary; its later collections succumb to the common comic-book failing of overpowered characters and overwrought story-stakes. The light-hearted, pun-laced Myth Adventures series concerns an inept would-be magician named Skeeve and the motley crew of allies, enemies, pets, and hangers-on he acquires during various adventures on his home world and in a motley multiverse.

> I think too many people try to distance themselves from the writing, because if it gets rejected, they don't want to hurt too much. They try to go with formula,

archetype or what-not—and wonder why it won't sell or, even if it does, why people don't respond to it. Again, if you don't care about it, why should anybody else?—(Robert Asprin, "No Quarter")

Major Works

Novels

Myth Adventures series: *Another Fine Myth* (1978), *Myth Conceptions* (1980), *Myth Directions* (1982), *Myth-Ing Persons* (1984), *Little Myth Marker* (1985), *M.Y.T.H. Inc. Link* (1986), *Myth-Nomers and Im-Pervections* (1987), *M.Y.T.H. Inc. in Action* (1990), *Sweet Myth-Tery of Life* (1993), *Myth-Ion Improbable* (2001), *Something M.Y.T.H. Inc* (2001), *Myth-Told Tales* (with Jody Lynn Nye, 2003), *Myth-Alliances* (with Jody Lynn Nye, 2003), *Myth-Taken Identity* (with Jody Lynn Nye, 2004), *Class Dis-Mythed* (with Jody Lynn Nye, 2005), *Myth-Gotten Gains* (with Jody Lynn Nye, 2006)

Graphic Novels

Thieves' World Graphics (with Lynn Abbey, art by Tim Sale; 1990)

Short Story Collections

Thieves' World series (edited, with Lynn Abbey): *Thieves' World* (1979), *Tales from the Vulgar Unicorn* (1980), *Shadows of Sanctuary* (1981), *Storm Season* (1982), *The Face of Chaos* (1983), *Wings of Omen* (1984), six others. Collected in a four-volume set: *Sanctuary* (1982), *Cross-Currents* (1984), *The Shattered Sphere* (1986), *The Price of Victory* (1990)

Research Sources

Encyclopedias and Handbooks: EF, HDF, SJGF

Biographies and Interviews

Ward, Jean Marie. "Robert Asprin and Eric Del Carlo: No Quarter." *Crescent Blues*. Interview dated 2001. http://www.crescentblues.com/4_5issue/int_asprin_delcarlo.shtml. Last visited January 25, 2008.

Criticism and Readers' Guides

Lindskold, Jane M. "Robert Asprin: The Man Behind the Myths." *Extrapolation* 35(1) (Spring 1994), pp. 60–67.

Web Sites

Nitpicker's Guide to Robert Asprin's Myth-series. http://www.sarangworld.com/mythpickf.php3. Last visited January 25, 2008. Fan-compiled errata.

Robert Lynn Asprin FAQ. http://www.olywa.net/cook/rlafaq.htm. Last visited January 25, 2008. Compiled by regulars of the Usenet newsgroup alt.fan.asprin. Contains detailed biographical information as well as regular updates on Asprin's output and spinoffs from Asprin material.

Lyman Frank Baum (L. Frank Baum) (1856–1919)

Biographical Sketch

Son of a wealthy oil magnate, Lyman Frank Baum grew up with strong interests in printing and theatre. Most of his theatrical efforts flopped, often causing him severe financial distress; after moving to South Dakota from New York in 1888, Baum bought and bankrupted a general store, turning instead to running a newspaper, which also failed. He then moved to Chicago with his wife Maud and their four sons, where he continued working on newspapers, and where Oz was born out of a fruitful partnership with illustrator W.W. Denslow.

The Oz books were immediately popular, sparking Baum's only successful theatrical effort (a musical *Wizard of Oz*) as well as other musicals, movies, and books by other hands. Baum tried to write other children's books (often under pseudonyms) after the Oz books rocketed to stardom, but fan demands and further financial difficulties repeatedly returned him to Oz and its wizards, witches, monarchs, and other fantastic denizens.

> Imagination has brought mankind through the dark ages to its present state of civilization. Imagination led Columbus to discover America. Imagination led Franklin to discover electricity.—(L. Frank Baum, Introduction, *The Lost Princess of Oz*)

Major Works

Children's/Young Adult Fiction

Oz series: *The Wonderful Wizard of Oz* (1900; often retitled *The Wizard of Oz*), *The Marvelous Land of Oz* (1904), *Ozma of Oz* (1907), *Dorothy and the Wizard in Oz* (1908), *The Road to Oz* (1909), *The Emerald City of Oz* (1910), *The Patchwork Girl of Oz* (1913), *Tik-Tok of Oz* (1914), *The Scarecrow of Oz* (1915), *Rinkitink in Oz* (1916), *The Lost Princess of Oz* (1917), *The Tin Woodman of Oz* (1918), *The Magic of Oz* (1919), *Glinda of Oz* (1920). These are all the Baum-authored Oz books; all other Oz books are by Ruth Plumly Thompson or other writers.

Royal Historians of Oz series: *Queer Visitors from the Marvelous Land of Oz* (1904–1905), *The Woggle-Bug Book* (1905), *Little Wizard Stories of Oz* (1913). All other Royal Historians of Oz books are by other authors.

Dot and Tot of Merryland (1901)
The Magical Monarch of Mo (1903)
Queen Zixi of Ix (1905)

Research Sources

Encyclopedias and Handbooks: EF, HDF, SJGF

Biographies and Interviews

Gardner, Martin and Russel B. Nye. *The Wizard of Oz and Who He Was.* East Lansing, MI: Michigan State University Press, 1994 (rev).

Rogers, Katharine M. *L. Frank Baum: Creator of Oz.* New York: St. Martin's Press, 2002.

Criticism and Readers' Guides

Baum, L. Frank, W.W. Denslow, and Michael Patrick Hearn. *The Annotated Wizard of Oz: The Wonderful Wizard of Oz.* New York: Norton, 2000.

Rahn, Suzanne. *L. Frank Baum's World of Oz: A Classic Series at 100.* Lanham, MD: Scarecrow Press, 2003.

Riley, Michael O'Neal. *Oz and Beyond: The Fantasy World of L. Frank Baum.* Lawrence, KS: University of Kansas Press, 1997.

Snow, Jack. *Who's Who in Oz.* New York: P. Bedrick Books, 1954.

Svartz, Mark Evan. *Oz before the Rainbow: The Wonderful Wizard of Oz on Stage and Screen to 1939.* Baltimore, MD: Johns Hopkins University Press, 2000.

Tuerk, Richard Carl. *Oz in Perspective: Magic and Myth in the L. Frank Baum Books.* Jefferson, NC: McFarland & Co, 2007.

Web Sites

Gjovaag, Eric. *The Wonderful Website of Oz.* http://thewizardofoz.info/. Last visited January 25, 2008. Fan site. Contains frequently asked questions about the Oz books and movie adaptations, Oz-related event calendar, digital art, lesson plans, more.

Peter S. Beagle (1939–)

Biographical Sketch

Born in the Bronx, Peter Soyer Beagle wrote his first novel *A Fine and Private Place* when he was 19. Since then, his difficult-to-pigeonhole written output, with its lyrical style and touches of magical realism and studied anachronism, has attracted fans, confused reviewers, and bewildered publishers. Beagle lives in Oakland, California; he often lectures at nearby colleges and appears at conventions.

A creative drought in the late 1990s arose from financial difficulties stemming from ill-advised professional relationships. Upon returning to fantasy, he won the 2006 Hugo best novelette award for *Two Hearts*. A guitarist and folksinger, Beagle has also written screenplays (including the animated adaptation of his own *The Last Unicorn*), an opera libretto, and folksongs of his own, one of which inspired *The Innkeeper's Song*.

> As for the world [of *The Innkeeper's Song*] itself . . . It's very much a playground for me. I like exploring it and finding out different parts of its folklore, geography, history, and so on. And the only way I can do that is to write the stories. I never find things out except by doing them.—(Peter S. Beagle, http://www.greenmanreview.com/book/interview_beagle.psb.html. Last visited January 25, 2008)

Major Works

Novels

A Fine and Private Place (1960)
The Last Unicorn (1968)
The Folk of the Air (1986)
The Innkeeper's Song (1993)
Tamsin (1999)
Summerlong (2006)

Children's/Young Adult Fiction

The Unicorn Sonata (1996)
I'm Afraid You've Got Dragons (2007)

Short Story/Novella Collections

The Fantasy Worlds of Peter S. Beagle (1978)
Giant Bones (1997; titled *The Magician of Karakosk* outside the United States)
The Line Between (2006)
The First Last Unicorn and Other Beginnings (2006)

Research Sources

Encyclopedias and Handbooks: EF, HDF, SJGF

Biographies and Interviews

Greenland, Colin. "Paradoxa Interview with Peter Beagle." *Paradoxa* 5(13–14) (1999–2000), pp. 288–302.

Hennessey-DeRose, Cristopher. "Peter S. Beagle Goes Back to his Fine and Private Place to Continue the Saga of *The Last Unicorn*." *Sci-Fi.com*. http://www.scifi.com/sfw/issue456/interview.html. Last visited January 25, 2008.

"Peter S. Beagle." *Fast Forward.* June 2006. http://www.fast-forward.tv/audio/audio191.m3u. Last visited January 25, 2008.

Criticism and Readers' Guides

Kelso, Sylvia. "Loces Genii: Urban Settings in the Fantasy of Peter Beagle, Martha Wells, and Barbara Hambly." *Journal of the Fantastic in the Arts* 13(1) (2002), pp. 13–32.

Norford, Don Parry. "Reality and Illusion in Peter Beagle's *The Last Unicorn*." *Critique* 19(2) (1977), pp. 93–104.

Palwick, Susan. "*The Last Unicorn*: Magic as Metaphor." *New York Review of Science Fiction* 6 (February 1989), pp. 1, 3–5.

Pennington, John. "Innocence and Experience and the Imagination in the World of Peter Beagle." *Mythlore* 15(4) (Summer 1989), pp. 10–16.

Stevens, David. "Incongruity in a World of Illusion: Patterns of Humor in Peter Beagle's *The Last Unicorn*." *Extrapolation* 20 (1979), pp. 230–237.

Tobin, Jean. "Werewolves and Unicorns: Fabulous Beasts in Peter Beagle's Fiction." Jan Hokenson, and Howard D. Pearce, eds., *Forms of the Fantastic*. Westport, CT: Greenwood, 1986, pp. 181–189.

Wolfe, Gary K. "Beagle and Eddison: A Special Issue." *Journal of the Fantastic in the Arts* 1(3) (1988).

Web Sites

"An Issue of Green Man Devoted to Peter S. Beagle." *Green Man Review*. http://www.greenmanreview.com/oneoffs/peterbeagle.html. Last visited January 25, 2008. Includes an interview, several reviews, essays, and poetry. Dated 19 July 2006.

(Unofficially) Peter S. Beagle. http://www.peterbeagle.com/. Last visited January 25, 2008. Fan site with considerable author access. Offers news, event notices, email newsletter.

Peter S. Beagle. http://www.myspace.com/petersbeagle. Last visited January 25, 2008. Author's official page. Contains fan comments, author Web log.

If you like Peter S. Beagle

Peter S. Beagle's beloved *The Last Unicorn* follows a mythical creature and her more mundane mortal friends through a world grimly determined to exploit and destroy myths. That not all myths are safe or wholesome is the theme of *The Innkeeper's Song* and its book of related stories *Giant Bones*. Beagle's lyrical prose tugs at heartstrings, even as his well-drawn characters win hearts.

Then you might like

Emma Bull

Bull has mostly written collaborative novels with other authors (the Liavek books with Will Shetterly, *Freedom and Necessity* with Steven Brust, and the Borderland books edited by Terry Windling). These, along with her original urban fantasy *War for the Oaks*, will reward the lover of works that cross between worlds.

Neil Gaiman

Gaiman shares Beagle's love for mixing the mundane and the magical, sometimes humorously, sometimes with serious intent. *Neverwhere* and *Stardust* will appeal to fans of Beagle's *The Last Unicorn*, whereas lovers of *The Innkeeper's Song* will be likely to enjoy Gaiman's *American Gods* and *Anansi Boys*.

Ellen Kushner

Swordspoint and its associated novels (*The Fall of the Kings*, *The Privilege of the Sword*) embed their characters firmly in a rigidly stratified society with intricate politics and real human costs. Her award-winning novel *Thomas the Rhymer* brings ancient British legend to new life. Kushner's eye for character and strong ethical sense will appeal to fans of Beagle.

Hope Mirrlees

Lud-in-the-Mist, a very early fantasy novel, explored the fear of the unfamiliar alongside the decay of the mundane. Her themes prefigure some of Beagle's, and her delicate prose is not unlike his.

James P. Blaylock (1950–)

Biographical Sketch

James P. Blaylock lives in Orange County, California, where he has spent almost all his life. He teaches English and comparative literature at Chapman University, and creative writing at the Orange County High School of the Arts.

Blaylock has two World Fantasy Awards and a Philip K. Dick Award to his credit. His protagonists are often brave, decent, sometimes self-centered, and he has claimed, strongly autobiographical. His writing style is inspired by classic English writers from Shakespeare to Dickens and Thackeray, and his settings range from biblical apocrypha to Victorian steampunk. With his teaching colleague Tim Powers, he created a poet named William Ashbless out of whole cloth so convincingly that many readers have tried in vain to research Ashbless.

To my mind there's absolutely nothing fantastic, imaginative or compelling about blue unicorns or flying cats or two-headed martial art experts with apostrophized names. I'm much more interested in writing about people who I sort of know and have an affection for, and who are much more authentic to my mind. —(James P. Blaylock, "Of Steam and Stuff: Conversations with James P. Blaylock")

Major Works

Novels

Balumnia trilogy: *The Elfin Ship* (1982), *The Disappearing Dwarf* (1983), *The Stone Giant* (1989)
St. Ives trilogy: *The Digging Leviathan* (1984), *Homunculus* (1986), *Lord Kelvin's Machine* (1992)
Christian trilogy: *The Last Coin* (1988), *The Paper Grail* (1991), *All the Bells on Earth* (1995)
Ghosts trilogy: *Night Relics* (1994), *Winter Tides* (1997), *The Rainy Season* (1999)
Land of Dreams (1987)

Children's/Young Adult Fiction

The Magic Spectacles (1991)

Short Story Collections

13 Phantasms (2000)
On Pirates (with Tim Powers, 2001)
The Devils in the Details (with Tim Powers, 2003)
In for a Penny (2003)

Research Sources

Encyclopedias and Handbooks: EF, HDF, SJGF

Biographies and Interviews

Berlyne, John. "Interview with James P. Blaylock." *Postscripts* 1 (June 2004).
Cox, Glen. "Of Steam and Stuff: A Conversation with James P. Blaylock." *NOVA Express* 2(2) (1988). Available online at http://www.sybertooth.com/blaylock/intervew.htm. Last visited January 25, 2008.

Criticism and Readers' Guides

Walker, Eric. "Science-Fiction and Fantasy Works: James Blaylock." *Great Science-Fiction and Fantasy Works.* http://greatsfandf.com/AUTHORS/JamesBlaylock.php. Last visited January 25, 2008.

Web Sites

James P. Blaylock Fantasy and Steampunk Author. http://www.sybertooth.com/blaylock/. Last visited January 25, 2008. Fan site, running since 1995. Offers brief book summaries, biography, discussion board.

Francesca Lia Block (1962–)

Biographical Sketch

Francesca Lia Block was born and currently lives in Los Angeles. Her parents, a poet and a painter, introduced her to Greek myth and fairy tales and encouraged her to write when she was young. She is married with two children, is active in the zine community, and is developing a television show for MTV.

Her urban fantasies, written for adults but often categorized as young adult despite overt sexuality and dark themes, draw heavily on her experience in Los Angeles as well as Latin American magic-realist authors such as Gabriel García-Márquez and Isabel Allende. Her work has received awards from the American Library Association among others.

> I usually begin with the poetry of the language and by trying to create vivid characters. Later, certain truths are revealed to me and I often go back and work on bringing them out more fully in the story.
>
> In some ways, starting with the fairy tales made my job easier because the truths are already inherent in the original work. I just had to find a way to apply it to my life. —(Francesca Lia Block, http://www.harperchildrens.com/hch/author/features/block/. Last visited January 25, 2008)

Major Works

Novels

Ecstasia (1993)
Primavera (1994)
Ruby (2006)
Psyche in a Dress (2006)

Children's/Young Adult Fiction

Weetzie Bat series: *Weetzie Bat* (1989), *Witch Baby* (1991), *Cherokee Bat and the Goat Guys* (1992), *Missing Angel Juan* (1993), *Baby Be-Bop* (1995), *Necklace of Kisses* (2005)
I Was a Teenage Fairy (1998)
Echo (2001)

Short Story Collections

The Rose and the Beast: Nine Fairy Tales (1993)
Girl Goddess #9: Nine Stories (1996)

Research Sources

Encyclopedias and Handbooks: EF, HDF

Biographies and Interviews

Levithan, David. "Wild Thing." *School Library Journal* 51(6) (June 2005), p. 44.

"Francesca Lia Block on The Rose and the Beast: Fairy Tales Retold." *HarperChildrens.com*. http://www.harperchildrens.com/hch/author/features/block/. Last visited January 25, 2008.

Criticism and Readers' Guides

Franzak, Judith. "The Mirror's New Message?: Gender in the Adolescent Postmodern Fairy Tale." *Canadian Children's Literature* 108 (Winter 2002), pp. 53–72.

Platzner, Rebecca. "Collage in Francesca Lia Block's Weetzie Bat Books." *The Alan Review* 25(2) (Winter 1998). http://scholar.lib.vt.edu/ejournals/ALAN/winter98/platzner.html. Last visited January 25, 2008.

Susina, Jan. "The Rebirth of the Postmodern Flâneur: Notes on the Postmodern Landscape of Francesca Lia Block's Weetzie Bat." *Marvels & Tales* 16(2) (2002), pp. 188–200. Available via Project MUSE.

Trites, Roberta Seelinger. "Narrative Resolution: Photography in Adolescent Literature." *Children's Literature* 27 (1999), pp. 129–149.

Web Sites

Official Website for Author Francesca Lia Block. http://francescaliablock.com/. Last visited January 25, 2008. News, biography, review list, contact information.

The Francesca Lia Block Shrine. http://www.glowinthedarkstars.com/. Last visited January 25, 2008. Extensive fan site with interviews, biographical and bibliographic information, book excerpts, discussion boards, and more.

Ray Bradbury (1920–)

Biographical Sketch

Novelist, poet, dramatist, designer, and essayist Ray Bradbury derived his initial writing impetus from growing up in small-town Waukegan, Illinois (despite two short stints in Tucson, Arizona). Voracious reading was all his education after high school. Bradbury became a full-time writer at the age of 22, after four years selling newspapers on street corners in Los Angeles. Bradbury married Marguerite McClure in 1947 and had four daughters with her. He still lives in California.

Even Bradbury's more science-fictionesque efforts often have a dreamlike, heavily symbolic tone of irreality that endears them to readers of fantasy and horror. Many of his works have been adapted to radio, stage, comic page, and screen, sometimes with his active participation, as with the long-running television series *The Ray Bradbury Theatre*. Of late his novels have mostly been mysteries.

> We were put here as witnesses to the miracle of life. We see the stars, and we want them. We are beholden to give back to the universe . . . If we make landfall on another star system, we become immortal. —(Ray Bradbury, "Speech to the National School Board Association," 1995)

Major Works

Novels

The Martian Chronicles (1950)
The Illustrated Man (1951)
Green Town trilogy: *Dandelion Wine* (1957), *Something Wicked This Way Comes* (1962), *Farewell Summer* (2006)
The Halloween Tree (1972)

Children's/Young Adult Fiction

Switch On the Night (1955)
With Cat for Comforter (1997)
Dogs Think that Every Day is Christmas (1997)

Short Story Collections

Dark Carnival (1947)
The October Country (1955)
A Medicine for Melancholy (1959)
I Sing the Body Electric (1969)
Quicker than the Eye (1996)
The Cat's Pajamas: Stories (2004)

Other Important Writings

Zen in the Art of Writing (1990)
Yestermorrow: Obvious Answers to Impossible Futures (1991)

Research Sources

Encyclopedias and Handbooks: EF, HDF

Biographies and Interviews

Aggelis, Steven L. *Conversations with Ray Bradbury*. Jackson, MS: University Press of Mississippi, 2004.

Eiler, Jonathan R. and William F. Touponce. *Ray Bradbury: The Life of Fiction*. Kent, OH: Kent State University Press, 2004.

Nolan, William F. *The Ray Bradbury Companion: A Life and Career History, Photolog, and Comprehensive Checklist of Writings*. New York: Gale Research: 1975.

Weist, Jerry. *Bradbury, an Illustrated Life: A Journey to Far Metaphor*. New York: William Morrow& Company, 2002.

Weller, Sam. *The Bradbury Chronicles: The Life of Ray Bradbury*. New York: Harper-Collins, 2005.

Criticism and Readers' Guides

Greenberg, Martin Harry and Joseph D. Olander, eds., *Ray Bradbury*. New York: Taplinger, 1980.

Lawson, Benjamin S. "Ray Bradbury Companions." *Utopian Studies* 12(1) (2001), pp. 133–136.

Rosenman, John B. "The Heaven and Hell Archetype in Faulkner's 'That Evening Sun' and Bradbury's *Dandelion Wine*." *South Atlantic Bulletin* 43(2) (May 1978), pp. 12–16.

Sullivan, Anita T. "Ray Bradbury and Fantasy." *English Journal* 61 (1972), pp. 1309–1314.

Touponce, William F. "Laughter and Freedom in Ray Bradbury's *Something Wicked This Way Comes*." *Children's Literature Association Quarterly* 13(1) (Spring 1988), pp. 17–21.

Web Sites

Ray Bradbury Online. http://raybradburyonline.com/. Last visited January 25, 2008. Fan site. Contains FAQ, biography, bibliography, news page, image gallery.

Ray Bradbury. http://raybradbury.com/. Last visited January 25, 2008. Official site maintained by publisher HarperCollins. Includes newsletter, active message boards, quotation list.

Marion Zimmer Bradley (1930–1999)

Biographical Sketch

Born near Albany, New York, Marion Zimmer Bradley graduated from college and attended graduate school in her thirties, already a published fantasy novelist.

She married and divorced twice, and had three children. She helped found the medieval-reenactment group called the Society for Creative Anachronism, and was active in gay and lesbian activism from the 1960s.

Her Darkover universe, which she later opened to contributions from other (often new and previously-unpublished) authors, explores women's difficult choices amidst social problems created by telepathy and species mixing. The long-running *Sword and Sorceress* series and the fantasy magazine Bradley edited introduced many female authors to fantasy publication, and kept feminist plots and characters alive in an often male-centric genre. Bradley's best-known fantasy work may be *The Mists of Avalon*, a feminist-revisionist take on Arthurian legend. She was honored with a World Fantasy lifetime achievement award in 2000.

> There is a very old spiritual law that says that you can have absolutely anything you want—but you must know how to ask for it, you must want it more than you want anything else, and nothing must be allowed to stand in its way.—(Marion Zimmer Bradley, "Why Prayer Is Not Answered")

Major Works

Novels

The Darkover series (omnibus editions listed): *The Children of Hastur* (1982), *The Oath of Renunciates* (1984), *The Darkover Saga* (1984), *The Ages of Chaos* (2002), *The Forbidden Circle* (2002), *Heritage and Exile* (2002), *The Saga of the Renunciates* (2002), *A World Divided* (2003), *First Contact* (2004), *To Save a World* (2004)
The Mists of Avalon (1979)
Night's Daughter (1985)
Warrior Woman (1987)

Short Story Collections

The Dark Intruder and Other Stories (1964)
Lythande (1986)
Jamie and Other Stories (1988)

Research Sources

Encyclopedias and Handbooks: EF, HDF, SJGF

Biographies and Interviews

Arbur, Rosemarie. *Marion Zimmer Bradley*. Mercer Island, WA: Starmont House, 1985.

Criticism and Readers' Guides

Benson, Gordon and Phil Stephensen-Payne. *Marion Zimmer Bradley: A Working Bibliography*. San Bernardino, CA: Borgo Press, 1991.

Breen, Walter H. *The Darkover Concordance: A Reader's Guide*. Berkeley, CA: Pennyfarthing Press, 1979.

McClain, Lee Tobin. "Gender Anxiety in Arthurian Romance." *Extrapolation: A Journal of Science Fiction and Fantasy* 38(3) (Fall 1997), pp. 193–199.

Russ, Joanna. "Recent Feminist Utopias." In Marleen S. Barr, ed., *Future Females: A Critical Anthology*. Bowling Green, OH: Bowling Green State University Press, 1981, pp. 71–75.

Schwartz, Susan M. "Marion Zimmer Bradley's Ethic of Freedom." In Tom Staicar, ed., *The Feminine Eye: Science Fiction and the Women Who Write It*. New York: Ungar, 1982, pp. 73–88.

Wood, Diane S. "Gender Roles in the Darkover Novels of Marion Zimmer Bradley." In Jane B. Weedman, ed., *Women Worldwalkers: New Dimensions of Science Fiction and Fantasy*. Lubbock, TX: Texas Tech Press, 1985, pp. 237–246.

Web Sites

Marion Zimmer Bradley Literary Works Trust. http://mzbworks.home.att.net/. Last visited January 25, 2008. Official page of Bradley's literary executors. Contains full-text essays by Bradley, biography, bibliography.

Terry Brooks (1944–)

Biographical Sketch

Terry Brooks was born in Sterling, Illinois. He earned a JD from Washington and Lee University and practiced as an attorney before leaving law to write full-time. He now lives in Seattle, Washington. He credits reading Tolkien's *Lord of the Rings* trilogy for his decision to write fantasy; his debt is evident in his characterization, plot structure, and even nomenclature.

> Fantasy is the only canvas large enough for me to paint on. It lets me capture the magic I felt reading my favorite books, and imagining my own worlds. A world in which elves exist and magic works offers greater opportunities to digress and explore.—(Terry Brooks, http://www.randomhouse.com/features/brooks/author/interview.html. Last visited January 25, 2008)

Major Works

Novels

Shannara series: *The Sword of Shannara* (1977), *The Elfstones of Shannara* (1982), *The Wishsong of Shannara* (1985), *The Scions of Shannara* (1990), *The Druid of*

Shannara (1991), *The Elf Queen of Shannara* (1992), *The Talismans of Shannara* (1993), *First King of Shannara* (1996), *Ilse Witch* (2000), *Antrax* (2001), *Morgawr* (2002), *Jarka Ruus* (2003), *Tanequil* (2004), *Straken* (2005), *Armageddon's Children* (2006), *The Elves of Cintra* (2007)

Magic Kingdom For Sale series: *Magic Kingdom For Sale – SOLD!* (1986), *The Black Unicorn* (1987), *Wizard at Large* (1988), *The Tangle Box* (1994), *Witches' Brew* (1995)

Word and Void series: *Running with the Demon* (1997), *A Knight of the Word* (1998), *Angel Fire East* (1999)

Graphic Novels

Dark Wraith of Shannara (forthcoming 2008)

Research Sources

Encyclopedias and Handbooks: EF, HDF, SJGF

Biographies and Interviews

Blaschke, Jayme Lynn. "An interview with Terry Brooks." *Science Fiction Chronicle* 24(11) (October 2002), pp. 42–47.

"Interview with Terry Brooks." *Hour 25*. Audio interview performed September 22, 2000. http://www.hour25online.com/Hour25_Previous_Shows_2000-5.html#Terry_Brooks_02. Last visited January 25, 2008.

Criticism and Readers' Guides

Brooks, Terry and Teresa Patterson. *The World of Shannara*. New York: Del Rey, 2001.

Web Sites

Gong, Minnie. *The Shannara Files*. http://www.alitheia.org/shannarafiles/. Last visited January 25, 2008. Extensive fan site containing character lists, book timelines, family trees, and news.

Speakman, Shawn (maintainer). *The Wondrous Worlds of Terry Brooks: The Official Author Website*. http://terrybrooks.net/. Last visited January 25, 2008. Contains biography, news, "Ask Terry" column, Web forum.

Steven K. Brust (1955–)

Biographical Sketch

Steven Karl Brust, who currently lives in Las Vegas, worked as a professional musician and as a computer programmer before turning to fiction. An active musician and filker, Brust is a frequent convention guest, particularly in the midwestern United States.

Most of Brust's novels take place in the sprawling world of Dragaera, featuring the confidence man Vlad Taltos. The Khaavren Romances could be easily dismissed as Dumas pastiche, but betray a sophisticated grasp of metanarrative as well as admirably light-handed humor. Brust is also fond of writing short stories in shared universes, such as that of *Thieves' World* or Neil Gaiman's *Sandman*.

> In an ideal world, I would write stories that could just be enjoyed as stories, enjoyed for a couple of hours, put down, and you're done with it, and also stories that reward a closer reading and examination, if you care to do it... An ideal book, in a sense, is one that can be read in two hours and talked about for two weeks. —(Steven Brust, http://www.scifi.com/sfw/issue224/interview.html. Last visited January 25, 2008)

Major Works

Novels

Vlad Taltos series: *Jhereg* (1983), *Yendi* (1984), *Teckla* (1987), *Taltos* (1988), *Phoenix* (1990), *Athyra* (1993), *Orca* (1996), *Dragon* (1998), *Issola* (2001), *Dzur* (2006)
Khaavren series: *The Phoenix Guards* (1991), *Five Hundred Years After* (1994), *The Paths of the Dead* (2002), *The Lord of Castle Black* (2003), *Sethra Lavode* (2004)
To Reign in Hell (1984)
The Sun, the Moon, and the Stars (1987)
The Gypsy (with Megan Lindholm, 1992)
Agyar (1993)
Freedom & Necessity (with Emma Bull, 1997)

Other Important Writings

Liavek stories: "An Act of Contrition," "An Act of Trust," "An Act of Mercy," "An Act of Love," "A Hot Night at Cheeky's." Liavek series edited by Emma Bull and Will Shetterly, published 1985–1990 by Ace Books.
"When the Bow Breaks." In Terry Windling and Delia Sherman, eds., *The Essential Bordertown*. New York: Tor, 1998.
"Valósaág and Élet." Neil Gaiman, and Edward E. Kramer, eds. *The Sandman Book of Dreams* (1996). New York: HarperTorch, 2002.

Research Sources

Encyclopedias and Handbooks: EF, HDF, SJGF

Biographies and Interviews

Robinson, Tasha. "Steven Brust Doesn't Take Himself Seriously—But His Readers Do." *Sci-Fi.com*. http://www.scifi.com/sfw/issue224/interview.html. Last visited January 25, 2008.

"Interview with Steven Brust." *Writing Forums*. November 25, 2006. http://www.writingforums.org/showthread.php?t=950. Last visited January 25, 2008.

Criticism and Readers' Guides

Mandel, Mark A. *Cracks and Shards: Observations on Dragaera*. http://www.speakeasy.org/~mamandel/Cracks-and-Shards/. Last visited January 25, 2008.

Tilendis, Robert M. "The Khaavren Romances." *Green Man Review*. http://www.greenmanreview.com/book/book_brust_khaavrenromances.html. Last visited January 25, 2008.

Web Sites

Brust, Steven. *A Bland and Deadly Courtesy*. http://skzbrust.livejournal.com/. Author's personal Web log. Last visited January 25, 2008.

Brust, Steven. *Dragaera: Dedicated to the works of Steven K. Zoltán Brust*. http://dragaera.info/. Last visited January 25, 2008. Author-sanctioned fan site. Includes pronunciation guide, targeted search of Dragaera-related Web sites, targeted search of the full text of the Dragaera books, mailing-list information and archives.

Brust, Steven. *The Dream Café*. http://dreamcafe.com/. Last visited January 25, 2008. Author's official Web site. Contains booklist, linklist.

The Lyorn Records. http://dragaera.wikia.com/wiki/Main_Page. Last visited January 25, 2008. Fan-maintained wiki covering the Dragaera novels.

Lois McMaster Bujold (1949–)

Biographical Sketch

Born in Columbus, Ohio, Lois McMaster Bujold now lives in Minneapolis. She wrote collaboratively with her friend Lillian Stewart Carl while in high school, toured East Africa to photograph wildlife while in college, and worked briefly as a pharmacy technician before quitting to raise her two children.

Bujold is best known for her long-running science-fiction Vorkosigan series, but the publication of *The Curse of Chalion* established her firmly among fantasy's best. The acclaimed, award-winning series offers an elaborate and well-thought-out religious system along with real insight into women's issues in a patriarchal society.

> So a novel, therefore, is a slice out of the writer's world-view. The slice in turn, if it is coherent, generates . . . a comment on the human condition, which is the book's theme. We experience theme . . . as a wonderful sense of meaning to the book. The book has succeeded in creating meaning inside the head of another person. And in my world-view, that's what art is for.—(Lois McMaster Bujold, "When World-Views Collide," http://www.dendarii.com/collide.html. Last visited January 25, 2008)

Major Works

Novels

The Spirit Ring (1993)
Chalion series: *The Curse of Chalion* (2001), *Paladin of Souls* (2003), *The Hallowed Hunt* (2005)
Sharing Knife series: *Beguilement* (2006), *Legacy* (2007)

Research Sources

Biographies and Interviews

Bernardi, Mike. "Interviews and Biographical Sketches." *The Bujold Nexus*. http://www.dendarii.com/interviews.html. Last visited January 25, 2008.
"Lois McMaster Bujold." *Fast Forward*. May 2005. http://www.fast-forward.tv/audio/audio178.m3u. Last visited January 25, 2008.
"Lois McMaster Bujold: On the Cusp." *Locus* 46(2) (February 2001), pp. 4, 84–85.
Levy, Michael M. "An Interview with Lois McMaster Bujold." *Kaleidoscope* 34 (Winter-Spring 1997), pp. 6–19.
Rand, Ken. "Talking with the Real Lois McMaster Bujold." *Science Fiction Chronicle* 17(1) (October–November 1995), pp. 7, 37–38, 40.
Sheridan, Barbara. "An interview with Lois McMaster Bujold." *Paranormal Romance*. http://paranormalromance.org/LoisMcMasterBujold.htm. Last visited January 25, 2008.
Sutton, Terry. "Between Planets." *Minneapolis/St. Paul City Pages* 25(1225) (May 26, 2004). http://citypages.com/databank/25/1225/article12152.asp. Last visited January 25, 2008.

Criticism and Readers' Guides

Monette, Sarah. "LMcMB, Paladin of Souls." http://truepenny.livejournal.com/225324.html. Last visited January 25, 2008.

Web Sites

Bernardi, Mike. *The Bujold Nexus*. http://www.dendarii.com/. Last visited January 25, 2008. Author-authorized fan site. Contains biography, news, maps and nomenclature lists, essays by Bujold, sample book chapters.

If you like Lois McMaster Bujold

Bujold's Chalion series (*The Curse of Chalion*, *Paladin of Souls*, *The Hallowed Hunt*) places likeable characters in a well-imagined world of military and religious conflict. Bujold draws her setting from the politics of medieval and Renaissance Europe, adding a unique and well-conceived original religion complete with heresies to the mix.

Then you might like

Steven Brust

Brust's lengthy, swashbuckling Vlad Taltos series (*Jhereg*, *Yendi*, *Teckla*, and many others) follows its scheming lead character through many reversals of fortune. Gloriously gung-ho action and sweeping settings feel like Bujold's science fiction translated into a fantasy setting.

Ursula K. Le Guin

Le Guin's fantasy, like Bujold's, pays clear-eyed attention to the status and choices of women in patriarchal societies. Among fantasists she is best known for her Earthsea series (*A Wizard of Earthsea*, *Tombs of Atuan*, *The Farthest Shore*, *Tehanu*, *The Other Wind*, *Tales of Earthsea*), which chronicles clashes between wizards and dragons, and the people caught up in them.

Barbara Hambly

Hambly's Darwath series (*The Time of the Dark*, *The Walls of Air*, *The Armies of Daylight*) follows a graduate-student philologist who uses her linguistic and historical training to unravel ancient mysteries in the otherworld she is transported to. Hambly's novels, like Bujold's, present tough ethical choices with severe consequences.

Elizabeth Moon

Moon's Paksenarrion series (*Sheepfarmer's Daughter*, *Divided Allegiance*, *Oath of Gold*) is the sweeping saga of a woman who leaves her home to follow her creed and her heart, becoming a great hero. Its epic scope, strong female lead, and upright characters recall Bujold.

James Branch Cabell (1879–1958)

Biographical Sketch

James Branch Cabell was born in Richmond, Virginia, and lived most of his life in Virginia until retiring to Florida. He worked as a journalist, a researcher and a genealogist, a bookkeeper, and a freelance writer as well as a novelist. He married twice and had one child.

Cabell's long-running series set in the fictitious French realm of Poictesme mix fantasy with satire, colored by linguistic inventiveness and involved symbolism. *Jurgen*, his eighth published work, was denounced for obscenity, leading to a drawn-out lawsuit that Cabell eventually won. The Poictesme series proved highly influential on later writers of fantasy and science fiction; such distinguished authors as Robert A. Heinlein and Neil Gaiman acknowledged his impact openly.

> For, as you of course perceive, the literary artist plays: he does nothing else, except with haste and grudgingly; and the sole end of his endeavor is to divert himself. —(James Branch Cabell, *Straws and Prayer Books*)

Major Works

Novels

Biography of the Life of Manuel (Jurgen, Poictesme) series: *Beyond Life* (1919), *Figures of Earth* (1921), *The Silver Stallion* (1926), *The Soul of Melicent* (1913; republished in 1920 under the title *Domnei*), *Chivalry* (1909), *Jurgen* (1919), *The Line of Love* (1905), *Gallantry* (1907), *The Certain Hour* (1916), *The Cords of Vanity* (1909), *From the Hidden Way* (1916), *The Rivet in Grandfather's Neck* (1915), *The Eagle's Shadow* (1904), *The Cream of the Jest* (1917), and several othcrs

Research Sources

Encyclopedias and Handbooks: EF, HDF, SJGF

Biographies and Interviews

Cabell, James Branch. *As I Remember It: Some Epilogues in Recollection*. New York: McBride, 1955.

Criticism and Readers' Guides

Flora, Joseph M. "From Virginia to Poictesme: The Early Novels of James Branch Cabell." *Missisippi Quarterly* 32 (1979), pp. 219–239.

Hall, James N. *James Branch Cabell: A Complete Bibliography*. New York: Revisionist Press, 1974.

Inge, M. Thomas and Edgar E. MacDonald. *James Branch Cabell: Centennial Essays*. Baton Rouge, LA: Louisiana State University Press, 1983.

Kalki: Studies in James Branch Cabell. (Journal of the Cabell Society, published from 1968 to 1996.)

Spencer, Paul. "Cabell: Fantasist of Reality." In Darrell Schweitzer, ed., *Exploring Fantastic Literature*. San Bernardino, CA: Borgo, 1985, pp. 97–106.

Web Sites

James Branch Cabell, 1879–1958. http://www.library.vcu.edu/jbc/speccoll/exhibit/cabell/jbclife.html. Last visited January 25, 2008. Online exhibit of Cabell-related materials from Virginia Commonwealth University, which named its main library after him. Includes links, guide to VCU's Cabell papers, biography, criticism.

Jacqueline Carey (1964–)

Biographical Sketch

Jacqueline Carey was born in Highland Park, Illinois. She holds a degree in psychology and English literature from Lake Forest College. After working in London for half a year and spending additional time touring, she returned to the United States and began writing. She lives near Saugatuck, Michigan with her partner Julie Abel and continues to travel widely.

The award-winning Kushiel's Legacy trilogy concerns a courtesan named Phèdre who carries the mark of the angel Kushiel, lord of justice and retribution, and experiences pleasure and pain as equivalent. The vicissitudes of service to Kushiel enslave her, make a spy and courtier of her, build her a household, and eventually earn her considerable political power. Carey's lush prose and skillful plotting continue to win readers and critical notice in the genre.

> Someone asked me if I wrote with a specific readership in mind, and I had to laugh. It would be impossible. When I began *Kushiel's Dart*, I was writing the book I wanted to read; a book with an epic scope that encompassed intrigue, adventure, sex, romance, sacrifice, redemption . . . everything but the kitchen sink. —(Jacqueline Carey, http://www.jacquelinecarey.com/archive06.html. Last visited January 25, 2008)

Major Works

Novels

Kushiel's Legacy trilogy: *Kushiel's Dart* (2001), *Kushiel's Chosen* (2002), *Kushiel's Avatar* (2003)

The Sundering: *Banewreaker* (2004), *Godslayer* (2005)

Imriel trilogy: *Kushiel's Scion* (2006), *Kushiel's Justice* (2007), *Kushiel's Mercy* (forthcoming in 2008)

Other Important Writings

"Bludemagic." *Inter-Text* #26, July–August 1995. http://www.intertext.com/magazine/v5n4/bludemagick.html. Last visited January 25, 2008.

"In the City." *Quanta*, July 1995. http://www.etext.org/Zines/Quanta/jul95/city.html. Last visited January 25, 2008.

Research Sources

Encyclopedias and Handbooks: HDF

Biographies and Interviews

"Interview with Jacqueline Carey." *SFFWorld.com*. June 10, 2006. http://www.sffworld.com/interview/189p0.html. Last visited January 25, 2008.

Oing, Beth. "Interview: Jacqueline Carey." *Strange Horizons*, (March 8, 2004). http://www.strangehorizons.com/2004/20040308/carey.shtml. Last visited January 25, 2008.

Tomio, Jay. "On the Spot at Fantasybookspot: Jacqueline Carey." July 26, 2005. http://www.fantasybookspot.com/node/217. Last visited January 26, 2008.

Criticism and Readers' Guides

"Jacqueline Carey: Existential BDSM." *Locus* 49(6) (December 2002), pp. 84–86.

Web Sites

Jacqueline Carey. http://www.jacquelinecarey.com/. Last visited January 26, 2008. Official author site. Contains bibliography, biography, news, sample chapters, fan art.

If you like Jacqueline Carey

The award-winning Kushiel's Legacy trilogy concerns a courtesan named Phèdre who carries the mark of the angel Kushiel, lord of justice and retribution, and experiences pleasure and pain as equivalent. The vicissitudes of service to Kushiel enslave her, make a spy and courtier of her, build her a household, and eventually earn her considerable political power.

Then you might like

Laurell K. Hamilton

The Anita Blake series of vampire novels (*Guilty Pleasures*, *The Laughing Corpse*, *Circus of the Damned*, others) earned Hamilton a considerable following with their tough heroine and crossover appeal to romance and mystery fans. This particular combination of genres will appeal to those who like Carey.

Ellen Kushner

Swordspoint and its associated novels (*The Fall of the Kings*, *The Privilege of the Sword*) embed their characters firmly in a rigidly-stratified society with intricate politics and real human costs. Like Carey, Kushner is well aware of the difficulties sexual politics cause women, and interested in exploring how women cope.

Tanith Lee

Lee's pulpier fiction will not appeal to Carey fans, but the Flat-Earth Cycle (*Night's Master*, *Death's Master*, *Delusion's Master*, *Delirium's Mistress*) is masterfully written, peopled with gods and mortals who suffer as much pain as they deal out.

Sarah Monette

Monette's Melusine series (*Melusine*, *The Virtu*, *The Mirador*, and the forthcoming *Corambis*) follows two half-brothers through a maze of treachery, madness, injury, and death; only their furtive loyalty can redeem them. Like Carey, Monette refuses to shy away from the darker aspects of sexuality.

Angela Carter (1940–1992)

Biographical Sketch

Angela Olive Stalker Carter was evacuated as a child from London to the Yorkshire countryside during World War II. After a brief career as a journalist, she studied English literature at the University of Bristol and began writing fiction, though she contributed freelance articles to major British magazines throughout her life. She married Paul Carter in 1960, divorcing him twelve years later, and eventually marrying Mark Pearce after over half a decade's travel in Japan, Europe, and the United States. That travel, in Japan especially, honed her feminism to a razor's edge. She died quite young of cancer.

Carter's work is dark, bizarre, baroquely-written, and disturbing. Her influences ranged from Shakespeare to de Sade to fairy tales; she often rethought and rewrote masculine work from a radical feminist's sensibility. Lush symbolism up to and including allegory, rewritten myth, sensuality, and an uneasy pairing of the real world with the fantastical characterize her short stories, and she was a major influence on later fantasists who rewrote fairy tales, especially from feminist perspectives.

> In a way all fiction starts off with "what if," but some "what ifs" are more specific. One kind of novel starts off with "What if I found out that my mother has an affair with a man that I thought was my uncle?" That's presupposing a different kind of novel from the one that starts off with "What if I found out my boyfriend had just changed sex?" If you read the *New York Times Book Review* a lot, you soon come to the conclusion that our culture takes more seriously the first kind of fiction, which is a shame in some ways. By the second "what if" you would actually end up asking much more penetrating questions.—(Angela Carter, in Katsavos, Angela, "An Interview with Angela Carter")

Major Works

Novels

Several Perceptions (1968)
Heroes and Villains (1969)

The War of Dreams (1972; published in the United Kingdom as *The Infernal Desire Machines of Dr. Hoffman*)
The Passion of New Eve (1977)
Nights at the Circus (1985)
Wise Children (1991)

Children's/Young Adult Fiction

The Donkey Prince (1970)
Miss Z, the Dark Young Lady (1970)
Comic and Curious Cats (1979)
The Music People (1980)
Moonshadow (1982)
Sleeping Beauty and Other Favourite Fairy Tales (1982)
Sea-Cat and Dragon King (2000)

Short Story Collections

Expletives Deleted: Selected Writings (1974)
The Bloody Chamber (1979)
Black Venus's Tale (1980)
Black Venus (1985; also published as *Saints and Strangers*)
Artificial Fire (1988; published in Canada as *Fireworks* and *Love*)
American Ghosts and Old World Wonders (1993)
Burning Your Boats: Collected Short Stories (1995)

Other Important Writings

The Curious Room: Plays, Film Scripts, and an Opera (1996)

Research Sources

Encyclopedias and Handbooks: EF, HDF, SJGF

Biographies and Interviews

Easton, Alison. *Angela Carter.* New York: St. Martin's Press, 2000.
Katsavos, Anna. "An Interview with Angela Carter." *Review of Contemporary Fiction* 14(3) (Fall 1994), pp. 11–17. Available online at http://www.centerforbookculture.org/interviews/interview_carter.html. Last visited January 26, 2008.
Lee, Alison. *Angela Carter*. New York: G.K. Hall, 1997.
Peach, Linden. *Angela Carter*. New York: St. Martin's Press, 1998.

Criticism and Readers' Guides

Bristow, Joseph and Trev Lynn Broughton, eds. *The Infernal Desires of Angela Carter: Fiction, Femininity, Feminism*. New York: Longman, 1997.

Brooke, Patricia. "Lyons and Tigers and Wolves-Oh My! Revisionary Fairy Tales in the Work of Angela Carter." *Critical Survey* 16(1) (2004), pp. 67–88.

Duncker, P. "Re-imagining the Fairytale." *Literature and History* 10:1 (Spring 1984), pp. 3–14.

Eaglestone, Robert. "The Fiction of Angela Carter: The Woman Who Loved to Retell Stories." In Richard J. Lane, Rod Mengham; and Philip Tew, eds., *Contemporary British Fiction.* Malden, MA: Blackwell Publishing, 2003.

Gamble, Sarah. *The Fiction of Angela Carter.* Cambridge, England: Icon Books, 2001.

Gass, Joanne M. "An Angela Carter Bibliography." *Review of Contemporary Fiction* 14(3) (Fall 1994), pp. 94–95.

Ikoma, Natsumi. "Impossible Love: Angela Carter and Her Analysis of the Sixties." *Studies in English Literature* 47 (2006), pp. 143–159.

Karpinsky, Eva C. "Signifying Passion: Angela Carter's Heroes and Villains as a Dystopian Romance." *Utopian Studies* 11(2) (2000), pp. 137–151.

Pearson, Jacqueline. "'These Tags of Literature': Some Uses of Allusion in the Early Novels of Angela Carter." *Critique* 40(3) (Spring 1999), pp. 248–256.

Roemer, Danielle M. and Cristina Bacchilega, eds. *Angela Carter and the Fairy Tale.* Detroit, MI: Wayne State University Press, 2001.

Sceats, Sarah. *Food, Consumption, and the Body in Contemporary Women's Fiction.* Cambridge, England: Cambridge University Press, 2000.

Tucker, Lindsey, ed. *Critical Essays on Angela Carter.* New York: G.K. Hall, 1998.

Yule, Jeffrey V. "Angela Carter." In Darren Harris-Fain, ed., *British Fantasy and Science-Fiction Writers Since 1960. (Dictionary of Literary Biography 261).* Detroit, MI: Gale, 2002, pp. 144–157.

Web Sites

VanderMeer, Jeff. *Angela Carter.* http://www.themodernword.com/scriptorium/carter.html. Last visited January 26, 2008. An extensive critical biography.

Carolyn Janice Cherryh (C.J. Cherryh) (1942–)

Biographical Sketch

Born in Missouri and raised in Oklahoma, Carolyn Janice Cherryh holds two degrees in classics along with many academic honors. She wrote her first novels in time spared from her job as a teacher of Latin in public schools. Living near Spokane, Washington, with fellow fantasy author and artist Jane Fancher, she is an energetic world traveler, avid studier of science, and figure skater.

Cherryh rejects many genre distinctions, emphasizing the shared roots of fantasy and science fiction, and her work blurs those boundaries convincingly. Her world building, for which she is justly famed, draws on expertise in archaeology and linguistics to create rounded cultures with their own rituals and philosophies.

The current generation of writers that never retypes, because there's always a computer file, might try re-entering an unsold novel or two and seeing if they can't be bettered with a thorough re-write. There's a certain mental trap inherent in knowing you've got a back-up, a certain laziness about really getting into the structure of a scene. —(C.J. Cherryh, *SFFWorld.com* interview)

Major Works

Novels

Morgaine series: *Gate of Ivrel* (1976), *Well of Shiuan* (1978), *Fires of Azeroth* (1979), *Exile's Gate* (1988)
Arafel series: *Ealdwood* (1979), *The Dreamstone* (1983), *The Tree of Swords and Jewels* (1983)
Rusalka series: *Rusalka* (1989), *Chernevog* (1990), *Yvgenie* (1991)
Tristan series: *Fortress in the Eye of Time* (1995), *Fortress of Eagles* (1998), *Fortress of Owls* (1998), *Fortress of Dragons* (2000), *Fortress of Ice* (2006)
The Paladin (1988)
The Goblin Mirror (1992)
Faery in Shadow (1993)

Short Story Collections

The Dreaming Tree (1997)
The Collected Short Fiction of C.J. Cherryh (2004)

Research Sources

Encyclopedias and Handbooks: EF, HDF, SJGF

Biographies and Interviews

Nicholls, Stan. "Interview with C.J. Cherryh." *Interzone* #31 (September–October 1989).
"Interview with C.J. Cherryh." *SFFWorld.com.* http://www.sffworld.com/interview/21p0.html. Last visited January 26, 2008.

Criticism and Readers' Guides

Beal, Rebecca S. "C.J. Cherryh's Arthurian Humanism." In Sally K. Slocum, ed., *Popular Arthurian Traditions*. Bowling Green, OH: Popular, 1992, pp. 56–67.
Carmien, Edward, ed. *A Cherryh Odyssey*. San Bernardino, CA: Borgo Press, 2004.
Heidcamp, Bernie. "Responses to the Alien Mother in Post-Maternal Cultures: C.J. Cherryh and Orson Scott Card." *Science-Fiction Studies* 23(3) (November 1996).
Raffel, Burton. "C.J. Cherryh's Fiction." *Literary Review* 44(3) (Spring 2001), pp. 578–591.

Web Sites

C.J. Cherryh's World. http://www.cherryh.com/. Last visited January 26, 2008. Author's Web site. Contains news, booklists, essays, Web log.

Susanna Clarke (1959–)

Biographical Sketch

Before she took the fantasy world by storm in 2004 with her ten-years-in-the-making debut novel, Susanna Mary Clarke spent eight years working in publishing, and two years teaching English in Italy and Spain. Her academic background is in politics, philosophy, and economics; before embarking on serious writing, she attended a fiction seminar held by the Arvon Foundation. She lives in Cambridge, England, with science-fiction novelist Colin Greenland (who taught the seminar), and is good friends with Neil Gaiman, citing him as a strong literary influence.

Written in the most byzantinely elegant Victorian prose imaginable and heavily footnoted, *Jonathan Strange and Mr. Norrell* is a masterpiece of historical fantasy. From the uneasy rapprochement of magic and the scientific method to the equally uneasy treatment of race, class, and gender, Clarke evokes an England that feels both unbearably familiar and unbearably bizarre. The novel inverts the common fantasy trope of a lost Golden Age, emphasizing instead the relentless modernization of magical practice via experiment.

> I don't want to write consciously about the present in a historical story . . . It's hard enough trying to will yourself and the reader back in time without dragging in contemporary issues and attitudes. I don't subscribe to this idea that's going round that what's interesting about the past is how similar it is to the present. What's interesting about the past is how different it is.—(Susanna Clarke, http://www.bookslut.com/features/2005_09_006537.php. Last visited January 26, 2008)

Major Works

Novels

Jonathan Strange and Mr. Norrell (2004)

Short Story Collections

The Ladies of Grace Adieu and Other Stories (2006)

Short Stories

"Stopp't-Clock Yard" (1996)

Research Sources

Encyclopedias and Handbooks: HDF

Biographies and Interviews

Goodwin, Geoffrey H. "An Interview with Susanna Clarke." *Bookslut*. September 2005. http://www.bookslut.com/features/2005_09_006537.php Last visited Janaury 28, 2008.

Kleffel, Rick. http://trashotron.com/agony/audio/susanna_clarke.mp3.Last visited January 30, 2008. Podcast interview (begins with Clarke reading from her novel *Jonathan Strange and Mr. Norrell*).

Miller, Laura. "Fantastic Friends." *Salon.com*. October 8, 2005. http://archive.salon.com/books/int/2005/10/08/gaiman_clarke/index.html. Last visited January 29, 2008.

Murphy, Peter. "Strange Tales and Practical Magic: Susanna Clarke." *The New Review*. http://www.laurahird.com/newreview/susannaclarke.html. Last visited January 27, 2008.

Silver, Steven H. "A Conversation with Susanna Clarke." *SF Site*. October 2004. http://www.sfsite.com/02a/su193.htm. Last visited January 27, 2008.

"Susanna Clarke." *Fast Forward*. November 2004. http://www.fast-forward.tv/audio/audio172.m3u. Last visited January 26, 2008.

"The Susanna Clarke Interview." BBC Nottingham, September 2004. http://www.bbc.co.uk/nottingham/content/articles/2004/09/15/entertainment_books_susanna_clarke_feature.shtml. Last visited January 26, 2008.

"The Three Susanna Clarkes." *Locus* (April 2005), pp. 6–7, 56–57. Excerpts available online at http://www.locusmag.com/2005/Issues/04Clarke.html. Last visited January 26, 2008.

Web Sites

JonathanStrange.com. http://www.jonathanstrange.com/. Last visited January 27, 2008. Author's official Web site. Includes biography, interview, a short story, and a reader's guide.

If you like Susanna Clarke

Written in the most byzantinely elegant Victorian prose imaginable and heavily footnoted, *Jonathan Strange and Mr. Norrell* evokes an England that feels both unbearably familiar and unbearably bizarre. The novel inverts the common fantasy trope of a lost Golden Age, emphasizing instead the relentless modernization of magical practice via experiment.

Then you might like

Lord Dunsany

Dunsany's beautiful, baroque language will appeal to Clarke fans. Any collection of his short stories will appeal, but look especially for stories of the gods of Peganá, a quarrelsome lot who almost prefigure Clarke's magicians.

Eric Rucker Eddison (E. R. Eddison)

The Worm Ouroboros, despite its unprepossessing opening, puts gloriously convoluted prose to the service of a brave quest story with several memorable, larger-than-life characters. Clarke fans will appreciate Eddison's Jacobean homage.

Tanith Lee

Lee's pulpier fiction and young adult works will not appeal to Clarke fans, but the Flat-Earth Cycle (*Night's Master, Death's Master, Delusion's Master, Delirium's Mistress*) is masterfully written, peopled with gods and mortals who suffer as much pain as they deal out.

Hope Mirrlees

Lud-in-the-Mist, a very early fantasy novel, explored the fear of the unfamiliar alongside the decay of the mundane. Its hidebound, unimaginative characters are reminiscent of some of Clarke's.

Mervyn Peake

Peake's Gormenghast series (*Gormenghast*, *Titus Groan*, *Titus Alone*) can compete with Clarke on characterization and adroit, meticulously-composed prose. Its unremitting bleakness and horror fits well alongside Clarke's dark vision of England.

Susan Cooper (1935–)

Biographical Sketch

Susan Mary Cooper grew up in England and holds an English degree from Oxford University. After college, she worked as a journalist while writing fiction in her spare time. She moved to the United States in 1963, expanding her literary output beyond her several novels to movie screenplays and picture books. In 1996 she married well-known actor Hume Cronyn; she currently lives in Fairfield, Connecticut.

Despite her many young adult fans and the young adult-specific honors her works have won, Cooper believes that publishers rather than authors draw boundaries around children's literature; she herself considers her work suitable for adults as well as teens. The much-loved Dark is Rising series catches four young English children up in a centuries-old battle between the forces of light and darkness, in an England that remembers King Arthur and Wayland Smith, Stonehenge and the Holy Grail. The books emphasize courage, loyalty, and kindness, though they do not shy away from unsentimentally cruel depictions of fear and betrayal.

> I start a book knowing it's a road. You know the beginning, you know who's going with you on the road, you know roughly where they're going, but you don't know anything at all (at least I don't) about what's going to happen on the way. You find out as you go along. —(Susan Cooper, online Thompson interview)

Major Works

Children's/Young Adult Fiction

The Dark Is Rising series: *Over Sea, Under Stone* (1965), *The Dark Is Rising* (1973), *Greenwitch* (1974), *The Grey King* (1975), *Silver on the Tree* (1977)
Boggart series: *The Boggart* (1993), *The Boggart and the Monster* (1997)
Seaward (1983)
King of Shadows (1999)
Green Boy (2002)
The Magician's Boy (2005)
Victory (2006)

Other Important Writings

Dreams and Wishes: Essays on Writing for Children (1996)
Dawn of Fear (1970)

Research Sources

Encyclopedias and Handbooks: EF, HDF, SJGF

Biographies and Interviews

Cooper, Susan. "How I Began . . . " *New Welsh Review* 2 (4) (Spring 1990), pp. 19–21.
Henneman, Heidi. "Just Like Magic, Susan Cooper Casts Another Captivating Spell." *Bookpage*. http://www.bookpage.com/0607bp/susan_cooper.html. Last visited January 27, 2008.

Thompson, Raymond H. "Interview with Susan Cooper." In Barbara Tepa Lupack, ed., *Adapting the Arthurian Legends for Children: Essays on Arthurian Juvenilia*. New York: Palgrave Macmillan, 2004, pp. 161–169.

Thompson, Raymond H. "Interview with Susan Cooper." *Interviews with Authors of Modern Arthurian Literature*. http://www.lib.rochester.edu/Camelot/intrvws/cooper.htm. Last visited January 27, 2008.

Criticism and Readers' Guides

Drout, Michael D.C. "Reading the Signs of Light: Anglo Saxonism, Education, and Obedience in Susan Cooper's *The Dark Is Rising*." *Lion and the Unicorn* 21(2) (April 1997), pp. 230–250.

Evans, Emrys. "Children's Novels and Welsh Mythology: Multiple Voices in Susan Cooper and Alan Garner." In Charlotte F. Otten and Gary D. Schmidt, eds., *The Voice of the Narrator in Children's Literature: Insights from Writers and Critics*. New York: Greenwood 1989, pp. 92–100.

Goodrich, Peter. "Magical Medievalism and the Fairy Tale in Susan Cooper's *The Dark Is Rising Sequence*." *Lion and the Unicorn* 12(2) (December 1988), pp. 165–177.

Kutzer, M. Daphne. "Thatchers and Thatcherites: Lost and Found Empires in Three British Fantasies." *Lion and the Unicorn* 22(2) (April 1998), pp. 196–210.

Plante, Raymond L. "Object and Character in *The Dark Is Rising*." *Children's Literature Association Quarterly* 11(1) (Spring 1986), pp. 37–41.

Rutledge, Amelia A. "Susan Cooper." *British Fantasy and Science-Fiction Writers Since 1960. (Dictionary of Literary Biography 261)*. Ed. Darren Harris-Fain. Detroit, MI: Gale, 2002, pp. 177–183.

Spivack, Charlotte. "Susan Cooper's *The Dark Is Rising*." In Barbara Tepa Lupack, ed., *Adapting the Arthurian Legends for Children: Essays on Arthurian Juvenilia*. New York: Palgrave Macmillan, 2004, pp. 139–159.

Web Sites

Scott, Mark. The Lost Land. http://www.thelostland.com/welcome.htm. Last visited January 28, 2008. Fan site. Contains biography, book lists, book descriptions, setting description.

If you like Susan Cooper

Cooper's much loved *Dark Is Rising* series catches four young English children up in a centuries-old battle between the forces of light and darkness, in an England that remembers King Arthur and Wayland Smith, Stonehenge and the Holy Grail. The books emphasize courage, loyalty, and kindness, though they do not shy away from unsentimentally cruel depictions of fear and betrayal.

Then you might like

Lloyd Alexander

Based on Welsh mythology, Alexander's Prydain series tells the story of Taran, an assistant pig keeper who is anxious to prove himself as a hero. The series starts with *The Book of Three*, and continues with *The Black Cauldron, The Castle of Llyr, Taran Wanderer,* and *The High King*. Alexander wrote a number of other fantasy books for young adults, including *The Cat Who Wished to Be a Man* and *The Wizard in the Tree*.

Robert Holdstock

Holdstock's highly allusive work seeks to ring changes on immortal archetypes (notably the Arthurian mythos), recognizing cultural commonalities while respecting the fresh perspectives brought to stock characters by every culture that treats of them. Cooper fans will enjoy *Mythago Wood* and its sequels (*Lavondyss*, *The Bone Forest*, *The Hollowing*, others).

Diana Wynne Jones

Jones' books are full of magic and humor; like Cooper, she pays close attention to the inner lives of young adults. She is probably best known for the Chrestomanci books, including *Charmed Life* and *The Lives of Christopher Chant*, but has written numerous other books, such as *The Merlin Conspiracy* and *Howl's Moving Castle*, which was recently adapted as a motion picture.

Linda Medley

Medley's *Castle Waiting* graphic-novel series shares Cooper's love of exploring and deepening myth and legend. Its characters pop off the page, ranging from Sleeping Beauty's ladies-in-waiting to a stork-headed chamberlain to a bearded-lady nun, brim-full of personality and humor.

Nnedi Okorafor-Mbachu

Like Cooper, Okorafor-Mbachu mines myth and legend for her young adult books, *The Shadow Speaker* and *Zahrah the Windseeker*. Her chosen legends, however, are those of West Africa, and her work will appeal to anyone wishing to expand horizons beyond standard European settings.

Patricia Wrede

Wrede's *Mairelon the Magician* and *Magician's Ward* follow young English guttersnipe Kim as she solves magical mysteries as well as the mysteries of well-bred English conduct alongside lordly magician Mairelon.

Lyon Sprague de Camp (L. Sprague de Camp) (1907–2000) and Catherine Crook (1907–2000)

Biographical Sketch

The extraordinarily prolific writer and editor Lyon Sprague de Camp was trained as an engineer and worked in the Philadelphia Naval Yard alongside Isaac Asimov and Robert E. Heinlein during World War II. He married writer and editor Catherine Crook in 1940 and frequently collaborated with her (particularly in nonfiction) beginning in the 1960s (because many of her collaborations were not credited at publication, we have included her as a coauthor on de Camp's main entry). His ashes are buried with hers in Arlington National Cemetery.

De Camp originally made his name writing the pulpiest of pulp science fiction, complete with bug-eyed monsters menacing bosomy women. His fantasy output divides neatly into light humorous fantasy exemplified by the feckless Howard Shea and sword-and-sorcery sequences modeled on Robert E. Howard, whose Conan series de Camp revived and extended. His biographies of Howard and H.P. Lovecraft (see those entries) are very much worth consulting.

> Most of all, imaginative fiction should be a window through which the reader can view the wonders of the world of today, the glories of the past, and the promise of the future. —(L. Sprague de Camp and Catherine Crook de Camp, *Science Fiction Handbook, Revised*)

Major Works

Novels

Harold Shea series (with Fletcher Pratt and Christopher Stasheff): *The Incomplete Enchanter* (1941), *The Castle of Iron* (1941), *Wall of Serpents* (1953, also published as *The Enchanter Completed*), *The Compleat Enchanter* (1975), *The Intrepid Enchanter* (1988), *Sir Harold and the Gnome King* (1991), *The Enchanter Reborn* (1992), *The Exotic Enchanter* (1995)

Krishna series: *The Tower of Zanid* (1958), *The Hand of Zei* (1963), *The Search for Zei* (1966; also published as *The Floating Continent*), *The Queen of Zamba* (1977), *The Hostage of Zir* (1977), *The Prisoner of Zhamanak* (1982)

Jorian series: *The Goblin Tower* (1968), *The Clocks of Iraz* (1971), *The Fallible Fiend* (1973), *The Unbeheaded King* (1983), *The Honorable Barbarian* (1989), *The Venom Trees of Sunga* (1992)

Short Story Collections

The Tritonian Ring and Other Pusanian Tales (1953)
The Reluctant Shaman: And Other Fantastic Tales (1970)
The Virgin of Zesh and the Tower of Zanid (1982)
Blond Barbarians and Noble Savages (1986)

Other Writings

Literary Swordsmen and Sorcerers: The Makers of Heroic Fantasy (1976)
Science Fiction Handbook (1953, revised edition 1975)

Research Sources

Encyclopedias and Handbooks: EF, HDF, SJGF

Biographies and Interviews

De Camp, L. Sprague and Catherine Crook de Camp. *Time and Chance: An Autobiography*. Hampton Falls, NH: Donald M. Grant, 1996.

Criticism and Readers' Guides

Locus 44(6) (June 2000). Issue dedicated to L. Sprague de Camp shortly after his death.

Laughlin, Charlotte and Daniel J. H. Levack. *De Camp: an L. Sprague de Camp Bibliography*. San Francisco, CA: Underwood/Miller, 1983.

Stableford, Brian M. "L. Sprague de Camp." In Bleiler, Everett Franklin, ed., *Science Fiction Writers: Critical Studies of the Major Authors from the Early Nineteenth Century to the Present Day*. New York: Scribner's, 1982, pp. 179–184.

Winthrop-Young, Geoffrey. "The Rise and Fall of Norse America: Vikings, Vínland, and Alternate History." *Extrapolation* 43(2) (Summer 2002), pp. 188–203.

Web Sites

L. Sprague de Camp.com. http://www.lspraguedecamp.com/. Last visited January 27, 2008. Authors' official Web site, now authorized by their estate. Contains biography, photos, obituaries, newsletter.

Charles de Lint (1951–)

Biographical Sketch

Born in the Netherlands, Charles de Lint has lived all but the first four months of life in various places in Canada; he currently lives in Ontario with artist wife Mary Ann Harris. He initially wanted to be a musician, with strong interest in Celtic music, but as that was not in vogue when he was young, he worked in record stores for well over a decade before his writing career took off. He now records albums with several friends, and dabbles in art as well.

His work, the Newford series in particular, helped establish the urban-fantasy genre, in which the everyday world has an otherworldly counterpart and some characters manage to split their lives between both. The basic theme of the Newford series is the duty and privilege of helping others through life's inevitable rough patches. The novels written under the pen name Samuel M. Key are much darker, intended to stir action against societal evils such as child molestation, against which de Lint is a tireless organizer.

> Write from the heart, what has meaning to you personally; have the patience and discipline to sit down and do it every day whether you're feeling inspired or not; never be afraid to take chances, in fact, make sure you take chances. As soon as you become complacent, you become boring. —(Charles de Lint, *Rose & Thorn* interview)

Major Works

Novels

Cerin Songweaver series: *The Oak King's Daughter* (1979), *A Pattern of Silver Strings* (1981), *Glass Eyes and Cotton Strings* (1982), *In Mask and Motley* (1983), *Laughter in the Leaves* (1984), *The Badger in the Bag* (1985), seven others
Moonheart series: *Moonheart* (1984), *Ascian in Rose* (1986), *Westlin Wind* (1989), *Ghostwood* (1990), *Spiritwalk* (1992)
Jack of Kinrowan series: *Drink Down the Moon* (1990), *Jack And the Giant Killer* (1990), *Jack of Kinrowan* (1995)
Newford series: *Memory and Dream* (1994), *The Ivory And the Horn* (1995), *Dreams Underfoot* (1993), *Trader* (1997), *Someplace to Be Flying* (1997), *Moonlight and Vines* (1998), *Tapping the Dream Tree* (2002), *The Hour Before Dawn* (2005), *The Onion Girl* (2001), *Widdershins* (2006), *Promises to Keep* (2007)
Angel of Darkness (1990) (writing as Samuel M Key)
From a Whisper to a Scream (1992) (writing as Samuel M Key)
Into the Green (1993)
I'll Be Watching You (1993) (writing as Samuel M Key)
Seven Wild Sisters (2001)
Spirits in the Wires (2003)
Medicine Road (2004)
The Blue Girl (2004)
Little (Grrl) Lost (2007)

Graphic novels

A Circle of Cats (with Charles Vess, 2003)

Short Story Collections

Hedgework and Guessery (1991)
Triskell Tales: 22 Years of Chapbooks (1993)
Waifs and Strays (2002)
A Handful of Coppers: Collected Early Stories, Heroic Fantasy (2003)

Quicksilver And Shadow: Collected Early Stories, Volume Two: Contemporary and Dark Fantasy and Science Fiction (2004)
Triskell Tales 2: Six More Years of Chapbooks (2006)

Research Sources

Encyclopedias and Handbooks: EF, HDF, SJGF

Biographies and Interviews

Brignall, Richard B. "Charles de Lint: Mythic Fiction." *Locus* 50(6) (June 2003), pp. 6–7, 73–74. Excerpts available online at http://www.locusmag.com/2003/Issue06/DeLint.html. Last visited January 27, 2008.

Fryer, Jason. "An Interview with Author Charles de Lint." *The Rose & Thorn Literary E-zine*. http://www.theroseandthornezine.com/Profile/CharlesdeLint.html. Last visited January 27, 2008.

Kleffel, Rick. *http://trashotron.com/agony/audio/charles_de_lint.mp3*. Last visited January 27, 2008. Podcast interview.

McCarty, Michael. "Someplace to Be Flying: An Interview with Charles de Lint." *Reflection's Edge*, April 2005. http://www.reflectionsedge.com/archives/apr2005/cdl_mm.html. Last visited Janaury 27, 2008.

McCarty, Michael. "Urbane Fantasist Charles de Lint pioneered the Urban-Fantasy Genre." *SciFi.com*. April 1, 2002. http://www.scifi.com/sfw/interviews/sfw8286.html. Last visited January 27, 2008.

Schellenberg, James and David M. Switzer. "Interview with Charles de Lint." *Challenging Destiny* (2000). http://www.challengingdestiny.com/interviews/delint.htm. Last visited January 27, 2008. Abridged interview previously published in *Challenging Destiny* #9.

Criticism and Readers' Guides

Kondratiev, Alexei. "Tales Newly Told." *Mythlore* 13(2) (Winter 1986), pp. 36, 54.

Mains, Christine. "Old World, New World, Otherworld: Celtic and Native American Influences in Charles de Lint's Moonheart and Forests of the Heart." *Extrapolation* 46(3) (Fall 2005), pp. 338–350.

Web Sites

"Charles de Lint." *SF Site*. http://www.sfsite.com/charlesdelint/index.html. Last visited Janaury 27, 2008. author's Web site. Includes interview reprints, news, reviews, link list.

"An Edition of Green Man Review on Charles de Lint." *Green Man Review*. http://www.greenmanreview.com/oneoffs/charlesdelint.html. Last visited January 27, 2008. Includes interview, reviews, criticism.

If you like Charles de Lint

Charles de Lint is best known for his Newford books (*Someplace to be Flying*, *Moonlight & Vines*, *The Onion Girl*, among others), which follows a varied cast of characters who straddle the divide between mundane Newford and the fantastic faerie realms only a thought away. For de Lint, the unreal is a guide and aid in dealing with the problems and sufferings of daily life.

Then you might like

Emma Bull

Bull has mostly written collaborative novels with other authors (the Liavek books with Will Shetterly, *Freedom and Necessity* with Steven Brust, the Borderland books edited by Terry Windling). These, along with her original urban fantasy *War for the Oaks*, will reward the lover of works that cross between worlds.

John M. Ford

Ford's *The Last Hot Time* follows a doctor with a guilty conscience into a gritty noirish world of motorcycle-riding elves and shifting alliances. His noir setting echoes de Lint's darker moments.

Neil Gaiman

Many of Gaiman's works evoke a similar sense of a mixed magical and mundane realities. Examples include *Neverwhere* and *Stardust*.

Gordon R. Dickson (1923–2001)

Biographical Sketch

Gordon Rupert Dickson spent his childhood in Canada, moving to the United States at age thirteen with his mother after his father's death. After serving in the army during World War II, he earned a BA in creative writing from the University of Minnesota. He wrote over 80 books and 100 short stories, and was a regular at science-fiction conventions, where he enjoyed playing guitar and talking with fans. He died of complications of asthma, which had restricted his activities for several years beforehand.

The humor-fantasy Dragon and the George series concerns a little-regarded scholar named Jim from our world who lands in a world of dragons and magic. The boundaries between that world and this turn out to be porous as real historical figures turn up to wreak amusing havoc. As the series progresses, Jim gains both political power and self-knowledge in his new domain. The much more serious "Call Him Lord," which won the 1966 Nebula for best novelette, crosses science-fiction concepts with a more fantastic milieu in an absorbing yarn about individual and collective responsibility.

> All my books are laboratory pieces. I'm trying something new in each one. They all have the same roots as the morality tale, but what I'm really tying into is something deeper. It's this human urge to reach out for something better and bigger that is driving us all the time as a race. —(Gordon R. Dickson, Minneapolis Star-Tribune obituary. http://www.startribune.com/466/story/34995.html. Last visited Janaury 27, 2008)

Major Works

Novels

Dragon and the George series: *The Dragon and the George* (1976), *The Dragon Knight* (1990), *The Dragon on the Border* (1992), *The Dragon at War* (1992), *The Dragon, the Earl, and the Troll* (1994), *The Dragon and the Djinn* (1995), *The Dragon and the Gnarly King* (1997), *The Dragon in Lyonesse* (1998), *The Dragon and the Fair Maid of Kent* (2000)

Jamie the Red (with Roland Green Eckert, 1984)

Short Story Collections

Beyond the Dar al-Harb (1985)

The Last Dream (1986)

Other Important Writings

"Call Him Lord" (1966)

"The Cloak and the Staff" (1980)

Research Sources

Encyclopedias and Handbooks: EF, SJGF

Criticism and Readers' Guides

Benson, Gordon and Phil Stephensen-Payne. *Gordon R. Dickson, First Dorsai: A Working Bibliography*. San Bernardino, CA: Borgo Press, 1992.

Healy, Kim Coleman. "Martial Illuminations: The Dorsai and the Bloodguard." *New York Review of Science Fiction* 14(12) (August 2002), pp. 1, 8–11.

Thompson, Raymond H. *Gordon R. Dickson: Primary and Secondary Bibliography*. Boston, MA: G.K. Hall, 1983.

Web Sites

Gordon Rupert Dickson Papers. http://special.lib.umn.edu/findaid/xml/mss039.xml. Last visited January 27, 2008. Finding aid for the University of Minnesota's collection of Dickson's private papers; includes biography, collection listing.

Stephen R. Donaldson (1947–)

Biographical Sketch

Stephen Reeder Donaldson lived in India as a child with his father, a medical missionary. After graduating college, he served two years as a conscientious objector in the Vietnam War earning an MA in literature and a karate black belt afterward. After the runaway success of the first Thomas Covenant novels, he stopped teaching and editing for pay. He now lives in Albuquerque, New Mexico.

The controversial but popular Thomas Covenant books surround a leper without faith who crosses over into a fantastic world, saving it several times in spite of his personal crimes and failings. Donaldson had not originally planned to write the Second Chronicles; he claims that editor Lester Del Rey sent him a lot of bad ideas that eventually sparked a good one. He is currently at work on the Last Chronicles.

> When I say that I only create what I need, I'm talking about... Races. Continents. Histories. Even characters and plot developments. But if we're talking about... how many words I should throw at a particular scene or landscape or interaction or emotion—my first-draft answer is: As many as possible... I don't want to risk blocking my creative flow, or missing the crucial detail which brings everything to life... Later, of course, I prune. Sometimes I prune a lot. But I would rather begin with the (easily corrected) mistake of too much than the (potentially fatal) mistake of too little. —(Stephen R. Donaldson, official Web site, January 2007)

Major Works

Novels

Chronicles of Thomas Covenant: *Lord Foul's Bane* (1977), *The Illearth War* (1977), *The Power That Preserves* (1977), *Gilden-Fire* (1981)

Second Chronicles of Thomas Covenant: *The Wounded Land* (1980), *The One Tree* (1982), *White Gold Wielder* (1983)

Last Chronicles of Thomas Covenant: *The Runes of the Earth* (2004), *Fatal Revenant* (2007), two more planned.

Mordant's Need series: *The Mirror of Her Dreams* (1986), *A Man Rides Through* (1987)

Short Story Collections

Daughter of Regals: And Other Stories (1984)
Reave the Just: And Other Tales (1998)

Other Important Writings

Epic Fantasy in the Modern World: A Few Observations (1986)

Research Sources

Encyclopedias and Handbooks: EF, HDF, SJGF

Biographies and Interviews

Adams, Andrew A. "An Interview with Stephen R. Donaldson." October 1991. http://www.personal.rdg.ac.uk/~sis00aaa/SD.html. Last visited January 27, 2008.

"Stephen R. Donaldson: Coming Back to Covenant." *Locus* 53(3) (September 2004), pp. 4–5, 74.

"Stephen R. Donaldson. Interview." *Bookreporter.com*, October 15, 2004. http://www.bookreporter.com/authors/au-donaldson-stephen.asp. Last visited Janaury 27, 2008.

Wilgus, Neal. "Stephen R. Donaldson: Chronicles of the Unbeliever." In Neal Wilgus, ed., *Seven by Seven: Interviews with American Science Fiction Writers of the West and Southwest*. San Bernardino, CA: Borgo, 1996, pp. 65–81.

Criticism and Readers' Guides

Barth, Melissa. *Stephen Donaldson*. Mercer Island, WA: Starmont House, 1991.

Healy, Kim Coleman. "Martial Illuminations: The Dorsai and the Bloodguard." *New York Review of Science Fiction* 14(12) (August 2002), pp. 1, 8–11.

Senior, W.A. "The Significance of Names: Mythopoesis in 'The First Chronicles of Thomas Covenant'." *Extrapolation* 31(3) (Fall 1990), pp. 258–269.

Senior, W.A. *Stephen R. Donaldson's Chronicles of Thomas Covenant: Variations on the Fantasy Tradition*. Kent, OH: Kent State University Press, 1995.

Slethaug, Gordon E. "No Exit: The Hero as Victim in Donaldson." *Mythlore* 11(2) (Autumn 1984), pp. 22–27.

Tiffin, Jessica. "Psychological Fantasy: Donaldson's Thomas Covenant and the Failure of Genre." *Inter Action* 3 (1995), pp. 134–141.

Web Sites

Kevin's Watch: The Official Stephen R. Donaldson Forum. http://kevinswatch.ihugny.com/. Last visited January 27, 2008. Active bulletin board surrounding Donaldson's works.

Steven R. Donaldson Home Page. http://speccoll.library.kent.edu/literature/prose/donaldson/donaldson.html. Last visited January 27, 2008. Inventory of Donaldson's papers, held by Kent State University. Also contains biographical information.

Stephen R. Donaldson: The Official Web Site. http://www.stephenrdonaldson.com/. Last visited January 27, 2008. Contains excerpts from criticism, reviews, bio, interviews, news.

Lord Dunsany (1878–1957)

Biographical Sketch

Irish Lord Edward John Moreton Drax Plunkett, 18th Baron Dunsany, split his time between London and Ireland. After graduating from the English military college Sandhurst, he served his country in the Boer War and both the World Wars. He married Beatrice Child Villiers, who aided him with the practical side of writing; they had one son. Dunsany enjoyed hunting, cricket, chess, and shooting, winning prizes in the latter two sports.

It may seem odd that a resolute atheist would write the entire myth cycle of Pegāna, but closer examination reveals that the gods of Pegāna (as well as in stories such as "The Exiles' Club") are often petty, vindictive, silly, or as powerless as mortals. A strong thread of city-hatred (which may well have influenced Tolkien, who shared it) runs through Dunsany as well. Dunsany's ornate, highly dramatic prose, common to his stories and his single novel as well as his actual plays, rewards reading aloud.

> The source of all imagination is here in our fields, and Creation is beautiful enough for the furthest flights of the poets. What is called realism only falls far from these flights because it is too meticulously concerned with the detail of material; mere inventories of rocks are not poetry; but all the memories of crags and hills and meadows and woods and sky that lie in a sensitive spirit are materials for poetry, only waiting to be taken out, and to be laid before the eyes of such as care to perceive them. —(Lord Dunsany, *Patches of Sunlight*)

Major Works

Novels

Don Rodriguez: Chronicles of Shadow Valley (1922)
The King of Elfland's Daughter (1924)
The Charwoman's Shadow (1926)
The Blessing of Pan (1927)
Curse of the Wise Woman (1933)
The Strange Journeys of Colonel Polders (1950)

Short Story Collections

The Gods of Peganá (1905)
Time and the Gods (1906)
The Sword of Welleran: And Other Tales of Enchantment (1908)
A Dreamer's Tales: And Other Stories (1910)
The Book of Wonder (1912)
Fifty-One Tales (1915)
The Last Book of Wonder (1916; published in the United Kingdom as *Tales of Wonder*)
Tales of Three Hemispheres (1919)
The Man Who Ate the Phoenix (1947)
The Little Tales of Smethers (1952)

Other Important Writings

Plays of Gods and Men (1917)
If (1922)
A Night at an Inn (1916)
Patches of Sunlight (1938)
While the Sirens Slept (1944)
The Sirens Wake (1945)

Research Sources

Encyclopedias and Handbooks: EF, HDF, SJGF

Biographies and Interviews

Amory, Mark. *Biography of Lord Dunsany*. London: Collins, 1972.

Criticism and Readers' Guides

Cantrell, Brent. "British Fairy Tradition in The King of Elfland's Daughter." *Romantist* 4(5) (1980–1981), pp. 51–53.

Davis, Hassoldt, Will Murray, and S.T. Joshi. "Lord Dunsany Divulges." *Studies in Weird Fiction* 25 (Summer 2003), pp. 22–24.

Duperray, Max. "Lord Dunsany Revisited." *Studies in Weird Fiction* 13 (Summer 1993), pp. 10–15.

Harris-Fain, Darren. "Lord Dunsany." In Darren Harris-Bain, ed., *British Fantasy and Science-Fiction Writers, 1918–1960 (Dictionary of Literary Biography 255)*. Detroit, MI: Gale, 2002., pp. 58–72.

Joshi, S.T. and Darrell Schweitzer. *Lord Dunsany: A Bibliography*. Lanham, MD: Scarecrow Press, 1993.

Joshi, S.T. *Lord Dunsany: Master of the Anglo-Irish Imagination*. Westport, CT: Greenwood Press, 1995.

Miller, Laura. "Minor Magus: The Fantastical Writings of Lord Dunsany." *New Yorker* 80(38) (December 6, 2004), pp. 110–116.
Pashka, Linda. "'Hunting for Allegories' in the Prose Fantasy of Lord Dunsany." *Studies in Weird Fiction* 12 (Spring 1993), pp. 19–24.
Saul, George Brandon. "Strange Gods and Far Places: The Short Stories of Lord Dunsany." *Arizona Quarterly* 19 (1963), pp. 197–210.
Schweitzer, Darrell. *Pathways to Elfland: The Writings of Lord Dunsany*. Philadelphia, PA: Owlswick Press, 1989.

Web Sites

Lord Dunsany (1878–1957), Edward John Moreton Drax Plunkett. http://www.dunsany.net/18th.htm. Last visited January 27, 2008. Dunsany family Web site's page for the 18th Earl. Contains bio, brief appreciation, list of in-print books.

David Eddings (1931–) and Leigh Eddings (1937–2007)

Biographical Sketch

Born and raised in Washington state, David Eddings worked as a buyer and analyst for the Boeing corporation, served in the military, and taught college English before turning to writing. Recently he acknowledged that the various series published under his name were coauthored by his wife Judith Leigh Schall Eddings, who died of stroke complications in January 2007. David Eddings refuses to use a computer. He burned his office and most of his manuscripts in an unfortunate accident in early 2007, though he himself was not hurt.

The Eddings' sprawling fantasy epics are coming-of-age tales, pitting mortal monarchs and heroes against gods and demons with fate governing all. Cycles of history form a somewhat artificial mechanism by which the later Malloreon can virtually mirror the plot of the earlier Belgariad.

> Fantasy takes people away from the real world and almost everybody dislikes the real world. —(David Eddings, interview at *sffworld.com*)

Major Works

Novels

Belgariad: *Pawn of Prophecy* (1982), *Queen of Sorcery* (1981), *Magician's Gambit* (1981), *Castle of Wizardry* (1984), *Enchanters' End Game* (1984), *Belgarath the Sorcerer* (1995), *Polgara the Sorceress* (1997), *The Rivan Codex* (1998)

Malloreon: *Guardians of the West* (1985), *King of the Murgos* (1988), *Demon Lord of Karanda* (1988), *Sorceress of Darshiva* (1989), *The Seeress of Kell* (1991)

Elenium: *The Diamond Throne* (1989), *The Ruby Knight* (1990), *The Sapphire Rose* (1991)
Tamuli: *Domes of Fire* (1992), *The Shining Ones* (1993), *The Hidden City* (1994)
The Redemption of Althalus (2000)

Research Sources

Encyclopedias and Handbooks: EF, HDF, SJGF

Biographies and Interviews

"Interview with David Eddings." *SFFWorld.com*. http://www.sffworld.com/interview/170p0.html. Last visited January 27, 2008.

Criticism and Readers' Guides

Douglas, Carole Nelson. "David Eddings." In E.A. Des Chenes and Diane Telgen, eds., *Authors & Artists for Young Adults*. New York: Gale Research, 1996.

Web Sites

Persson, Jack. *Jack's David and Leigh Eddings Site*. http://www.eddingschronicles.com/. Last visited January 27, 2008. Fan site. Contains booklists, news, forums, links, character lists.

Eric Rucker Eddison (E.R. Eddison) (1882–1945)

Biographical Sketch

Eric Rucker Eddison grew up writing; at college in Cambridge, he taught himself Icelandic so that he could read sagas. He worked at the Board of Trade, achieving several promotions and honors, until 1938, when he left London for Marlborough to devote all his time to his writing and his family.

He is most famed for *The Worm Ouroboros*, an aristocratic saga written in meticulously-composed faux-Jacobean prose, which is about four brothers who risk their lives and their lands for the glory of war and quest, and their sometimes-evil, sometimes-honorable enemies. Notable as well for its unabashedly bellicose philosophy and two or three intriguing characterizations, the book impressed Tolkien and C.S. Lewis and is a lasting favorite. The Zimiamvia trilogy is an extensive elaboration of Eddison's philosophies, less plotted and less elaborately written; *Styrbiorn the Strong* and *Egil's Song* are fantasy recreations of the Icelandic sagas Eddison loved.

> I had rather a hundred people should read my books again and again than a million read them once and be done with them. —(E.R. Eddison, personal letter)

Major Works

Novels

The Worm Ouroboros (1922)
Styrbiorn the Strong (1926)
Egil's Song (1930)
Zimiamvia trilogy: *Mistress of Mistresses: A Vision of Zimiamvia* (1935), *A Fish Dinner in Memison* (1941), *The Mezentian Gate* (1958)

Research Sources

Encyclopedias and Handbooks: EF, HDF, SJGF

Criticism and Readers' Guides

Flieger, Verlyn. "The Man Who Loved Women: Aspects of the Feminine in Eddison's Zimiamvia." *Mythlore* 13(3) (Spring 1987), pp. 29–32.
Flieger, Verlyn. "The Ouroboros Principle: Time and Love in Zimiamvia." *Mythlore* 15(4) (Summer 1989), pp. 43–46.
Harris-Fain, Darren. "E.R. Eddison." In Darren Harris-Bain, ed., *British Fantasy and Science-Fiction Writers, 1918–1960 (Dictionary of Literary Biography 255).* Detroit, MI: Gale, 2002., pp. 73–81.
Oakes, David A. "The Eternal Circle: The Beginning and Ending of E.R. Eddison's The Worm Ouroboros." *Extrapolation* 40(2) (Summer 1999), pp. 125–128.
Pesch, Helmut W. "The Sign of the Worm: Images of Death and Immortality in the Fiction of E.R. Eddison." In Carl B. Yoke and Donald M. Hassler, eds., *Death and the Serpent: Immortality in Science Fiction and Fantasy*. Westport, CT: Greenwood, 1985, pp. 91–101.
Schuyler, William M., Jr. "E.R. Eddison's Metaphysics of the Hero." *New York Review of Science Fiction* 31 (March 1991), pp. 12–17.
Wolfe, Gary K. "Beagle and Eddison: A Special Issue." *Journal of the Fantastic in the Arts* 1(3) (1988).

Web Sites

Walker, Eric. "Science Fiction and Fantasy Books by E.R. Eddison." http://greatsfandf.com/AUTHORS/EREddison.php. Last visited January 27, 2008. Extensive literary appreciation by a fan.

Kate Elliott (1958–)

Biographical Sketch

Alis A. Rasmussen grew up in Oregon, moving to California to attend Mills College. She took up karate, as well as broadsword combat in the Society for

Creative Anachronism, in which group she met archaeologist Jay Silverstein, whom she married and with whom she has three children. They now live in Hawaii, traveling in Europe and Mesoamerica. After the Highroad series did not sell as well as her publisher would have liked, Rasmussen adopted her pen name, and her book sales took off. Her books are well-researched and credibly imagined, with complex and layered cultures. The Crown of Stars series chronicles a terrible magical and religious culture-clash between two races, which a prince, a sorceress, and a foster child must navigate to make lives for themselves.

> Everything I write is based in real-world research in the sense that the cultural and technological details have to be consistent with the level of social organization and the level of technology available to the various societies within the novel. It's also important to make an imaginary culture seem "real" in the sense that it should all hold together without elements that jump out at the reader as being out of place or anachronistic.—(Kate Elliott, http://www.arwz.com/zineinterviewKE.html. Last visited January 27, 2008)

Major Works

Novels

Crown of Stars series: *King's Dragon* (1997), *Prince of Dogs* (1998), *The Burning Stone* (1999), *Child of Flame* (2000), *The Gathering Storm* (2003), *In the Ruins* (2005), *The Crown of Stars* (2006)

Highroad series: *A Passage of Stars* (1990), *Revolution's Shore* (1990), *The Price of Ransom* (1990)

The Labyrinth Gate (1988)

The Golden Key (with Melanie Rawn and Jennifer Roberson, 1996)

Spirit Gate (2007)

Short stories

"My Voice Is In My Sword" (1994)

"With God to Guard Her" (1995)

"A Simple Act of Kindness" (1996)

"The Gates of Joriun" (1997)

"Making the World Live Again" (1997)

Research Sources

Encyclopedias and Handbooks: EF, HDF

Biographies and Interviews

Allen, Moira. "An Eye for Detail: An Interview with Kate Elliot." *Writing World*. http://www.writing-world.com/sf/elliott.shtml. Last visited January 30, 2008.

Allen, Moira. "What's In a Name?" *Writing World*, 2000. http://www.writing-world.com/sf/name.shtml. Last visited January 27, 2008.

Kleffel, Rick. http://trashotron.com/agony/audio/elliott_rawn_2006_1.mp3 and http://trashotron.com/agony/audio/elliott_rawn_2006_2.mp3. Last visited January 30, 2008. Podcast interview with Elliott and Melanie Rawn.

Slevinski, Sarah K. "A New Series Brings New Horizons from Contemporary Fantasist, Kate Elliott." *Alternative Reality Web Zine*. http://www.arwz.com/zineinterviewKE.html. Last visited Janaury 28, 2008.

Web Sites

Kate Elliott. http://www.sff.net/people/Kate.Elliott/world.html. Last visited January 27, 2008. Author's official Web site. Contains book news, essays, reviews by the author, links.

The Official Kate Elliott Online Forums. http://p199.ezboard.com/bkateelliott. Last visited January 27, 2008.

Author-approved fan site. *But Enough About Me*. http://kateelliott.livejournal.com. Last visited January 27, 2008. Author's personal Web log.

DeepGenre. http://www.deepgenre.com/wordpress/. Last visited January 27, 2008.

A collaborative authors' and artists' web log including Kate Elliott.

Carol Emshwiller (1921–)

Biographical Sketch

Carol Fries Emshwiller grew up in Michigan—where her father was professor of English and linguistics—and in France. She was stationed in Italy with the Red Cross during World War II. She met and married artist and science-fiction illustrator Ed Emshwiller in art school, and with him participated heavily in the 1960s avant-garde artistic movement. Emshwiller winters in New York City, where she teaches at New York University School of Continuing Education, and spends her summers in the Sierra Mountains in California.

The satirical *Carmen Dog*, described by Ursula K. LeGuin as "perhaps the funniest and the cruellest of her books, a sort of feminist *Candide*," inspired the creation of the James M. Tiptree Award for gender-aware speculative fiction. In it, women are becoming animals and vice versa; the innocent heroine Pooch, formerly a golden setter, must learn to protect herself and her children in the human world. Her award-winning short stories combine Borgesian magical realism with a feminist sensibility.

> About my writing, a lot of people don't seem to understand how planned and plotted even the most experimental of my stories are. I'm not interested in stories where anything can happen at any time. I set up clues to foreshadow what will happen and what is foreshadowed does happen. I try to have all, or most

of the elements in the stories, linked to each other. —(Carol Emshwiller, http://www.sfwa.org/members/emshwiller/. Last visited January 27, 2008)

Major Works

Novels

Carmen Dog (1988)
Venus Rising (1992)
Mister Boots (2005)

Short Story Collections

Verging on the Pertinent (1989)
The Start of the End of It All: And Other Stories (1990)
Joy in Our Cause: Short Stories (1990)
Report to the Men's Club: Stories (2002)
I Live with You (2005)

Research Sources

Encyclopedias and Handbooks: EF, SJGF

Biographies and Interviews

Finn, Joseph J. "An Interview with Carol Emshwiller." *Bookslut.* http://www.bookslut.com/features/2003_07_000135.php. Last visited January 27, 2008.

Holliday, Liz. "Carol Emshwiller." *Science Fiction Chronicle* 14(4) (January 1993), pp. 5, 26–27.

Weekes, Patrick. "Interview: Carol Emshwiller." *Strange Horizons* (April 30, 2001). http://www.strangehorizons.com/2001/20010430/interview.shtml. Last visited January 27, 2008.

Wexler, Robert Freeman. "Carol Emshwiller Interview." *Fantastic Metropolis.* http://www.fantasticmetropolis.com/i/emshwiller/full/. Last visited January 28, 2008.

Criticism and Readers' Guides

Duchamp, L. Timmel. "Carol Emshwiller: An Appreciation." May 2003. http://ltimmel.home.mindspring.com/emshwiller.html. Last visited January 28, 2008.

Helford, Elyce Rae. "'I'm Wondering What Sort of Misunderstanding Is Happening Right Now': Poststructuralism, French Feminism, and Carol Emshwiller's 'The Start of the End of It All.'" *Foundation* 74 (Autumn 1998), pp. 67–79.

Martini, Adrienne. "The Most Virginia Woolf of SF Writers." *Bookslut* (May 2005). http://www.bookslut.com/specfic_floozy/2005_05_005636.php. Last visited January 28, 2008.

Wheeler, Pat. "Metamorphoses of the Female Subject: Bodily Transformations in Carol Emshwiller's *Carmen Dog* and Linda Jaivin's *Rock N Roll Babes from Outer Space*." *Foundation* 31(84) (Spring 2002), pp. 36–47.

Web Sites

Carol Emshwiller's Official Web Page. http://www.sfwa.org/members/emshwiller/. Contains biography, bibliography, essays, reviews, fiction. Last visited January 28, 2008.

Raymond E. Feist (1945–)

Biographical Sketch

Raymond Elias Feist was born and raised in Southern California, and currently lives in San Diego with his children. He was educated at the University of California, San Diego, where he graduated with honors in Communication Arts. He is a collector of wine, biographies, history, and football memorabilia.

His novels about Midkemia grew out of a long-running Dungeons and Dragons role-playing campaign, in which Feist expanded the setting because he found the given game settings too constricting. The initial series chronicles the invasion of Midkemia by the expansionistic Tsurani through a rift between worlds; later, that rift is closed, abandoning many Tsurani in Midkemia. The central character Pug grows from an unheeded castle servant to a mighty magician.

> I don't write fantasy; I write historical novels about an imaginary place. At least that's how I look at it. —(Raymond E. Feist, http://www.raymondfeistbooks.com/midkemia.htm. Last visited January 28, 2008)

Major Works

Novels

Riftwar series: *Magician: Apprentice* (1982), *Magician: Master* (1982), *Silverthorn* (1985), *A Darkness at Sethanon* (1985), *Prince of the Blood* (1989), *The King's Buccaneer* (1989)

Serpentwar Saga: *Shadow of a Dark Queen* (1994), *Rise of a Merchant Prince* (1995), *Rage of a Demon King* (1995), *Shards of a Broken Crown* (1998)

Riftwar Legacy series: *Krondor: The Betrayal* (1998), *Krondor: The Assassins* (1999), *Krondor: Tear of the Gods* (1999)

Conclave of Shadows series: *Talon of the Silver Hawk* (2002), *King of Foxes* (2003), *Exile's Return* (2004)

Darkwar series: *Flight of the Nighthawks* (2005), *Into a Dark Realm* (2006), *Wrath of a Mad God* (2007)

Faerie Tale (1988)

Short Story Collections

The Wood Boy/The Burning Man (with Tad Williams, Sean J. Jordan, and Robin Gillespie, 2005)

Research Sources

Encyclopedias and Handbooks: EF, HDF, SJGF

Biographies and Interviews

Auden, Sandy. "A Feisty Temperament: An Interview with Raymond E. Feist." *SFSite.com*. http://www.sfsite.com/12b/sarf214.htm. Last visited January 29, 2008.

Brunton, Michael. "Raymond E. Feist Interview." http://www.crydee.com/?q=node/2420. Last visited January 29, 2008.

White, Claire E. "A Conversation with Raymond Feist." *Writers Write: The Internet Writing Journal*. http://www.writerswrite.com/journal/mar00/feist.htm. Last visited January 28, 2008.

Web Sites

Askren, R.M. *Elvandar*. http://www.elvandar.com/. Last visited January 28, 2008. Contains maps and a gazetteer of Feist's world of Midkemia.

The Hall of Worlds. http://www.hallofworlds.net/. Last visited January 28, 2008. Contains a fan forum and a news/events Web log.

The Raymond E. Feist Reference Pages. http://www.crydee.com/. Last visited January 28, 2008. Contains biography, events, forum, interviews, mailing-list archives.

Raymond Feist Books. http://www.raymondfeistbooks.com/. Last visited January 28, 2008. Official author site, maintained by publisher HarperCollins.

John M. Ford (1957–2006)

Biographical Sketch

Polymath and wordplay artist John M. Ford was born and raised in Indiana. He worked for *Isaac Asimov's Science Fiction Magazine* in New York for several years before moving to Minneapolis, where he lived with partner Elise Matthesen until his death in 2006. Ford also worked as a game designer and computer consultant; he enjoyed science-fiction conventions as long as his health permitted his attendance.

Ford's "Winter Solstice, Camelot Station," which recasts the Round Table as a train station, is the only poem to ever win the World Fantasy Award for best short fiction. His poignant response to the September 11, 2001, terrorist attacks, "110

Stories," has been multiply reprinted. His genre-defying novels' central theme is growing up, learning one's place in the world and accepting responsibility for one's actions and predilections.

> [F]antasy doesn't make different stories possible, but sometimes it makes different outcomes possible, through the literalization of metaphor that is one of the key things fantasy does. Moral strength can change the real world—and a good thing, too—but in a fantastic story it can make dramatic, transformative, immediate changes. The idea that such transformations always have a price is what keeps fantasy from being morally empty—magic may save time and reduce staff requirements, but it offers no discounts.—(John M. Ford, http://www.well.com/conf/inkwell.vue/topics/126/John-M-Ford-The-Last-Hot-Time-page01.html. Last visited January 28, 2008)

Major Works

Novels

Web of Angels (1980)
The Princes of the Air (1982)
The Dragon Waiting (1983)
The Last Hot Time (2000)

Short Story Collections

Casting Fortune (1989)
From the End of the Twentieth Century (1997)
Heat of Fusion: And Other Stories (2004)

Other Important Writings

Timesteps (1993)

Research Sources

Encyclopedias and Handbooks: EF, SJGF

Biographies and Interviews

Castellani, Linda. "John M. Ford: The Last Hot Time." *The Well*, October 2001. http://www.well.com/conf/inkwell.vue/topics/126/John-M-Ford-The-Last-Hot-Time-page01.html. Last visited January 28, 2008.

Mohanraj, Mary Anne and Fred Bush. "Interview: John M. Ford." *Strange Horizons* (April 29, 2002). http://www.strangehorizons.com/2002/20020429/interview.shtml. Last visited January 28, 2008.

Criticism and Readers' Guides

Miller, Chris L. "Image and Plot: An Anatomy of John M. Ford's 'Green Is the Color.'" *New York Review of Science Fiction* 6 (February 1989), pp. 15–17.

Web Sites

Against Entropy. http://community.livejournal.com/nemesis_draco/. Last visited January 28, 2008. Memorial community, containing news, tributes, and discussion of Ford's work.

Nielsen Hayden, Teresa, Patrick Nielsen Hayden, and Jim Macdonald. "Mike Ford: Occasional Works." http://nielsenhayden.com/makinglight/archives/008735.html. Last visited January 28, 2008. Compilation of Ford's comments to the *Making Light* web log. Includes poetry, politics, observations on writing.

Alan Dean Foster (1946–)

Biographical Sketch

Alan Dean Foster grew up in California, and has a bachelor's degree in political science and a master's in cinema. He worked briefly as an advertising copywriter before August Derleth unexpectedly published a fan letter Foster wrote as a short story, launching a career that went full-time in 1978. Since then, Foster has occasionally taught screenwriting, film history, and literature. Foster and his wife JoAnn Oxley currently live in Prescott, Arizona, and are avid world travelers.

The Spellsinger series, Foster's major foray into humorous fantasy, lands a University of California, Los Angeles law student in a world of talking bipedal animals. Budding musician "Jon-Tom" learns to use his voice to work magic. Foster is also popular for his movie novelizations.

> I'm the direct descendent of the itinerant yarn-spinner who traveled from camp to camp, telling tales for his supper. A great majority of my novels, if not my short fiction, is designed to entertain. Not to preach, not to lecture, but to transport the audience to another place and time and make them forget the often numbing and disheartening events of everyday life.—(Alan Dean Foster, http://www.scifi.com/sfw/issue251/interview.html. Last visited January 28, 2008)

Major Works

Novels

Spellsinger series: *Spellsinger* (1983), *The Hour of the Gate* (1983), *The Day of the Dissonance* (1984), *The Moment of the Magician* (1984), *The Paths of the Perambulator* (1985), *The Time of the Transference* (1986), *Chorus Skating* (1994), *Son of Spellsinger* (1993)

Journeys of the Catechist series: *Carnivores of Light and Darkness* (1998), *Into the Thinking Kingdoms* (1998), *A Triumph of Souls* (2000)
Clash of the Titans (1981)
Krull (1983)
Shadowkeep (1984)
Maori (1988)
Kingdoms of Light (2001)

Research Sources

Encyclopedias and Handbooks: EF, HDF, SJGF

Biographies and Interviews

Cobb, Stephen Euin. *The Future and You.* http://www.thefutureandyou.libsyn.com/?search_string=foster&Submit=Search&search=1. Last visited January 28, 2008. Series of podcasts involving Alan Dean Foster.
Hennessey-DeRose, Cristopher and Michael McCarty. "Interview." *Sci-Fi.com.* http://www.scifi.com/sfw/issue251/interview.html. Last visited January 28, 2008.
Hunt, Stephen. "Fostering Science Fiction: Alan Dean Foster Interviewed." *SFCrowsnest.comi* (August 2002). http://www.sfcrowsnest.com/sfnews2/02_aug/news0802_4.shtml. Last visited January 28, 2008.
White, Claire E. "A Conversation with Alan Dean Foster." *Writers Write: The Internet Writing Journal* (April 2002). http://www.writerswrite.com/journal/apr02/foster.htm. Last visited January 28, 2008.

Web Sites

Alan Dean Foster. http://www.alandeanfoster.com/. Last visited January 28, 2008. Author's official web site. Contains biography, news, maps, links.

Esther Friesner (1951–)

Biographical Sketch

Esther Mona Friesner-Stutzman holds a PhD in Spanish from Yale, and taught there for several years until writing and editing became her full-time endeavor. She is a regular guest at conventions (where she practices "divination" by hamster-wheel, which she calls "cheeblemancy"), and wrote a long-running advice column for *Pulphouse* magazine. She lives in Connecticut with her husband and two children.

Friesner is best known for her humorous tales. While never savage, her humor is often pointed, requiring readers to question their cultural assumptions. When she chooses to be serious, Friesner's stories are often poignantly emotional. She is also an indefatigable editor of anthologies, most notably the lighthearted Chicks in Chainmail series.

I'm not a funny writer or a serious writer or a fantasy writer or a poet or a playwright. I'm a writer. Either I write in the vein that a particular story demands or I wind up writing a less than satisfactory (for me) story. —(Esther Friesner, http://www.fmwriters.com/Visionback/issue7/Interview.htm. Last visited January 28, 2008)

Major Works

Novels

Twelve Kingdoms series: *Mustapha and His Wise Dog* (1985), *Spells of Mortal Weaving* (1986), *The Witchwood Cradle* (1987), *The Water King's Laughter* (1989),

Demon series: *Here Be Demons* (1988), *Demon Blues* (1989), *Hooray for Hellywood* (1990)

Tim Desmond series: *Gnome Man's Land* (1991), *Harpy High* (1991), *Unicorn U* (1992)

Majyk series: *Majyk by Accident* (1993), *Majyk by Hook or Crook* (1993), *Majyk by Design* (1994)

Harlot's Ruse (1986)
The Silver Mountain (1986)
Druid's Blood (1988)
It's Been Fun (1991)
Ecce Hominid (1991)
Yesterday We Saw Mermaids (1992)
The Wishing Season (1993)
The Sherwood Game (1994)
The Psalms of Herod (1995)
Child of the Eagle (1996)
The Sword of Mary (1996)
Nobody's Princess (2007)

Short Story Collections

Up the Wall: And Other Stories (1999)
Death and the Librarian: And Other Stories (2002)
Bit Players (with Jay Caselberg, 2005)

Research Sources

Encyclopedias and Handbooks: EF, HDF, SJGF

Biographies and Interviews

Gifford, Lazette. "An Interview with Esther Friesner." *Vision: A Resource for Writers*. 2002. http://www.fmwriters.com/Visionback/issue7/Interview.htm. Last visited January 28, 2008.

Starr, Richard. "A Conversation with Esther Friesner." *Science Fiction Chronicle* 16(4) (February–March 1995), pp. 5, 30–32.

Web Sites

Esther Friesner. http://www.sff.net/people/e.friesner/. Last visited January 28, 2008. Author's official Web site. Contains events, biography, bibliography, link to newsgroup.

Neil Gaiman (1960–)

Biographical Sketch

Born in Portchester, Hampshire, England, and now residing in the Great Lakes region of the United States, Neil Gaiman came to prominence with the award-studded publication of the comic series *The Sandman*, whose title character, an anthropomorphic personification of dreams and stories, struggles to accept love and change. Gaiman began his writing career as an interview journalist, shifting to comics after forming a friendship with well-known British comics writer Alan Moore. Since then, Gaiman has written novels, children's books, screenplays, poetry, and short fiction, as well as several other short comics series. Gaiman tours extensively to meet and speak to fans, and maintains a popular web log chronicling those travels as well as his writing life. He is married and has three children.

Gaiman's work has won too many awards to list. Most notably, *Sandman* won nine Eisner Awards and the World Fantasy Award for best short story. *American Gods* won both the Hugo and Nebula awards for best novel.

> Don't mistake the opinions of characters in a book for either the opinions of the author or for any kind of objective truth. —(Neil Gaiman, http://www.neilgaiman.com/faqs/completefaq. Last visited January 28, 2008)

Major Works

Novels

Good Omens (with Terry Pratchett 1990)
Neverwhere (1997)
American Gods (2001)
Anansi Boys (2005)

Graphic Novels

The Sandman #1–75. With various artists (1991–1997)
Books of Magic. With various artists (1993)
Death: The High Cost of Living. (1994, with Chris Bachalo)

Death: The Time of Your Life. (1997, with Chris Bachalo)
Stardust (Being a Romance of the Realm of Faerie). (1998, with Charles Vess)
Sandman: The Dream Hunters. (1999, with Yoshitaka Amano)
Endless Nights. With various artists (2003)

Short Story Collections

Angels and Visitations (1993)
Smoke and Mirrors (1998)
Fragile Things: Short Fictions and Wonders (2006)

Children's/Young Adult Fiction

Stardust (1999)
Coraline (2002)
The Wolves in the Walls. With Dave McKean. (2003)

Other Important Writings

Gaiman, Neil and Kim Newman. *Ghastly Beyond Belief: The Science Fiction and Fantasy Book of Quotations*. London: Newman, 1985.

Research Sources

Encyclopedias and Handbooks: EF, HDF

Biographies and Interviews

Marnell, Blair. "Eternal Dreaming." *All the Rage*, October 2005. http://www.silverbulletcomicbooks.com/rage/112897468846116.htm. Last visited January 28, 2008.

McCabe, Joseph. "Hanging Out with the Dream King: Neil Gaiman on Comics." *Science Fiction Chronicle* 24(11) (October 2002), pp. 42–47.

"Neil Gaiman." *Fast Forward*. September/October 2006. http://www.fast-forward.tv/audio/audio194.m3u. Last visited January 28, 2008.

Olson, Ray. "The Booklist Interview: Neil Gaiman." *Booklist*, August 2003, p. 19.

Rabinovitch, Dina. "A writer's Life: Neil Gaiman." *The Daily Telegraph*, December 11, 2005. http://www.telegraph.co.uk/arts/main.jhtml?xml=/arts/2005/12/11/bokgaiman.xml. Last visited January 30, 2008-

Criticism and Readers' Guides

Allen, Bruce. "The Dreaming of Neil Gaiman." In *Contemporary Literary Criticism*. Farmington Hills, MI: Thomson Gale, 2004, p. 195

Bender, Hy. *The Sandman Companion*. DC Comics, 1999.

D'Elia, Jenifer. "Sometimes There Is Nothing You Can Do: A Critical Summary of Neil Gaiman's Neverwhere." *Studies in Fantasy Literature: A Scholarly Journal for the Study of the Fantasy Genre*, 1 (2004), pp. 29–37.

Ekman, Stefan. "Down, Out and Invisible in London and Seattle." *Foundation: The International Review of Science Fiction* 34(94) (Summer 2005), pp. 64–74.
Kwitney, Alisa. *The Sandman: King of Dreams*. Introduction by Neil Gaiman. San Francisco, CA: Chronicle Books, 2003.
McConnell, Frank. "Epic Comics: Neil Gaiman's Sandman." *Commonweal* 122(18) (October 20, 1995), pp. 21–22.
"Neil Gaiman: Of Monsters and Miracles." *Locus: The Newspaper of the Science Fiction Field*, 42(4)5April 1999), pp. 4, 66–68.
Pratt, Tim. "Of Explorers and Button Eyes: Neil Gaiman's Coraline." *Strange Horizons* (online magazine) (July 1, 2002). http://strangehorizons.com/2002/20020701/coraline.shtml. Last visited January 28, 2008.
Sanders, Joe. "Neil Gaiman." In Darren Harris-Fain, ed., *British Fantasy and Science-Fiction Writers Since 1960. (Dictionary of Literary Biography 261).* Detroit, MI: Gale, 2002, pp. 196–204.
Sanders, Joe. "Of Storytellers and Stories in Gaiman and Vess's 'A Midsummer Night's Dream.'" *Extrapolation: A Journal of Science Fiction and Fantasy*, 45(3) (Fall 2004), pp. 237–248.
Worcester, Kent. "The Graphic Novels of Neil Gaiman." *In Contemporary Literary Criticism*. Farmington Hills, MI: Thomson Gale, 2004, p. 195.
Zaleski, Jeff. "Comics! Books! Films!: The Arts and Ambitions of Neil Gaiman." *Publishers Weekly* 250(30) (July 28, 2003), pp. 46–57.

Web Sites

The Dreaming: The Neil Gaiman Page. March 21, 2006. http://www.holycow.com/dreaming/. Last visited January 28, 2008. Fan site. Includes news, extensive bibliography, and linklists.

Neil Gaiman's Official Website. March 21, 2006. http://www.neilgaiman.com/. Last visited January 28, 2008. Includes author's Web log, FAQs, biography.

If you like Neil Gaiman

Gaiman leapt to prominence with his *Sandman* series for Vertigo Comics, which wove the DC comics universe together with Gaiman's unique vision of the seven Endless, personifications of eternal human verities. He then turned to writing fantasies with unique twists on traditional or otherwise well-known characters and situations (*Stardust, Neverwhere, American Gods, Anansi Boys*).

Then you might like

Peter S. Beagle

Peter S. Beagle's beloved *The Last Unicorn* follows a mythical creature and her more mundane mortal friends through a world grimly determined to exploit and destroy myths. That not all myths are safe or wholesome is the theme of *The Innkeeper's Song* and its book of related stories *Giant Bones*. The intersection and interactions of the mundane and the fantastic is a central conceit in both Gaiman and Beagle.

Emma Bull

Bull has mostly written collaborative novels with other authors (the Liavek books with Will Shetterly, *Freedom and Necessity* with Steven Brust, and the Borderland books edited by Terry Windling). These, along with her original urban fantasy *War for the Oaks*, will reward the lover of works that cross between worlds.

John M. Ford

Ford's *The Last Hot Time* follows a doctor with a guilty conscience into a gritty noirish world of motorcycle-riding elves and shifting alliances. His cross of horror with mundanity will appeal to fans of *Sandman*.

Linda Medley

Medley's *Castle Waiting* graphic-novel series shares Gaiman's themes of self-exploration and self-acceptance. Its characters pop off the page, ranging from Sleeping Beauty's ladies-in-waiting to a stork-headed chamberlain to a bearded-lady nun, brim-full of personality and humor.

Philip Pullman

Pullman's fantasy books are often enjoyed by adults as well. The His Dark Materials trilogy, which is set partly in an alternate universe (*The Golden Compass, The Subtle Knife*, and *The Amber Spyglass*), mirrors Gaiman's sense of responsibility.

Randall Garrett (1927–1987), and Vicki Ann Heydron (1945–)

Biographical Sketch

Gordon Randall Philip David Garrett used a tremendous number of pseudonyms throughout his writing career, several of them combinations of his given names. Born in Missouri, he entered the Marine Corps and after his time there worked as an industrial chemist. He lived in New York, California, and Texas before settling in the San Francisco area with his second wife and writing collaborator, author Vicki Ann Heydron. He was one of the founders of the Society for Creative Anachronism. Garrett became ill with encephalitis in 1979, was institutionalized two years later, and died of his illness in 1987.

The Lord Darcy series penned by Garrett inhabits an alternate history in which Great Britain and France, united originally by Richard the Lion-Hearted, formed an empire that persists into the twentieth century; magic in this world is the chief scientific endeavor. The novels and stories are mysteries, Lord Darcy being the Chief Criminal Investigator of Normandy. The Gandalara Cycle, much of which was written by Heydron according to outlines by Garrett, concerns a language professor who shares a telepathic link with a not-quite-human individual in an Arabian-Nights-like setting far in the earth's past.

Major Works

Novels

Lord Darcy series: *Too Many Magicians* (1966), *The Napoli Express* (1979), *Lord Darcy Investigates* (1981)

Gandalara Cycle: *The Steel of Raithskar* (1981), *The Glass of Dyskornis* (1982), *The Bronze of Eddarta* (1983), *The Well of Darkness* (1983), *The Search for Ka* (1984), *The River Wall* (1986)

Research Sources

Encyclopedias and Handbooks: EF, SJGF

Web Sites

Willick, George C. "Spacelight: Randall Garrett." http://www.gcwillick.com/Spacelight/garrett.html. Last visited January 30, 2008. Substantial biography.

Zweig, Dani. "Belated Reviews PS #6: Randall Garrett and Lord Darcy." http://www-users.cs.york.ac.uk/susan/sf/dani/PS_006.htm. Last visited January 28, 2008. Extended review of the Lord Darcy books.

Mary Gentle (1956–)

Biographical Sketch

Mary Rosalyn Gentle was born in Sussex, England. She worked several odd jobs before becoming a writer; shortly thereafter, she returned to school, eventually earning a master's degree in 17th-century studies and another in war studies. She now lives with her amateur-historian partner Dean Wayland.

Gentle's work is heavily influenced by her research interests. "Scientific" magic in the Rat Lords series follows very closely on seventeenth-century ideas about alchemy and magic, and the books contain many literary and historical allusions, obvious and obscure alike. Her books are hard-edged and sometimes cynical or even outright pessimistic; the Golden Witchbreed series ends with a hint of the destruction of the world. She is also frustrated with by-the-numbers fantasy tropes, as her parody *Grunts!*, which reverses the usual hero and villain racial roles found in post-Tolkien fantasy, makes clear.

> It is pure technique: almost never, in these books, will you read where a character 'thinks' or 'feels' something. You see what they do, and you hear what they say. How you judge them, thereafter, is up to you . . . If I've done it right, there is more space for the reader to work out why what happened, happened. More than with the writer leaning over your shoulder going *poke! that was immoral!* or *prod! that was heroic*. It isn't my business to give you moral certainty. Any more than any other kind of certainty. —(Mary Gentle, http://web.archive.org/web/20060510011431/http://www.philm.demon.co.uk/Baroquon/MaryGentleArticle.html. Last visited January 28, 2008)

Major Works

Novels

Golden Witchbreed series: *Golden Witchbreed* (1983), *Ancient Light* (1987)
Rat Lords series: *Rats and Gargoyles* (1990), *The Architecture of Desire* (1991), *Left to His Own Devices* (1994)
Book of Ash series: *A Secret History* (1999), *Carthage Ascendant* (2000), *The Wild Machines* (2000), *Lost Burgundy* (2000)
Ilario series: *The Lion's Eye* (2006), *The Stone Golem* (2007)
A Hawk in Silver (1977)
Moon at Midday (1989)
Grunts! (1992)
1610: A Sundial In a Grave (2003)

Short Story Collections

Scholars and Soldiers (1989)
Villains! Book 1 (1992)
Soldiers and Scholars (1995)
White Crow (2003)
Cartomancy (2004)

Other Important Writings

Under the Penitence (2004)

Research Sources

Encyclopedias and Handbooks: EF, HDF, SJGF

Biographies and Interviews

Gevers, Nick. "The Joy of Knowledge, the Clash of Arms: An Interview with Mary Gentle." *Infinity Plus*. http://www.infinityplus.co.uk/nonfiction/intmg.htm. Last visited January 28, 2008.

McDonald, Paul. "Explication and Investigation: Mary Gentle." *The Zone* 6.
McVeigh, Kev. "Mary Gentle Interview. *Vector* 160 (1991), pp. 6–11.
Turner, Rodger. "Conversation With Mary Gentle." *SFSite.com.* July 2000. http://www.sfsite.com/10b/mg91.htm. Last visited January 28, 2008.

Web Sites

Gentle, Mary. "Hunchbacks, Sadists, and Shop-Soiled Heroes, or 'SF Author's Hunchback Fetish – The True Story." http://web.archive.org/web/20041208222320/http://www.rastus.force9.co.uk/CS14Gentle.html. Last visited January 28, 2008.
Gentle, Mary. "Gargoyles, Architecture, and Devices, Or: Why Write Science Fiction As If It Wasn't?" *Baroquon.* (1), available online at http://web.archive.org/web/20060510011431/http://www.philm.demon.co.uk/Baroquon/MaryGentleArticle.html. Last visited January 28, 2008.

Charlotte Perkins Gilman (1860–1935)

Biographical Sketch

Charlotte Anna Perkins Gilman was born in Connecticut and raised by her mother and her aunts, among whom were *Uncle Tom's Cabin* author Harriet Beecher Stowe and prominent suffragists Isabella Beecher Hooker and Catharine Beecher. She attended design school and worked as a greeting-card designer afterwards. Despite a number of passionate affairs with women, she married fellow artist Charles Walter Stetson, separating from him later, after the birth of their one daughter. She lived with Adele Knapp for a time before marrying New York lawyer George Houghton Gilman. After a life spent struggling with depression, she committed suicide after learning that she had an inoperable cancer of the breast.

Herland is the ancestor of feminist fantasy and utopian fiction. It treats of a world without men, in which women reproduce by parthenogenesis. The society thus created is ideal, free of war and struggles for dominance. Three men who happen upon Herland react in different ways to it, but all three eventually come to value it so greatly and find it so superior to their own male-dominated cultures that they wish to remain there. There is an unfortunate racist aspect to the book; all inhabitants of Herland are avowedly Aryan.

> There is no female mind. The brain is not an organ of sex. As well speak of a female liver. —(Charlotte Perkins Gilman, *Women and Economics*)

Major Works

Novels

Herland series: *Herland* (1915), *With Her in Ourland* (1916)
The Yellow Wallpaper (1899)

Moving the Mountain (1911)
Benigna Machiavelli (1914)

Short Story Collections

The Charlotte Perkins Gilman Reader: The Yellow Wallpaper and Other Fiction (1980)
The Yellow Wallpaper: And Other Writings (1980)

Research Sources

Biographies and Interviews

Gilman, Charlotte Perkins. *The Diaries of Charlotte Perkins Gilman.* Charlottesville, VA: University of Virginia Press, 1994.

Gilman, Charlotte Perkins. *The Living of Charlotte Perkins Gilman: An Autobiography.* New York: D. Appleton-Century Co., 1935.

Gough, Val and Jill Rudd. *Charlotte Perkins Gilman: Optimist Reformer.* Iowa City: University of Iowa Press, 1999.

Hill, Mary Armfield. *Charlotte Perkins Gilman: The Making of a Radical Feminist, 1860–1896.* Philadelphia, PA: Temple U P, 1980.

Lane, Ann J. *To Herland and Beyond: The Life and Work of Charlotte Perkins Gilman.* New York: Pantheon, 1990.

Perkins, Charlotte Gilman and Mary Armfield Hill. *A Journey from Within: The Love Letters of Charlotte Perkins Gilman, 1897–1900.* Lewisburg, PA: Bucknell University Press, 1995.

Criticism and Readers' Guides

Auerbach, Nina. *Communities of Women: An Idea in Fiction.* Cambridge, MA: Harvard University Press, 1978.

Davis, Cynthia J. and Denise D. Knight. *Charlotte Perkins Gilman and Her Contemporaries: Literary and Intellectual Contexts.* Tuscaloosa: University of Alabama Press, 2004.

Donaldson, Laura E. "The Eve of De-Struction: Charlotte Perkins Gilman and the Feminist Recreation of Paradise." *Women's Studies: An Interdisciplinary Journal,* 16 (1989), pp. 373–387.

Gough, Val. "Lesbians and Virgins: The Motherhood in Herland." In David Seed, ed., *Anticipations: Essays on Early Science Fiction and Its Precursors.* Syracuse, NY: Syracuse University Press, pp. 195–215.

Karpinski, Joanne B., ed. *Critical Essays on Charlotte Perkins Gilman.* New York: G. K. Hall, 1992.

Web Sites

The Charlotte Perkins Gilman Society. http://web.cortland.edu/gilman/. Last visited January 28, 2008. Includes newsletter, listserv, conference information, links.

"Charlotte Perkins Gilman." *Domestic Goddesses.* http://www.womenwriters.net/domesticgoddess/gilman1.html. Last visited January 28, 2008. Includes bibliography, criticism, biography, links.

Lisa Goldstein (1953–)

Biographical Sketch

Lisa Goldstein is the daughter of two Holocaust survivors who emigrated to the United States in 1947. She was born in Los Angeles, holds a degree in English from the University of California, Los Angeles, and now lives in Oakland with her husband. She grew up reading science fiction and knowing that she wanted to be a writer. When not writing, she has worked part-time in a library and has done freelance proofreading.

Goldstein has resisted pigeon-holing; her early books are startlingly different both from each other and from other fantasy. This commercially-unviable distinctiveness led to the publication of *Daughter of Exile* and *The Divided Crown*, both of which are more conventional high fantasy, under the pseudonym Isabel Glass. Goldstein has said that her early critical successes caused her to disregard advice from editors and publishers, advice she now regrets not heeding.

> Myths are tremendously important, something people need to survive and to understand the world around them . . . So no, I don't see fantasy as escapism—quite the opposite. —(Lisa Goldstein, http://www.furiousspinner.com/2004/06/interview-with-lisa-goldstein. Last visited January 28, 2008)

Major Works

Novels

The Red Magician (1981)
The Dream Years (1985)
Tourists (1989)
Strange Devices of the Sun and Moon (1993)
Summer King, Winter Fool (1994)
Walking the Labyrinth (1996)
The Alchemist's Door (2002)
Daughter of Exile series: *Daughter of Exile* (2004), *The Divided Crown* (2005)

Short Story Collections

Daily Voices (1989)
Travellers In Magic (1994)

Research Sources

Encyclopedias and Handbooks: EF, HDF, SJGF

Biographies and Interviews

Antieau, Kim. "Interview with Lisa Goldstein." *Furious Spinner* (June 1, 2004). http://www.furiousspinner.com/2004/06/interview-with-lisa-goldstein. Last visited January 28, 2008.

Awl, Dave. "Lisa Goldstein." http://www.brazenhussies.net/Goldstein/Interview.html. Last visited January 28, 2008.

Hartwell, David G. "Lisa Goldstein Interview." *Marion Zimmer Bradley's Fantasy Magazine* 30.

"Lisa Goldstein: Underground Connections." *Locus* 42(5) (May 1999), pp. 6, 76.

White, Lori Ann. "Interview: Lisa Goldstein." *Strange Horizons* (July 28, 2003). http://www.strangehorizons.com/2003/20030728/goldstein.shtml. Last visited January 28, 2008.

Web Sites

Lisa Goldstein. http://www.brazenhussies.net/goldstein/. Last visited January 28, 2008. Author's official site. Includes reviews of and by the author, links, bibliography, news, excerpts.

Terry Goodkind (1948–)

Biographical Sketch

Terry Goodkind was raised in Omaha, Nebraska. He dropped out of college owing to frustration stemming from dyslexia. He worked as a wildlife painter, violin maker, and restorer of antique furniture before turning to writing. He now alternates between homes on an island off the coast of Maine and in the Nevada desert.

Goodkind considers himself an objectivist, a follower of Ayn Rand, and his intent is for his books to inspire individual action. The Sword of Truth series is unusual among epic-fantasy series in that its novels are largely self-contained, although themes and threads still work themselves out over the course of the series. The main character is a young man named Richard whose steadfast loyalty to his beliefs in spite of significant setbacks inspires others to follow his example.

> The issues I write about are firmly rooted in reality, as are the characters. I often hear people say that they read to escape reality, but I believe that what they're really doing is reading to find reason for hope, to find strength. While a bad book leaves readers with a sense of hopelessness and despair, a good novel, through stories of values realized, of wrongs righted, can bring to readers a connection to the wonder of life. A good novel shows how life can and ought to be

lived. It not only entertains but energizes and uplifts readers. —(Terry Goodkind, http://www.prophets-inc.com/communicate/q_and_a.html. Last visited January 28, 2008)

Major Works

Novels

Sword of Truth series: *Wizard's First Rule* (1994), *Stone of Tears* (1995), *Blood of the Fold* (1996), *Temple of the Winds* (1997), *Soul of the Fire* (1999), *Faith of the Fallen* (2000), *The Pillars of Creation* (2001), *Debt of Bones* (2001), *Naked Empire* (2003), *Chainfire* (2005), *Phantom* (2006), *Confessor* (2007)

Research Sources

Encyclopedias and Handbooks: EF, HDF, SJGF

Biographies and Interviews

Kleffel, Rick. httphttp://trashotron.com/agony/audio/terry_goodkind.mp3. Last visited January 30, 2008.

Podcast interview.Snider, John C. "Interview: Terry Goodkind." *SciFiDimensions.com* (2003). http://www.scifidimensions.com/Aug03/terrygoodkind.htm. Last visited January 28, 2008.

Criticism and Readers' Guides

Perry, William E. "The Randian Fantasies of Terry Goodkind." *The Atlas Society*. http://www.objectivistcenter.org/ct-1695-Goodkind.aspx. Last visited January 28, 2008.

Web Sites

Terry Goodkind: The Official Web Site. http://www.terrygoodkind.com/. Last visited January 28, 2008. Contains news, book list, author information and photos, chat room.

Terry Goodkind. http://www.terrygoodkind.net/. Last visited January 28, 2008. Fan site with considerable author access. Includes forums, chat room, links, news.

Henry Rider Haggard (H. Rider Haggard) (1856–1925)

Biographical Sketch

Sir Henry Rider Haggard's education ended at age seventeen, when his parents withdrew him from school for daydreaming. He was sent to South Africa to serve the lieutenant governor of Natal. On his return to England, he successfully passed the bar, though by then he strongly preferred his writing career. He was made a Knight Commander of the Order of the British Empire in 1919.

Inspired by adventurers he met in Africa, Haggard pioneered the genre of the "lost continent" adventure novel with his Allan Quatermain books, which despite their obviously imperialist perspective often contain considerable sympathy for native African characters. The title character of *She* and *Ayesha* was cited by Freud and Jung as a paradigmatic example of womanhood.

> Truly the universe is full of ghosts, not sheeted churchyard spectres, but the inextinguishable elements of individual life, which having once been, can never die, though they blend and change, and change again for ever. —(H. Rider Haggard, *King Solomon's Mines*)

Major Works

Novels

Allan Quatermain series: *King Solomon's Mines* (1885), *Allan Quatermain* (1887), *Allan's Wife* (1887), *A Tale of Three Lions* (1887), *Maiwa's Revenge: or, The War of the Little Hand* (1888), *Marie* (1912), *Child of Storm* (1913), *The Holy Flower* (1915), *The Ivory Child* (1916), *Finished* (1917), *The Ancient Allan* (1920), *She and Allan* (1920), *Heu-heu: or The Monster* (1924), *The Treasure of the Lake* (1926), *Allan and the Ice-gods* (1927)

Ayesha series: *She* (1886), *Ayesha: The Return of She* (1905), *Wisdom's Daughter: The Life and Love Story of She-Who-Must-Be-Obeyed* (1923)

The Witch's Head (1884)

The World's Desire (with Andrew Lang, 1890)

The Saga of Eric Brighteyes (1891)

The Wizard (1896)

A Winter Pilgrimage (1901)

Stella Fregelius: A Tale of Three Destinies (1903)

Benita: An African Romance (1906)

The Way of the Spirit (1906)

The Ghost Kings (1908)

Morning Star (1910)

Red Eve (1911)

Love Eternal (1918)

When the World Shook (1919)

The Missionary and the Witch-doctor (1920)

Short Story Collections

Black Heart and White Heart, and Other Stories (1893)

Smith and the Pharaohs and Other Tales (1920)

The Works of H. Rider Haggard (1928)

Research Sources

Encyclopedias and Handbooks: EF, HDF, SJGF

Biographies and Interviews

Cohen, Morton N. *Rider Haggard: His Life and Work.* London: Macmillan, 1968.

Higgins, D.S. *Rider Haggard: A Biography*. New York: Stein and Day, 1981.

Higgins, D.S. and H. Rider Haggard. *The Private Diaries of Sir H. Rider Haggard, 1914–1925*. New York: Stein and Day, 1980.

Criticism and Readers' Guides

Chrisman, Laura. *Rereading the Imperial Romance: British Imperialism and South African Resistance in Haggard, Schreiner, and Plaatje*. Oxford: Clarendon, 2000.

Fraser, Robert. *Victorian Quest Romance: Stevenson, Haggard, Kipling, and Conan Doyle*. Plymouth, MA: Northcote House, 1998.

Hammer, Jóna E. "Eric Brighteyes: Rider Haggard Rewrites the Sagas." *Studies in Medievalism* 12 (2002), pp. 137–170.

Katz, Wendy Roberta. *Rider Haggard and the Fiction of Empire: A Critical Study of British Imperial Fiction.* New York: Cambridge University Press, 1988.

Monsman, Gerald Cornelius. *H. Rider Haggard on the Imperial Frontier: The Political and Literary Contexts of His African Romances*. Greensboro, NC: ELT Press, 2006.

Mullen, Richard D. "The Prudish Prurience of H. Rider Haggard and Edgar Rice Burroughs." *Riverside Quarterly* 5 (1974), pp. 14–19, 6 (1974), pp. 134–146.

Murphy, Patricia. "The Gendering of History in She." *Studies in English Literature, 1500–1900*, 39(4) (Autumn 1999), pp. 747–772.

Siemens, Lloyd. *The Critical Reception of Sir Henry Rider Haggard: An Annotated Bibliography, 1882–1991*. Greensboro, NC: University of North Carolina at Greensboro Press, 1991.

Stiebel, Lindy. *Imagining Africa: Landscape in H. Rider Haggard's African Romances.* Westport, CN: Greenwood Press, 2001.

Whatmore, D.E. *H. Rider Haggard: A Bibliography*. Westport, CN: Meckler Publishing, 1987.

Web Sites

Cox, Noel. "Summaries and Reviews of Books by H. Rider Haggard." http://www.geocities.com/noelcox/Haggard.htm. Last visited January 28, 2008.

Weinberg, Robert. "Works by H. Rider Haggard—An Appreciation." http://www.robertweinberg.net/haggard.htm. Last visited January 28, 2008.

Zweig, Dani. "Dani Zweig's Belated Reviews #26: H. Rider Haggard." http://www-users.cs.york.ac.uk/susan/sf/dani/026.htm. Last visited January 28, 2008. Extended reviews of Haggard's books.

Barbara Hambly (1951–)

Biographical Sketch

Barbara Joan Hambly was born and raised in California, and currently lives in Los Angeles. L. Frank Baum's and J.R.R. Tolkien's books drew her into fantasy, and she has been a longtime participant in the Society for Creative Anachronism. She holds two degrees in medieval history from the University of California, Riverside. In order to find time to write during her early career, she worked several different jobs, from karate instructor to high-school teacher. She was married to writer George Alec Effinger until his death in 2002.

Hambly's Darwath novels speak of her academic background; the first trilogy's main character is a graduate-student philologist who uses her linguistic and historical training to unravel ancient mysteries in the otherworld she is transported to. Hambly's novels, unusually for the genre, tend to eschew purely happy endings in favor of tough ethical choices with severe consequences.

> Fiction, like any form of make-believe, is a way of processing fear and exploring the roads of hope: both reading it and writing it. I tend to like to write about situations that are a little ragged, that don't have obvious solutions: part of the solution is seeing how much of the situation is livable-with, how much of the situation isn't what you originally thought it was. I like to explore the different shapes that "Happily Ever After" takes. —(Barbara Hambly, http://www.andromedaspaceways.com/issue21.htm. Last visited January 28, 2008)

Major Works

Novels

Darwath series: *The Time of the Dark* (1982), *The Walls of Air* (1983), *The Armies of Daylight* (1996), *Mother of Winter* (1996), *Icefalcon's Quest* (1998)

Sun Wolf and Starhawk series: *The Ladies of Mandrigyn* (1984), *The Witches of Wenshar* (1987), *The Dark Hand of Magic* (1990)

Winterlands series: *Dragonsbane* (1985), *Dragonshadow* (1999), *The Knight of the Demon Queen* (2000), *Dragonstar* (2002)

Windrose series: *The Silent Tower* (1986), *The Silicon Mage* (1988), *Dog Wizard* (1992)

Sun-Cross series: *The Rainbow Abyss* (1991), *The Magicians of Night* (1991)

Sisters of the Raven series: *Sisters of the Raven* (2002), *Circle of the Moon* (2005)

Stranger at the Wedding (1994) aka *Sorcerer's Ward*

Magic Time (with Marc Scott Zicree, 2001)

Research Sources

Encyclopedias and Handbooks: EF, HDF, SJGF

Biographies and Interviews

Amberstone, Celu. “An Interview with Barbara Hambly.” *SF Canada* (Autumn 2006). http://www.sfcanada.ca/autumn2006/hambly.htm. Last visited January 28, 2008.

Cook, Ben. “Barbara Hambly Interview.” *Andromeda Spaceways* 21 (October/November 2005). Available online at http://www.andromedaspaceways.com/issue21.htm. Last visited January 28, 2008.

“Corridors of Communication.” May 16, 1999. http://www.geocities.com/Area51/Shadowlands/3932/intervbh.html. Last visited January 28, 2008.

Criticism and Readers' Guides

Kelso, Sylvia. “Loces Genii: Urban Settings in the Fantasy of Peter Beagle, Martha Wells, and Barbara Hambly.” *Journal of the Fantastic in the Arts* 13(1) (2002), pp. 13–32.

Monk, Patricia. “Dragonsaver: The Female Hero in Barbara Hambly's Dragonsbane.” *Journal of the Fantastic in the Arts* 4(4) (1991), pp. 60–82.

Web Sites

Hambly, Barbara. *The Official Barbara Hambly Page*. http://www.barbarahambly.com/. Last visited January 28, 2008. Author's official site, fan-maintained. Contains news, interview list, biography, FAQ, fan feedback, message board.

If you like Barbara Hambly

Hambly's Darwath novels speak of her academic background; the first trilogy's main character is a graduate-student philologist who uses her linguistic and historical training to unravel ancient mysteries in the otherworld she is transported to. Hambly's novels, unusually for the genre, tend to eschew purely happy endings in favor of tough ethical choices with severe consequences.

Then you might like

Lois McMaster Bujold

Bujold's Chalion series (*The Curse of Chalion*, *Paladin of Souls*, *The Hallowed Hunt*) places likeable characters in a well-imagined world of military and religious conflict. Like Hambly, Bujold draws her setting and its many details from the politics of medieval and Renaissance Europe.

Cherry Janice Cherryh (C.J. Cherryh)

Cherryh rejects many genre distinctions, emphasizing the shared roots of fantasy and science fiction, and her work blurs those boundaries convincingly. Her world building, like Hambly's, draws on expertise in archaeology and linguistics to create rounded cultures with their own rituals and philosophies.

Guy Gavriel Kay

Kay's later books (*Tigana, A Song for Arbonne, The Lions of Al-Rassan*) are a step away from alternate history, set in fantasy worlds that strongly resemble medieval Spain or Italy or France or Turkey. This historical grounding will appeal to fans of Hambly.

Elizabeth Moon

Moon's Paksenarrion series (*Sheepfarmer's Daughter, Divided Allegiance, Oath of Gold*) is the sweeping saga of a woman who leaves her home to follow her creed and her heart, becoming a great hero. Its epic scope and upright characters recall Hambly's.

Tracy Hickman (1955–)

Biographical Sketch

Tracy Raye Hickman was born in Salt Lake City, Utah. After serving a church mission in Indonesia, he got married to his wife Laura, who had introduced him to roleplaying games.

Hickman started working with Margaret Weis at TSR, a company that produced roleplaying games. Hickman was a newly hired game module designer and Weis was an editor in the books division. TSR had contracted with professional writers to write tie-in novels for Hickman's Dragonlance game modules, but none of them quite seemed to get it. Frustrated, Hickman and Weis started writing their own. The books were a huge hit, even among non roleplayers. They continue to collaborate on a number of Dragonlance series, as other fantasy novels and series.

Hickman has since written other books both on his own and in collaboration with his wife Laura. He and his family currently reside in Utah.

> Epic fantasy has heros who must conquer the foe. We all want to see ourselves as heros of some kind, vanquishing the bad things around us. We identify strongly with the hero or heroine in these adventures because we want to be them. It is this desire that makes fantasy such an appealing genre. —(Tracy Hickman, "Ethics in Fantasy: Morality and D&D." Available online at http://www.trhickman.com/Intel/Essays/Ethic3.html. Last visited January 28, 2008)

Major Works

Dragonlance Novels

Dragonlance Chronicles series, with Margaret Weis: *Dragons of Autumn Twilight* (1984), *Dragons of Winter Night* (1985), *Dragons of Spring Dawning* (1985), *Dragons of Summer Flame* (1995), *The Annotated Chronicles* (1999)

Dragonlance Legends series, with Margaret Weis: *Test of the Twins* (1986), *War of the Twins* (1986), *Time of the Twins* (1986), *The Annotated Legends* (2003)

Dragonlance War of Souls series, with Margaret Weis: *Dragons of a Fallen Sun* (2000), *Dragons of a Lost Star* (2001), *Dragons of a Vanished Moon* (2002)

Dragonlance Dark Chronicles series, with Margaret Weis: *Dragons of the Dwarven Depths* (2006), *Dragons of the Highlord Skies* (2007)

Other Series and Novels

Darksword series, with Margaret Weis: *Forging the Darksword* (1987), *Darksword Adventures* (1988), *Doom of the Darksword* (1988), *Triumph of the Darksword* (1988), *Legacy of the Darksword* (1997)

Rose of the Prophet series, with Margaret Weis: *The Will of the Wanderer* (1988), *The Paladin of the Night* (1989), *The Prophet of Akharan* (1989)

Death Gate series, with Margaret Weis: *Dragon Wing* (1990), *Elven Star* (1990), *Fire Sea* (1991), *The Serpent Mage* (1992), *The Hand of Chaos* (1993), *Into the Labyrinth* (1993), *The Seventh Gate* (1994), *The Immortals*, 1996

Sovereign Stone series, with Margaret Weis: *Well of Darkness* (2000), *Guardians of the Lost* (2001) *Journey into the Void* (2003)

Bronze Canticles series, with Laura Hickman: *Mystic Warrior* (2004), *Mystic Quest* (2005), *Mystic Empire* (2006)

Children's/Young Adult Fiction

Dragonlance: Young Adult Chronicles, with Margaret Weis: *Night of the Dragons* (2003), *A Rumor of Dragons* (2003), *The Nightmare Lands* (2003), *To the Gates of Palanthas* (2003), *Hope's Flame* (2004), *A Dawn of Dragons* (2004)

Other Important Writings

Dragonlance Adventures, with Margaret Weis (1987)

Research Sources

Encyclopedias and Handbooks: EF

Biographies and Interviews

Hunt, Stephen. "Dragon' On." *SF Crowsnest.com*. http://www.sfcrowsnest.com/sfnews/newsd0102.htm. Joint interview with Weis and Hickman. Last visited January 28. 2008.

"Interview with Tracy Hickman." *SFFWorld.com.* May 21, 2006. http://www.sffworld.com/interview/187p0.html. Last visited January 28, 2008.

Tonjes, Wayne. "Interview with Tracy Hickman." *GamingReport.com*, September 29, 2005. http://www.gamingreport.com/modules.php?op=modload&name=Sections&file=index&req=viewarticle&artid=162. Last visited January 28, 2008.

Criticism and Readers' Guides

Weis, Margaret and Hickman, Tracy, eds. *Leaves from the Inn of the Last Home: The Complete Krynn Source Book.* Lake Geneva, WI: TSR, 1987.

Weis, Margaret and Hickman, Tracy, eds. *Realms of Dragons: The Worlds of Weis and Hickman.* New York: HarperPrism, 1999.

Web Sites

The Dragonlance Nexus. http://www.dlnexus.com. Last visited January 28, 2008.

The Worlds and Works of Tracy Raye Hickman. http://www.trhickman.com. Last visited January 28, 2008. Hickman's Web site.

If you like Tracy Hickman

Hickman's love of epic adventure is evident in his many books and series. The Dragonlance books, written with Margaret Weis, have been especially popular and enduring.

Then you might like

David and Leigh Eddings

The Eddings' Belgariad series tells the story of young Garion as he slowly realizes his long prophesied destiny. They are comprised of *Pawn of Prophecy*, *Queen of Sorcery*, *Magician's Gambit*, *Castle of Wizardry*, and *Enchanters' End Game*.

Kate Elliott

Elliot's epic fantasies are based on a densely thought out alternate world that seems reminiscent from European myth, but not quite. Her interest in political and religious conflict is evident in her Crown of Stars series (*King's Dragon*, *Prince of Dogs*, *The Burning Stone*, *Child of Flame*, *The Gathering Storm*, *In the Ruins*, and *The Crown of Stars*).

Robert Jordan

Jordan's multi-volume Wheel of Time series takes place in a world that cycles through periods of war between essential good and evil forces in the universe (the first three books are *The Eye of the World*, *The Great Hunt*, and *The Dragon Reborn*).

George R.R. Martin

Martin's epic Song of Ice and Fire series encompasses a broad tapestry of characters and kingdoms. So far, it includes *A Game of Thrones*, *A Clash of Kings*, *A Storm of Swords*, *A Feast for Crows*, and *A Dance with Dragons*.

John Ronald Reuel Tolkien (J.R.R. Tolkien)

Tolkien's Middle Earth fantasies reflect his scholarly interests in languages and myth. Beginning with prequel *The Hobbit*, they continue with *The Fellowship of the Ring*, *The Two Towers*, and *The Return of the King*.

Robert Holdstock (1948–)

Biographical Sketch

Born and raised in Kent, England, Robert Holdstock trained as a medical zoologist before starting to write in the mid-1970s. He currently lives with his wife in London, but visits woodlands and other wild areas in England and mainland Europe (particularly France) whenever he can.

Holdstock has written under a number of pseudonyms, including Chris Carlsen, Ken Blake, and Robert Faulcon. His highly allusive work seeks to ring changes on immortal archetypes (notably the Arthurian mythos), recognizing cultural commonalities while respecting the fresh perspectives brought to stock characters by every culture that treats of them. The Mythago series, nominally set in England after World War II, features a "wildwood" containing hundreds of archetypal characters, some well-known, some all but forgotten.

> Everybody's creating and this is a metaphor for the oral tradition, in that different people in different communities always tell the story slightly differently. The evolution is affected by who told it, where and when, and to what sort of an audience. We all have our own way of expressing a character; we all have different definitions of heroism; we all have different ideas of how much stamina a person can have. —(Robert Holdstock, http://www.lib.rochester.edu/camelot/intrvws/holdst.htm. Last visited January 28, 2008)

Major Works

Novels

Berserker series: *Shadow of the Wolf* (1977), *The Horned Warrior* (1979)
Raven Series: *Swordsmistress of Chaos* (1978), *A Time of Ghosts* (1978), *Lords of the Shadows* (1979)

Mythago Wood series: *Mythago Wood* (1984), *Lavondyss* (1988), *The Bone Forest* (1991), *The Hollowing* (1993), *Merlin's Wood* (1994), *Gate of Ivory, Gate of Horn* (1997)
Merlin Codex series: *Celtika* (2001), *The Iron Grail* (2002), *The Broken Kings* (2006)
Necromancer (1985)
The Emerald Forest (1985)
Ancient Echoes (1986)
The Fetch (1991)

Short Story Collections

In the Valley of the Statues and Other Stories (1982)

Other Important Writings

Realms of Fantasy: An Illustrated Exploration of the Most Famous Worlds in Fantasy Fiction (with Malcolm Edwards, 1983)
Lost Realms: An Illustrated Exploration of the Lands Behind the Legends (with Malcolm Edwards, 1984)

Research Sources

Encyclopedias and Handbooks: EF, HDF, SJGF

Biographies and Interviews

Auden, Sandy. "Fantasy Theme Park: An Interview with Robert Holdstock." *SF-Site.com*. 2005. http://www.sfsite.com/11b/sarh212.htm. Last visited January 28, 2008.
Brown, Carroll. "Robert Holdstock." *Science Fiction Chronicle* 16(2) (December 1994), pp. 5, 44–48.
Hall, Melissa Mia. "Robert Holstock Takes on the Greek Gods." *SciFi.com*. http://www.scifi.com/sfw/issue356/interview.html. Last visited January 28, 2008.
"Interview with Robert Holdstock." *Fantastinet*. 2006. http://fantastinet.com/auteurs.php?id=130. Last visited January 28, 2008.
Thompson, Raymond H. "Interview with Robert Holdstock." *Interviews with Authors of Modern Arthurian Literature*. http://www.lib.rochester.edu/camelot/intrvws/holdst.htm. Last visited January 28, 2008.

Criticism and Readers' Guides

Brown, Carroll. "The Flame in the Heart of the Wood: The Integration of Myth and Science in Robert Holdstock's Mythago Wood." *Extrapolation* 34(2) (Summer 1993), pp. 158–172.

Web Sites

Mythago Wood. http://www.robertholdstock.com/. Last visited January 28, 2008. Author's official site. Contains news, links, essays, reviews and criticism, excerpts, biography, mailing list.

Nalo Hopkinson (1960–)

Biographical Sketch

Born in Jamaica to Guyanese poet Abdur Rahman Slade Hopkinson and named after a dancer in the African ballet, Nalo Hopkinson grew up reading fantastical fiction, from the *Iliad* to folk and fairy tales. She holds a master's degree in writing from Seton Hall University. Although she experienced considerable culture shock when she moved to Toronto, Canada, at age sixteen, she still lives there, and works odd jobs to supplement her income from writing, editing, and teaching.

Fascinated by the process of creolization in language, the rapprochement of the colonizer's language with that of the colonized, Hopkinson blends elements of several Caribbean creoles in her narration and character voices. Her themes include urban decay (*Brown Girl in the Ring*), exile and subsequent self-actualization through story (*Midnight Robber*), and the intersection of the mundane and the divine (*Salt Roads*). The many awards and critical accolades her writing has earned speak to its freshness, power, and courage.

> We experience many flavors of not being included. One of the flavors I tasted was when it finally occurred to me that the science fiction and fantasy I'd been enthusiastically reading for decades didn't particularly reflect people like me in its pages. —(Nalo Hopkinson, http://www.scifi.com/sfw/issue232/interview2.html. Last visited January 28, 2008)

Major Works

Novels

Brown Girl in the Ring (1998)
Midnight Robber (2000)
Le Ronde des Esprits (2001)
The Salt Roads (2003)
The New Moon's Arms (2007)

Short Story Collections

Skin Folk (2001)
Under Glass (2001)

Research Sources

Encyclopedias and Handbooks: HDF

Biographies and Interviews

Batty, Nancy. "'Caught by a . . . Genre': An Interview with Nalo Hopkinson." *ARIEL* 33(1) (January 2002), pp. 175–201.

"A Conversation with Nalo Hopkinson." *SFSite.com*. 2000. http://www.sfsite.com/03b/nh77.htm. Last visited January 28, 2008.

Gaines, Luan. "An Interview with Nalo Hopkinson." *Curled Up with a Good Book*. http://www.curledup.com/naloint.htm. Last visited January 28, 2008.

Glave, Dianne D. "An Interview with Nalo Hopkinson." *Callaloo* 26(1) (Winter 2003), pp. 146–159.

Grant, Gavin J. "Nalo Hopkinson." *BookSense.com*. http://www.booksense.com/people/archive/hopkinsonnalo.jsp. Last visited January 28, 2008.

"Interview: Nalo Hopkinson." http://www.hachettebookgroupusa.com/authors/84/1272/interview9730.html. Last visited January 28, 2008.

"Interview with Nalo Hopkinson." *SFFWorld.com*. March 13, 2003. http://www.sffworld.com/interview/76p0.html. Last visited January 28, 2008.

Mohanraj, Mary Anne. "Interview: Nalo Hopkinson." *Strange Horizons* (September 1, 2000). http://www.strangehorizons.com/2000/20000901/NaloHopkinson_Interview.shtml. Last visited January 28, 2008.

"Nalo Hopkinson." *Fast Forward* 154. May 2003. http://www.fast-forward.tv/audio/audio154c.m3u. Last visited January 30, 2008.

Rutledge, Gregory E. "Speaking in Tongues: An Interview with Science Fiction Writer Nalo Hopkinson." *African American Review* 33(4) (Winter 1999), pp. 589–601. Available online at http://findarticles.com/p/articles/mi_m2838/is_4_33/ai_59024880/pg_1. Last visited January 28, 2008.

Schellenberg, James and David M. Switzer. "Interview with Nalo Hopkinson." *Challenging Destiny* 12 (2001), available in expanded form online at http://www.challengingdestiny.com/interviews/hopkinson.htm. Last visited January 28, 2008.

Soyka, David. "Interview." *SciFi.com*( ). http://www.scifi.com/sfw/issue232/interview2.html. Last visited January 28, 2008.

Watson-Aifah, Jen. "A Conversation with Nalo Hopkinson." *Callaloo* 26(1) (Winter 2003), pp. 160–169.

Criticism and Readers' Guides

Anatol, Giselle Liza. "A Feminist Reading of Soucouyants in Nalo Hopkinson's *Brown Girl in the Ring* and *Skin Folk*." *Mosaic* 37(3) (September 2004), pp. 33–50.

Clemente, Bill. "Tan-Tan's Exile and Odyssey in Nalo Hopkinson's *Midnight Robber*." *Foundation* 33(91) (Summer 2004), pp. 10–24.

Collier, Gordon. "Spaceship Creole: Nalo Hopkinson, Canadian-Caribbean Fabulist Fiction, and Linguistic/Cultural Syncretism." *Matatu* 27–28(2003), pp. 443–456.

Ramraj, Ruby. "Power Relationships and Femininity in Nalo Hopkinson's *The Salt Roads*." *Foundation* 33(91) (Summer 2004), pp. 25–35.

Reid, Michelle. "Crossing the Boundaries of the 'Burn': Canadian Multiculturalism and Caribbean Hybridity in Nalo Hopkinson's *Brown Girl in the Ring*." *Extrapolation* 46(3) (Fall 2005), pp. 297–314.

Rutledge, Gregory E. "Nalo Hopkinson's Urban Jungle and the Cosmology of Freedom: How Capitalism Underdeveloped the Black Americas and Left a Brown Girl in the Ring." *Foundation* 30(81) (Spring 2001), pp. 22–39.

Wood, Sarah. "'Serving the Spirits': Emergent Identities in Nalo Hopkinson's *Brown Girl in the Ring*." *Extrapolation* 46(3) (Fall 2005), pp. 315–326.

Web Sites

Nalo Hopkinson. http://nalohopkinson.com/. Last visited January 28, 2008.
Author's official site. Contains biography, news, links, essays, and a blog.

If you like Nalo Hopkinson

Fascinated by the process of creolization in language, the rapprochement of the colonizer's language with that of the colonized, Hopkinson blends elements of several Caribbean creoles in her narration and character voices. Her themes include urban decay (*Brown Girl in the Ring*), exile and subsequent self-actualization through story (*Midnight Robber*), and the intersection of the mundane and the divine (*Salt Roads*).

Then you might like

John M. Ford

Ford's *The Last Hot Time* follows a doctor with a guilty conscience into a gritty noirish world of motorcycle-riding elves and shifting alliances. His unflinching grasp of human nature will appeal to Hopkinson fans.

Charles de Lint

Charles de Lint is best known for his Newford books (*Someplace to be Flying*, *Moonlight & Vines*, *The Onion Girl* among others), which follows a varied cast of characters who straddle the divide between mundane Newford and the fantastic faerie realms only a thought away. For de Lint as for Hopkinson, the unreal is a guide and aid in dealing with the problems and sufferings of daily life.

Ursula K. Le Guin

Le Guin's fantasy is invariably sensitive to culture clashes and the struggle to survive despite oppression. Among fantasists she is best known for her Earthsea series (*A Wizard of Earthsea*, *Tombs of Atuan*, *The Farthest*

Shore, *Tehanu*, *The Other Wind*, *Tales of Earthsea*), which chronicles clashes between wizards and dragons, and the people caught up in them.

Linda Medley

Medley's *Castle Waiting* graphic-novel series shares Hopkinson's ability to create sympathy for the extraordinary and the forgotten alike. Its characters pop off the page, ranging from Sleeping Beauty's ladies-in-waiting to a stork-headed chamberlain to a bearded-lady nun, brim-full of personality and humor.

Nnedi Okorafor-Mbachu

Okorafor-Mbachu mines myth and legend for her young adult books, *The Shadow Speaker* and *Zahrah the Windseeker*. Her chosen legends, however, are those of West Africa, and her work will appeal to anyone wishing to expand horizons beyond standard European settings. Look for her work in anthologies edited by Hopkinson.

Robert E. Howard (1906–1936)

Biographical Sketch

Robert Ervin Howard spent a peripatetic childhood in Texas; his mother Hester was instrumental in instilling a love of literature in him even as bad experiences in school taught him that life was often brutal and unfair. He began writing quite young, learning from his initial rejections to study his markets carefully. At the same time, he trained hard in boxing and maintained a keen interest in other sports. As an older teenager, he found himself forced to work odd jobs for money. His early writing and recollections from friends indicate that he suffered from depression from his mid-teens; minutes after learning that his mother was soon to die, he shot himself to death.

Howard's Conan stories demonstrate their author's near-obsession with bodily perfection and physical combat as well as his lonely, gloomy outlook on life. Conan's "Hyborian Age," however, is only one part of Howard's imagined alternate-world history; other characters set therein include King Kull, Solomon Kane, and Cormac Mac Art. Periods of history in this world are separated by horrible cataclysms that efface almost all memory of the past.

> I became a writer in spite of my environments. Understand, I am not criticizing those environments. They were good, solid, and worthy. The fact that they were not inducive to literature and art is nothing in their disfavor. Nevertheless, it is no light thing to enter into a profession absolutely foreign and alien to the people

among which one's lot is cast; a profession which seems as dim and faraway and unreal as the shores of Europe. —(Robert E. Howard, personal letter, 1933)

Major Works

Novels

The Hour of the Dragon (1935)
Almuric (1964)

Short Story Collections

Conan series: *The Sword of Conan* (1952), *The Coming of Conan* (1953), *King Conan* (1953), *Conan the Barbarian* (1954)
Skull-Face: And Other Stories (1946)
The Dark Man and Others (1963)
Red Shadows (1968)
King Kull (1969)

Research Sources

Encyclopedias and Handbooks: EF, HDF, SJGF

Biographies and Interviews

De Camp, L. Sprague, Catherine Crook de Camp, and Jane Whittington Griffin. *Dark Valley Destiny: The Life of Robert E. Howard.* New York: Bluejay Books, 1983.

De Camp, L. Sprague. *The Miscast Barbarian: A Biography of Robert E. Howard.* Saddle River, NJ: Gerry de la Ree, 1975.

Finn, Mark. *Blood & Thunder: The Life & Art of Robert E. Howard.* Austin, TX: Monkey Brain Books, 2006.

Holley, Joe and Mark Finn. "Robert E. Howard." In Frances Leonard, *Ramona Cearley*, eds., *Conversations with Texas Writers.* Austin: University of Texas Press, 2005, pp. 168–175.

Criticism and Readers' Guides

Coffman, D. Franklin "Frank" Jr. "Moral Law, Secondary Worlds, and Crossed Planes: Some Thoughts upon the Nature of Fantasy." *Studies in Fantasy Literature* 3 (2005), pp. 13–18.

Dark Man: The Journal of Robert E. Howard Studies. West Warwick, RI: Necronomicon Press.

Dotommaso, Lorenzo. "Robert E. Howard's Hyborian Tales and the Question of Race in Fantastic Literature." *Extrapolation* 37(2) (Summer 1996), pp. 151–170.

Herman, Paul and Glenn Lord. *The Neverending Hunt: A Bibliography of Robert E. Howard.* Holicong, PA: Wildside, 2007.

Herron, Don, ed. *The Dark Barbarian: The Writings of Robert E. Howard: A Critical Anthology*. Westport, CT: Greenwood, 1984.

Web Sites

The Cimmerian. http://www.thecimmerian.com/. Last visited January 28, 2008. Web site of the *Cimmerian* journal. Includes blog, print journal information, frequently asked questions list.

Herman, Paul and Todd A. Woods. *The Works of Robert E. Howard*, 2000. http://www.howardworks.com/howard.htm. Last visited January 28, 2008. Immense bibliography of Howard's writings; also includes secondary sources.

REH Two-Gun Raconteur: The Definitive Howard Fanzine. http://www.rehtwogunraconteur.com/. Last visited January 28, 2008. Includes journal, issue index, links.

Robert E. Howard. http://rehoward.com/. Last visited January 28, 2008. Author's official Web site. Contains biography, book descriptions, links, reviews, essays about the author.

Robert E. Howard Foundation. http://rehfoundation.org/. Last visited January 28, 2008. Site dedicated to reviving Howard's memory. Contains news, museum information, links.

Robert E. Howard United Press Association. http://rehupa.com/. Last visited January 28, 2008. Amateur press devoted to Howard's work. Contains criticism, links, news, biography.

Waterman, Edward E. *Barbarian Keep*. http://www.barbariankeep.com/. Last visited January 28, 2008. Fan site. Contains bibliography, art, links.

Kij Johnson (1960–)

Biographical Sketch

Born in Iowa, Kij Johnson received her bachelor's degree from St. Olaf College in Minnesota, and now lives in Seattle, Washington. She is very active in publishing, having been an editor for Tor Books as well as the roleplaying game publisher Wizards of the Coast and comics publisher Dark Horse. She also worked for a time on the electronic-book development team at Microsoft. Currently, she serves as associate director of the J. Wayne and Elsie McGunn Center for the Study of Science Fiction at the University of Kansas. Johnson enjoys rock-climbing and is a frequent convention guest and teacher at writing workshops.

Johnson modeled her carefully researched Heian Japan novels after Japanese pillow-books and folklore, adding a notably feminist sensibility; her heroines are complex and capable women who actively work to change their situations despite the often stifling social conditions in which they find themselves.

> I have these moments of clarity, when some combination of event and sense and mood combine to make me feel as though I have been permitted a glimpse at

the machinery behind the world's operation, a field trip to the meaning of life. We all have them, I suppose; for me, it's almost always a combination of light and music and feeling. —(Kij Johnson, http://kijjohnson.livejournal.com/. Last visited January 30, 2008.)

Major Works

Novels

The Fox Woman (2000)
Fudoki (2003)

Short Story Collections

Tales for the Long Rains (2001)

Research Sources

Biographies and Interviews

Sargent, Pamela. "Interview between Kij Johnson and Pamela Sargent." *Mundane-SF*. July 2006. http://mundane-sf.blogspot.com/2006/07/interview-between-kij-johnson-and.html. Last visited January 28, 2008.

Walters, Trent. "A Conversation with Kij Johnson." *SFSite.com*. December 2000. http://www.sfsite.com/02a/kj97.htm. Last visited January 28, 2008.

Web Sites

Johnson, Kij. *Kij Johnson main page*. http://www.sff.net/people/kij-johnson/. Last visited January 28, 2008. Author's official site. Contains writing updates, news, links to online excerpts.

The wall/muscle/gravity puzzle. http://kijjohnson.livejournal.com/. Last visited January 30, 2009. Author's personal journal.

Diana Wynne Jones (1934–)

Biographical Sketch

Born in England to a distant father and frankly neglectful mother and raised during the chaos of World War II, Diana Wynne Jones began writing adventure stories as a child to amuse her two younger sisters; she began writing fantasy later in life to amuse her sons. She went to university at Oxford, where she attended lectures by J.R.R. Tolkien and C.S. Lewis. She moved from Oxford when her husband John Burrow received a professorship in Bristol; they have three sons. The University of Bristol awarded her an honorary doctorate in literature in 2006.

Wynne Jones's work places high value on originality; she despises cliché. Joyfully absurd situations abound in her books. Her characters are often children and young adults struggling through adversity to find their personal strengths and fit themselves into their worlds. Perhaps her best loved work, the Chrestomanci series, chronicles a number of magicians who must keep a multiverse of England-like lands in magical order.

> Fantasy for me as a kid was real, and I had a fantasy about what life was, whether it was sort of wicked and dire, or wholly normal, or whatever. Anything really close to home is not, it seems to me, what a good book should be about. —(Diana Wynne Jones, http://www.misrule.com.au/dwjones.html. Last visited January 28, 2008)

Major Works

Novels

Magids series: *Deep Secret* (1997), *The Merlin Conspiracy* (2003)
Derkholm series: *Dark Lord of Derkholm* (1998), *Year of the Griffin* (2000)
A Sudden Wild Magic (1992)

Children's/Young Adult Fiction

Chrestomanci series: *Charmed Life* (1977), *The Magicians of Caprona* (1980), *Witch Week* (1982), *The Lives of Christopher Chant* (1988), *Mixed Magics* (collection) (2000), *Stealer of Souls* (2002), *Conrad's Fate* (2005), *The Pinhoe Egg* (2006)
Dalemark series: *Cart and Cwidder* (1975), *Drowned Ammet* (1977), *The Spellcoats* (1979), *Crown of Dalemark* (1993)
Castle series: *Howl's Moving Castle* (1986), *Castle in the Air* (1992)
Wilkins' Tooth (aka Witch's Business) (1973)
The Ogre Downstairs (1974)
Eight Days of Luke (1975)
Dogsbody (1975)
Power of Three (1976)
The Homeward Bounders (1981)
The Time of the Ghost (1981)
Archer's Goon (1984)
Fire and Hemlock (1984)
*Black Maria (*aka *Aunt Maria)* (1991)
Hexwood (1993)
Puss in Boots (1999)
The Game (2007)

Short Story Collections

Warlock at the Wheel and Other Stories (1984)
Stopping for a Spell (1993)

Everard's Ride (1994)
Minor Arcana (1996)
Believing is Seeing: Seven Stories (1999)
Unexpected Magic (2002)

Other Important Writings

The Tough Guide to Fantasyland (1996)

Research Sources

Encyclopedias and Handbooks: EF, HDF, SJGF

Biographies and Interviews

"Author Interview: Diana Wynne Jones." *BookBrowse.com*. http://www.bookbrowse.com/author_interviews/full/index.cfm?author_number=908. Last visited January 28, 2008.

Craig, Amanda. "Diana Wynne Jones Interview." March 2005. http://www.amandacraig.com/pages/journalism/interviews/diana_wynne_jones.htm. Last visited January 28, 2008.

Gay, Anne. "The Line One Interview with Diana Wynne Jones." http://www.herebedragons.co.uk/gay/dwj.htm. Last visited January 28, 2008.

Jones, Diana Wynne. "The Heroic Ideal—A Personal Odyssey." *The Lion and the Unicorn* 13(1) (June 1989), pp. 129–140.

Parsons, Caron. "Going Out in Bristol." *BBC.com*. March 2003. http://www.bbc.co.uk/bristol/content/goingout/2003/03/05/books.shtml. Last visited January 28, 2008.

Ridge, Judith. "Interview with Diana Wynne Jones." http://www.misrule.com.au/dwjones.html. Last visited January 28, 2008.

Criticism and Readers' Guides

Hixon, Martha P., Sharon M. Scapple, and Donna R. White, eds. *Diana Wynne Jones: An Exciting and Exacting Wisdom*. New York: Peter Lang, 2002.

Mendlesohn, Farah and Jack Zipes. "Diana Wynne Jones: Children's Literature and the Fantastic Tradition." *Children's Literature and Culture*. New York: Routledge, 2005.

Perry, Evelyn M. "The Ever-Vigilant Hero: Revaluing the Tale of Tam Lin." *Children's Folklore Review* 19(2) (Spring 1997), pp. 31–49.

Turner, Alice K. "Reading Diana Wynne Jones." *New York Review of Science Fiction* 15(11) (July 2003), pp. 1, 4–5.

White, Donna R. "Diana Wynne Jones." In Caroline C. Hunt, ed., *British Children's Writers Since 1960: First Series* (Dictionary of Literary Biography)Detroit, MI: Gale, 1996, pp. 225–232.

Web Sites

HarperCollins. *The Many Worlds of Diana Wynne Jones.* http://www.harpercollins.co.uk/authors/default.aspx?id=2989 Last visited January 28, 2008. Publisher's site. Contains book information, biography.

Kaplan, Deborah. *Chrestomanci Castle: The Diana Wynne Jones Homepage.* http://www.suberic.net/dwj/index.html. Last visited January 28, 2008. Fan site. Contains news, bibliography, links, quotes, mailing list, wiki, and Kaplan's thesis on Wynne Jones.

MacArdle Meredith and Helen Scott. *The Diana Wynne Jones Fansite.* http://www.leemac.freeserve.co.uk/. Last visited January 28, 2008.

If you like Diana Wynne Jones

Wynne Jones despises cliché. Joyfully absurd situations abound in her books. Her characters are often children and young adults struggling through adversity to find their personal strengths and fit themselves into their worlds. Perhaps her best loved work, the Chrestomanci series chronicles a number of magicians who must keep a multiverse of England-like lands in magical order.

Then you might like

Lloyd Alexander

Based on Welsh mythology, Alexander's Prydain series tells the story of Taran, an assistant pig keeper who is anxious to prove himself as a hero. The series starts with *The Book of Three*, and continues with *The Black Cauldron*, *The Castle of Llyr*, *Taran Wanderer*, and *The High King*. Alexander wrote a number of other fantasy books for young adults, including *The Cat Who Wished to Be a Man* and *The Wizard in the Tree*.

Susan Cooper

Cooper's The Dark Is Rising series is a grand saga of the efforts of the Light to defeat the Dark. Like Wynne Jones's work, it explores friendship and growing up under threatening circumstances. Other Cooper fantasies include *Seaward* and *The Boggart*.

Linda Medley

Medley's *Castle Waiting* graphic-novel series shares Alexander's themes of self-exploration and self-acceptance. Its characters pop off the page, ranging from Sleeping Beauty's ladies-in-waiting to a stork-headed chamberlain to a bearded-lady nun, brim-full of personality and humor.

Edith Nesbit (E Nesbit)

One of the first children's fantasy writers, Nesbit wrote several magically humorous books, including *Five Children and It*, *The Phoenix and the Carpet*, and *The Enchanted Castle*. Like Jones, Nesbit injected humor and personality into her child characters. Nesbit also wrote less magical (but still humorous) books such as *The Wouldbegoods*.

Nnedi Okorafor-Mbachu

Okorafor-Mbachu mines myth and legend for her young adult books, *The Shadow Speaker* and *Zahrah the Windseeker*. Her chosen legends, however, are those of West Africa, and her work will appeal to anyone wishing to expand horizons beyond standard European settings.

Patricia Wrede

Wrede's *Mairelon the Magician* and *Magician's Ward* follow young English guttersnipe Kim as she solves magical mysteries as well as the mysteries of well-bred English conduct alongside lordly magician Mairelon.

Robert Jordan (1948–2007)

Biographical Sketch

James Oliver Rigney Jr. lived his entire life in South Carolina, graduating from the Citadel military college with a degree in physics. He served two tours in the U.S. Army in Vietnam, where he earned the Distinguished Flying Cross and Bronze Star, and after college worked for the U.S. Navy as a nuclear engineer. He died in 2007 from complications of amyloidosis, a rare blood disease.

The immense, sprawling Wheel of Time series takes place in a world that cycles through periods of war between essential good and evil forces in the universe. In the latest conflict in the cycle, dark forces have tainted the major source of magical and spiritual power of the forces of light, such that the cycle's savior may turn out too insane to fight. Hundreds of characters and their intricate relationships bolster the main plot.

> Some stories need to be told in certain genres, and fantasy allows the writer to explore good and evil, right and wrong, honour and duty without having to bow to the mainstream belief that all of these things are merely two sides of a coin. —(Robert Jordan, http://www.sffworld.com/interview/51p0.html. Last visited January 28, 2008)

Major Works

Novels

Conan series: *Conan the Defender* (1982), *Conan the Invincible* (1982), *Conan the Triumphant* (1983), *Conan the Unconquered* (1983), *Conan the Destroyer* (1984), *Conan the Magnificent* (1984), *Conan the Victorious* (1984)

Wheel of Time series: *The Eye of the World* (1990), *The Great Hunt* (1990), *The Dragon Reborn* (1991), *The Shadow Rising* (1992), *The Fires of Heaven* (1993), *Lord of Chaos* (1994), *A Crown of Swords* (1996), *The Path of Daggers* (1998), *Winter's Heart* (2000), *Crossroads of Twilight* (2002), *Knife of Dreams* (2005)

Research Sources

Encyclopedias and Handbooks: EF, HDF, SJGF

Biographics and Interviews

Lilley, Ernest. "SFRevu Interview: Robert Jordan." *SFRevu*. January 21, 2003. http://www.sfrevu.com/ISSUES/2003/0301/Feature%20Interview%20-%20Robert%20Jordan/Interview.htm. Last visited January 28, 2008.

McCarthy, Michael and Mark McLaughlin. "The Big Wheel of Time Keeps On Turning for Fantasist Robert Jordan." *SciFi.com* 362. 2004. http://www.scifi.com/sfw/issue362/interview.html. Last visited January 28, 2008.

"'New Spring': Fantasy writer Robert Jordan." *USA Today* (January 5, 2004). http://cgi1.usatoday.com/mchat/20040106007/tscript.htm. Last visited January 28, 2008.

Orbit. "Interview with Robert Jordan." *SFFWorld.com*. 2000. http://www.sffworld.com/interview/50p0.html. Last visited January 28, 2008.

"Robert Jordan." *Fast Forward*. March 2003. http://www.fast-forward.tv/audio/audio152.m3u. Last visited January 28, 2008.

"Robert Jordan Chats About His 'Wheel of Time' Series." *CNN.com* (December 12, 2000). http://www.cnn.com/chat/transcripts/2000/12/12/jordan/index.html. Last visited January 28, 2008.

"Robert Jordan: The Name Behind the Wheel." *Locus* 44(3) (March 2000), pp. 6–7, 76.

Criticism and Readers' Guides

Attrill, Heather. "Lore, Myth, and Meaning for Postmoderns: An Introduction to the Story World of Robert Jordan's Wheel of Time Sequence." *Australian Folklore* 18 (November 2003), pp. 37–76.

Butler, Leigh, Pamela Korda, and Erica Sadun. "Wheel of Time FAQ." http://www.steelypips.org/wotfaq/. Last visited January 28, 2008.

Ryan, J.S. "Neglected Repositories for Folk Memory and Timeless Folk Attitudes." *Australian Folklore* 18 (November 2003), pp. 35–106.

Web Sites

Dragonmount: A Wheel of Time Community. http://www.dragonmount.com/News/. Last visited January 28, 2008. Fan site. Contains news, art gallery, forums, mailing list, book information.

Robert Jordan's Official Blog. http://www.dragonmount.com/RobertJordan/. Last visited January 28, 2008.

Seven Spokes: A Wheel of Time Chronology. http://www.sevenspokes.com/. Last visited January 28, 2008. Fan site. Also contains interview list (through 2004) and index.

Theoryland of the Wheel of Time. http://www.theoryland.com/. Last visited January 28, 2008. Fan site. Contains forum, essays, and guesses about the book's future plotlines.

Guy Gavriel Kay (1954–)

Biographical Sketch

Guy Gavriel Kay was born in Weyburn, Saskatchewan, Canada, and raised in Winnipeg, Manitoba. After college at the University of Manitoba, he moved to Oxford to help Christopher Tolkien with the editing of J.R.R. Tolkien's *The Silmarillion*. On his return to Canada, he earned a law degree from the University of Toronto, later passing the bar. In addition to his fiction, he has written for radio series. He lives with his wife Laura and their two sons in Toronto, typically writing his books while living abroad.

Kay's Fionavar Tapestry series follows the well-known fantasy trope of abandoning this world characters in a fantasy world, where they become powerful in their separate ways and must save their adopted home. His later books are a step away from alternate history, set in fantasy worlds that strongly resemble medieval Spain or Italy or France or Turkey. Kay researches and plots his novels carefully, and their intricate detail endears them to fans.

> What I do believe is that the quiet, steady accumulation of detail and complexity reach out to readers in an almost subliminal way. Readers end up with a measure of trust in the author and the book, without necessarily being able to point to anything specific, and that trust is invaluable. —(Guy Gavriel Kay, http://www.sfsite.com/09a/ggk88.htm. Last visited January 28, 2008)

Major Works

Novels

Fionavar Tapestry series: *The Summer Tree* (1984), *The Wandering Fire* (1986), *The Darkest Road* (1986)

Sarantine Mosaic series: *Sailing to Sarantium* (1998), *Lord of Emperors* (2000)

Tigana (1990)
A Song for Arbonne (1992)
The Lions of Al-Rassan (1995)
The Last Light of the Sun (2003)
Ysabel (2007)

Research Sources

Encyclopedias and Handbooks: EF, HDF, SJGF

Biographies and Interviews

Auden, Sandy. "Historical Significance: An Interview with Guy Gavriel Kay." *Infinity Plus*. http://www.infinityplus.co.uk/nonfiction/intggk.htm. Last visited January 28, 2008.

Auden, Sandy. "A Question of Character: An Interview with Guy Gavriel Kay." *SF-Site.com*. 2005. http://www.sfsite.com/04b/sagk198.htm. Last visited January 28, 2008.

Grant, Glenn M. "An Interview with Guy Gavriel Kay." *New York Review of Science Fiction* 33 (May 1991), pp. 16–19.

"Guy Gavriel Kay: Lord of Fantasy." *Locus* 44(5) (May 2000), pp. 6–7, 63–64.

"Guy Gavriel Kay: View from the North." *Locus* 52(4) (April 2004), pp. 6–7, 54, 56.

Halasz, Peter. "An Interview with Guy Gavriel Kay." *New York Review of Science Fiction* 13(5) (January 2001), pp. 17–19.

Holliday, Liz. "Guy Gavriel Kay." *Science Fiction Chronicle* 13(3) (December 1991), pp 5, 24–26.

Turner, Rodger. "A Conversation with Guy Gavriel Kay." *SFSite.com*. June 2000. http://www.sfsite.com/09a/ggk88.htm. Last visited January 28, 2008.

Criticism and Readers' Guides

Cobb, Christopher. "Guy Gavriel Kay and the Psychology of History." *Foundation* 34(94) (Summer 2005), pp. 87–99.

Francis, Diana Pharaoh. "Paradigms of Colonization: Exploring Themes of Imperialism in Guy Gavriel Kay's *Tigana*." *Journal of the Fantastic in the Arts* 13(2) (2002), pp. 114–133.

Patton, Andy. "We See By Jad's Light Alone: Guy Gavriel Kay and the New Sanctuary Mosaicist." *New York Review of Science Fiction* 14(5) (January 2002), pp. 15–18.

Webb, Janeen. "Post-Romantic Romance: Guy Gavriel Kay's *Tigana* and *A Song for Arbonne*." *New York Review of Science Fiction* 7(5) (January 1995), pp. 17–19.

Web Sites

Bright Weavings: The Worlds of Guy Gavriel Kay. http://brightweavings.com/. Last visited January 28, 2008. Author's official Web site. Contains news, reviews, journal, excerpts, bibliography, essays, and links.

If you like Guy Gavriel Kay

Kay's Fionavar Tapestry series (*The Summer Tree*, *The Wandering Fire*, *The Darkest Road*) follows the well-known fantasy trope of abandoning this world characters in a fantasy world, where they become powerful in their separate ways and must save their adopted home. His later books (*Tigana*, *A Song for Arbonne*, *The Lions of Al-Rassan*) are a step away from alternate history, set in fantasy worlds that strongly resemble medieval Spain or Italy or France or Turkey. Kay researches and plots his novels carefully, and their intricate detail endears them to fans.

Then you might like

Steven K. Brust

Brust's lengthy, swashbuckling Vlad Taltos series (*Jhereg*, *Yendi*, *Teckla*, and many others) follows its scheming lead character through many reversals of fortune. Gloriously gung-ho action and sweeping settings mirror Kay's dramatic, romantic storytelling.

Lois McMaster Bujold

Bujold's Chalion series (*The Curse of Chalion*, *Paladin of Souls*, *The Hallowed Hunt*) places likeable characters in a well-imagined world of military and religious conflict. Like Kay, Bujold draws her setting from the politics of medieval and Renaissance Europe.

Barbara Hambly

Hambly's Darwath series (*The Time of the Dark*, *The Walls of Air*, *The Armies of Daylight*) follows a graduate-student philologist who uses her linguistic and historical training to unravel ancient mysteries in the otherworld she is transported to. Hambly's novels, like Kay's, present tough ethical choices with severe consequences.

Robert Holdstock

Holdstock's highly allusive work seeks to ring changes on immortal archetypes (notably the Arthurian mythos), recognizing cultural commonalities while respecting the fresh perspectives brought to stock characters by every culture that treats of them. Kay fans will enjoy *Mythago Wood* and its sequels (*Lavondyss*, *The Bone Forest*, *The Hollowing*, and others).

Ellen Kushner

Swordspoint and its associated novels (*The Fall of the Kings*, *The Privilege of the Sword*) embed their characters firmly in a rigidly stratified society with intricate politics and real human costs. Her award-winning novel *Thomas the Rhymer* brings ancient British legend to new life. Like Kay, Kushner's settings and characters reflect real European cultures.

Elizabeth Moon

Moon's Paksenarrion series (*Sheepfarmer's Daughter, Divided Allegiance, Oath of Gold*) is the sweeping saga of a woman who leaves her home to follow her creed and her heart, becoming a great hero. Its epic scope and upright characters recall Kay's.

Naomi Novik

Novik burst on the fantasy scene with the Temeraire series, the story of Napoleonic Europe with talking dragons. Its political intrigue and romantic flair will appeal to fans of Kay's works.

Katharine Kerr (1944–)

Biographical Sketch

Born Nancy Brahtin in Cleveland, Ohio, of British parents, Katharine Kerr grew up in Santa Barbara, moving to the San Francisco Bay area as a young adult. She dropped out of Stanford during the 1960s and worked odd jobs while educating herself in history, antiquities, and languages. She and her husband Howard are avid baseball fans. She also enjoys roleplaying games; she edited a major industry publication for a time and wrote several adventure modules. The publication of her third Deverry series was delayed owing to serious illness.

Celtic influences show in Kerr's work. The Deverry series, which when it is complete will divide into three "quartets" of novels, investigates the past as well as the present of the world of Annwn, which contains several races with distinct (and well-drawn) cultures. The central setting is the kingdom of Deverry, which undergoes considerable political intrigue and upheaval; the central characters, Lord Rhodry Maelwaedd and his beloved Jill, endure separation, slavery, and exile.

> The careful building up of an alien culture in order to make the actions of alien characters comprehensible is not filler; no more is the creation of a historical background for a culture in order to give the events that happen their depth; and finally, the depiction of relationships between characters in these exotic contexts is to many readers and writers the core of a book, not "romantic fluff" or more filler.—(Katharine Kerr, http://deverry.com/roman3.html. Last visited January 28, 2008)

Major Works

Novels

Deverry series: Daggerspell (1986), *Darkspell* (1987), *The Bristling Wood* (1989), *The Dragon Revenant* (1990), *A Time of Exile* (1991), *A Time of Omens* (1992), *Days of Blood and Fire* (1993), *A Time of Justice* (1994), *The Red Wyvern* (1997), *The Black Raven* (1998), *The Fire Dragon* (2000), *The Gold Falcon* (2006), *The Spirit Stone* (2007)

Research Sources

Encyclopedias and Handbooks: EF, HDF, SJGF

Biographies and Interviews

Allen, Moira. "What's in a Name?" *Writing World.* 2000. http://www.writing-world.com/sf/name.shtml. Last visited January 28, 2008.

"An Interview with Katharine Kerr." *Amaranth* 1 (September/October 1990), pp. 32–35.

King, T. Jackson. "Katharine Kerr." *Science Fiction Chronicle* 14(11) (August 1993), pp. 5, 31–34.

Web Sites

DeepGenre. http://www.deepgenre.com/wordpress/. Last visited January 28, 2008. A collaborative authors' and artists' web log including Katharine Kerr. Last visited March 20, 2007.

Katharine Kerr's Home Page. http://www.deverry.com/. Last visited January 28, 2008. Author's official web site. Includes news, bibliography, biography, essays, links.

KatherineKerr Mailing List. http://groups.yahoo.com/group/KatharineKerr/. Last visited January 28, 2008.

Gregory Keyes (1963–)

Biographical Sketch

Gregory Keyes holds a master's degree in anthropology from the University of Georgia. He has also studied Russian, French, Mandarin, Japanese, and Old Norse. He is bilingual in Navajo after having lived on a Navajo reservation as a child because of his father's job. He enjoys fencing and lives in Savannah, Georgia.

Keyes' novels are strongly influenced by his interest in mythology, history, and story telling. For instance, his Children of the Changeling series was influenced by several ancient water controlling cultures such as the Egyptians and the Mesopotamians, while his Age of Reason series is set in an fantasy alternate history and features characters such as Benjamin Franklin, Cotton Mather, and Isaac Newton. Keyes also publishes as "Greg Keyes" and "J. Gregory Keyes."

> I have a hard time believing in Fantasy that is completely unconnected to our world. I've said before if you've got running around with Christian names running around in a Fantasy world and there was never a Christ it seems very odd to me. Or for that matter, people running around in a world that's not Ireland or not originally from Ireland who have Irish names. —(Gregory Keyes, *sffworld.com* interview. Available online at http://www.sffworld.com/interview/28p1.html. Last visited January 28, 2008)

Major Works

Novels

Children of the Changeling series: *The Waterborn* (1996), *The Blackgod* (1997)

Age of Unreason series: *Newton's Cannon* (1998), *A Calculus of Angels* (1999), *Empire of Unreason* (2000), *The Shadows of God* (2001)

Kingdoms of Thorn and Bone series: *The Briar King* (2002), *The Charnel Prince* (2004), *The Blood Knight* (2006)

Research Sources

Encyclopedias and Handbooks: HDF

Biographies and Interviews

Bedford, Rob. "Interview with Greg Keyes." *sffworld.com*. February 11, 2003. http://www.sffworld.com/interview/28p0.html. Last visited January 28, 2008.

Web Sites

Greg Keyes. http://www.gregkeyes.com. Last visited January 28, 2008. Author's official web site.

Rosemary Kirstein (1953–)

Biographical Sketch

Rosemary Kirstein was born in Massachussets and raised in Connecticut. She discovered science fiction and fantasy through her older sister. Kirstein has worked as a singer-songwriter, a computer programmer, and various other jobs. She currently lives near Boston. Kirstein has won critical and popular acclaim for her Steerswomen cycle, in which she plays with the conventions of fantasy and magic.

> Fiction gives us a sense of perspective, a sense of purpose. We don't have to turn our lives into stories; we just have to dig out the story that's there as a natural result of living. —(Rosemary Kirstein, "Rosemary Kirstein: Steering Through Life." *Locus* interview, 2005)

Major Works

Novels

The Steerswomen series: *The Steerswoman* (1989), *The Outskirter's Secret* (1992), *The Lost Steersman* (2003), *The Language of Power* (2004)

Research Sources

Encyclopedias and Handbooks: EF

Biographies and Interviews

Kirstein, Rosemary. "Rosemary Kirstein: Steering Through Life." *Locus* 54(5) (May 2005), pp. 74–75.

Laurie J. Marks. "Interview with Rosemary Kirstein." *SFRevu*, August 2003. http://www.sfrevu.com/ISSUES/2003/0308/Rosemary%20Kirstein%20Interview/Review.htm. Last visited January 28, 2008.

Ellen Kushner (1955–)

Biographical Sketch

Ellen Kushner grew up in Cleveland, Ohio. She attended Bryn Mawr College and Barnard College, and then worked in the New York publishing industry for some years. She is currently the host for "Sound and Spirit," a public radio program. Kushner is also a performance artist, and has taught at several writing workshops. She currently lives in New York City.

Many of Ellen Kushner's fantasy novels and short stories have been described as "Mannerpunk." Together with several other artists and writers, Ellen Kushner has been active in the so called "interstitial" movement—a movement which strives to integrate and cross boundaries between various forms of art, music, and literature.

> I like the fact that we don't all have the same hallucinations. What happens when your book gets out there and people actually read it, and it turns out to a completely different object from what you made. I love that. Nobody is having the same hallucination I am, even when I read it to you. —(Ellen Kushner, "Ellen Kushner." Available online at http://web.mit.edu/m-i-t/science_fiction/profiles/kushner.html. Last visited January 28, 2008)

Major Works

Novels

Swordspoint: A Melodrama of Manners (1987)
Thomas the Rhymer (1990)
The Fall of the Kings (with Delia Sherman, 2002)
The Privilege of the Sword (2006)

Children's/Young Adult Fiction

From the Choose Your Own Adventure series: *Outlaws of Sherwood Forest* (1985), *The Enchanted Kingdom* (with Judith Mitchell, 1986), *Statue of Liberty Adventure* (1986), *The Mystery of the Secret Room* (1986) *Knights of the Round Table* (1989)

Other

Host, "Sound & Spirit," a weekly National Public Radio show. http://www.wgbh.org/pages/pri/spirit. Last visited January 28, 2008.

Research Sources

Encyclopedias and Handbooks: EF, HDF, SJGF

Biographies and Interviews

Adams, John Joseph. "*Privilege* Isn't Just For Teens." *SciFi.com*. March 30, 2007. http://www.scifi.com/scifiwire/index.php?category=5&id=40794. Last visited January 28, 2008.

"Author Interview: Ellen Kushner." *Science Fiction Book Club*. http://www.sfbc.com/doc/full_site_enrollment/detail/fse_product_detail_plus.jhtml?section_name=Author%20Interview&repositoryId=982646B510. Last visited January 28, 2008.

Berkwits, Jeff. "Blowing the Horns of Elfland—Ellen Kushner and the Magic of Music." *ASTERISM: The Journal of Science Fiction, Fantasy and Space Music* (Fall 1996). Available online at http://www.wgbh.org/pages/pri/spirit/specials/asterism.html. Last visited January 28, 2008.

Berman, Steve. "Interview: Ellen Kushner." *Strange Horizons*, (November 11, 2002). http://www.strangehorizons.com/2002/20021111/interview.shtml. Last visited January 28, 2008.

"Ellen Kushner: True Fantasy." *Locus* 28(4) (April 1992), pp. 5, 65–66.

Haldeman, Joe. "Ellen Kushner/Sarah Zettel." *Media in Translation*, September 3, 1998. http://web.mit.edu/m-i-t/science_fiction/transcripts/kushner_zettel_index.html. Joint interview with Kushner and Zettel. Last visited January 28, 2008.

Mathew, David. "Dividing The Rewards: An Interview with Ellen Kushner and Delia Sherman." *SF Site*. http://www.sfsite.com/11b/dm69.htm. Last visited January 28, 2008.

Scalzi, John. "Your Wednesday Author Interview: Ellen Kushner." *By the Way. . . .* July 25, 2006. http://journals.aol.com/johnmscalzi/bytheway/entries/2006/07/26/your-wednesday-author-interview-ellen-kushner/6253. Last visited January 28, 2008.

Schweitzer, Darrell. "Interview with Ellen Kushner." *Marion Zimmer Bradley's Fantasy Magazine* 34 (Winter 1997), pp. 38–43.

Web Sites

Ellen Kushner. http://www.sff.net/people/kushnerSherman/Kushner. Author's official Web site. Last visited January 28, 2008.

Puggy's Hill. http://ellen-kushner.livejournal.com. Last visited January 28, 2008. Author's personal journal.

Mercedes Lackey (1950–)

Biographical Sketch

Mercedes Lackey was born in Chicago, Illinois, and graduated from Purdue University. She worked at a variety of jobs prior to writing full time, including waitressing, serving as an artist's model, and computer programming. She lives in Tulsa, Oklahoma, and is active in wildlife rehabilitation.

She has written novels in a variety of genres, including fantasy, science fiction, horror, and detective, but is probably most popular for her Valdemar books. Lackey has also written the lyrics for several science-fiction folk songs, and music plays a prominent role in many of her novels.

> I'm a storyteller; that's what I see as 'my job.' My stories come out of my characters; how those characters would react to the given situation. Maybe that's why I get letters from readers as young as thirteen and as old as sixty-odd. —(Mercedes Lackey, http://www.mercedeslackey.com/biography.html. Last visited January 30, 2008)

Major Works

Novels

Heralds of Valdemar series: *Arrows of the Queen* (1987), *Arrow's Flight* (1987), *Arrow's Fall* (1988), *By the Sword* (1991), *Take a Thief* (2001), *Exile's Honor* (2002), *Exile's Valor* (2003)

Vows & Honor series: *The Oathbound* (1988), *Oathbreakers* (1989), *Oathblood* (1998)

Last Herald Mage trilogy: *Magic's Pawn* (1989), *Magic's Promise* (1990), *Magic's Price* (1990)

The Mage Winds trilogy: *Winds of Fate* (1991), *Winds of Change* (1992), *Winds of Fury* (1993)

Elemental Masters series: *The Fire Rose* (1994), *The Serpent's Shadow* (2001), *The Gates of Sleep* (2002), *Phoenix and Ashes* (2004), *The Wizard of London* (2005)
Mage Wars trilogy (with Larry Dixon): *The Black Gryphon* (1994) *The White Gryphon* (1995), *The Silver Gryphon*, 1996
The Owl Mage trilogy (with Larry Dixon): *Owlflight* (1997), *Owlsight* (1998), *Owlknight* (1999)
Dragon Jousters series: *Joust* (2003), *Alta* (2004), *Sanctuary* (2005) *Aerie* (2006)
Tales of Five Hundred Kingdoms series: *The Fairy Godmother* (2004), *One Good Knight* (2006), *Fortune's Fool* (2007)
By the Sword (1991)
Brightly Burning (2000)

Short Story Collections

Fiddler Fair (1998)
Werehunter (1998)

Other Important Writings

Lackey, Mercedes. "Harry Potter and the Post-Traumatic Stress Disorder Counselor." *Mapping the World of Harry Potter: Science Fiction and Fantasy Authors Explore the Bestselling Fantasy Series of All Time*. Ed., Mercedes Lackey. Dallas, TX: BenBella Books, 2005, pp. 157–162.

Research Sources

Encyclopedias and Handbooks: EF, HDF, SJGF

Biographies and Interviews

"Mercedes Lackey Interview." *Ebon Tower*. http://www.telisphere.com/~davidl/inkmouse/lackeyqna.htm. Last visited January 28, 2008.
Waters, Elizabeth. "Interview With Mercedes Lackey." *Marion Zimmer Bradley's Fantasy Magazine* 19 (Spring 1993), pp. 50–52.

Criticism and Readers' Guides

Helfers, John and Denise Little. *The Valdemar Companion: A Guide to Mercedes Lackey's World of Valdemar*. New York: DAW Books, 2001.

Web Sites

Mercedes Lackey Homepage. http://www.mercedeslackey.com. Last visited January 28, 2008. Author's official Web site.
Queen's Own: The Official Mercedes Lackey Fan Club. http://www.dragonlordsnet.com/qo.htm. Last visited January 28, 2008.

If you like Mercedes Lackey

Although she has written in a variety of genres, Lackey is probably best known for her long-running epic fantasy Valdemar books.

Then you might like

Lois McMaster Bujold

Bujold's Chalion series (*The Curse of Chalion*, *Paladin of Souls*, *The Hallowed Hunt*) places likeable characters in a well-imagined world of military and religious conflict.

Kate Elliott

Elliott's epic fantasies are based on a densely thought out alternate world reminiscent from European myth. Elliott's interest in religious and political conflict is evident in her Crown of Stars series (*King's Dragon*, *Prince of Dogs*, *The Burning Stone*, *Child of Flame*, *The Gathering Storm*, *In the Ruins*, and *The Crown of Stars*).

Katharine Kerr

Kerr's Deverry books, set in the world of Annwn, include political intrigue and a rich tapestry of characters. The first "quartet" of books includes *Daggerspell*, *Darkspell*, *The Bristling Wood*, and *The Dragon Revenant*.

Anne McCaffrey

McCaffrey's Dragonriders books feature a rich and diverse cast of characters and history. A good place to start is her "Dragonriders of Pern" series (*Dragonflight*, *Dragonquest*, and *The White Dragon*).

Patricia McKillip

McKillip's Riddle Master of Hed trilogy follows Morgan, Prince of Hed, as he journeys far from his home and finds himself embroiled in a war beyond his imaginings (*The Riddle-Master of Hed*, *Heir of Sea and Fire*, and *Harpist in the Wind*).

Diana Paxson

Paxson's Westeria series, set in a far future Californian landscape, is another classic epic fantasy (*Lady of Light*, *Lady of Darkness*, *Silverhair the Wanderer*, *The Earthstone*, *The Sea Star*, *The Wind Crystal*, *The Jewel of Fire*, and *The Golden Hills of Westria*).

Stephen R. Lawhead (1950–)

Biographical Sketch

Stephen Lawhead was born in Nebraska. He was associated with *Campus Life Magazine* for several years, and wrote or cowrote numerous books on Christian themes. He also used to work as a rock band manager and owned a music label.

Many of Lawhead's novels are set in a medieval fantasy setting, including his *Pendragon Cycle*, a retelling of the story of King Arthur. He also writes historical fiction and science fiction. At one time, he lived in Oxford, England, which greatly aided his access to Arthurian research materials, but he currently lives in Austria.

> To the extent that fantasy books paint a picture of a world that is in some way more heroic, more humane, more beautiful and hopeful than this one... that is something that people really respond to, and I'm all for it.—(Stephen Lawhead, "Fact and Fiction—Stephen Lawhead Interviewed." Available online at http://mewsingonbooks.blogspot.com/2006_10_01_archive.html. Last visited January 28, 2008)

Major Works

Novels

Dragon King Trilogy: *In the Hall of the Dragon King* (1982), *The Warlords of Nin* (1983), *The Sword and the Flame* (1984)

Pendragon Cycle: *Taliesin* (1987), *Merlin* (1988), *Arthur* (1989), *Pendragon* (1994), *Grail* (1997)

Song of Albion series: *The Paradise War* (1991), *The Silver Hand* (1992), *The Endless Knot* (1993)

Avalon: The Return of King Arthur (1999)

Other Important Writings

After You Graduate: A Guide to Life After High School. Grand Rapids, MI: Zondervan Pub. House, 1978.

Rock of this Age: The Real & Imagined Dangers of Rock Music. Downers Grove, IL: InterVarsity Press, 1987.

Research Sources

Encyclopedias and Handbooks: EF, HDF, SJGF

Biographies and Interviews

Barrett, David V. "Bloody History: Stephen Lawhead Interviewed." *Interzone* 112 (October 1996), pp. 23–26.

"Fact and Fiction—Stephen Lawhead Interviewed." *Through the Looking Glass (Or Musings on Books): A Blog About Genre Fiction*, October 4, 2006.

http://mewsingonbooks.blogspot.com/2006_10_01_archive.html. Last visited January 28, 2008.

Grantham, Madeleine. "A Nebraska Yankee in King Arthur's Court: An Interview with Stephen Lawhead." *Vector*. 199 (May/June 1998), pp. 6–8.

Grey, Ciara. "Interview with Stephen Lawhead." *Fiction Factor: The Online Magazine for Fiction Writers*. http://www.fictionfactor.com/interviews/stephenlawhead.html. Last visited January 30, 2008.

Markowitz, John. "Stephen R. Lawhead." *Science Fiction Chronicle* 18(1) October 1996, pp. 11, 66–70.

"Stephen Lawhead: Author of Hood." *The Frequency Podcast: A Christian Perspective on Pop-Culture*. http://audio.calvaryabq.org/m88/interviews/Lawhead_interview.mp3. Last visited January 28, 2008. Audio podcast interview with Lawhead.

Criticism and Readers' Guides

Doherty, John J. "'A Land Shining with Goodness': Magic and Religion in Stephen R. Lawhead's *Taliesin*, *Merlin*, and *Arthur*." *Arthuriana* 9(1) (Spring 1999), pp. 57–66.

Hildebrand, Kristina. "The Female Reader at the Round Table: Religion and Women in Three Contemporary Arthurian Texts." *Acta Universitatis Upsaliensis, Studia Anglistica Upsaliensia*. Uppsala, Sweden: Uppsala University, 2001, p. 115.

Kobler, Turner S. "King Arthur and Popular Culture." In William E. Tanner, ed., *The Arthurian Myth of Quest and Magic: A Festschrift in Honor of Lavon B. Fulwiler*. Dallas, TX: Caxton's Mod. Arts, 1993, pp. 107–114.

Web Sites

Stephen Lawhead. http://www.stephenlawhead.com. Last visited January 28, 2008. Author's official Web site.

Stephen R. Lawhead Mailing List. http://www.aracnet.com/~petercj/srl. Last visited January 28, 2008.

E-mail list for discussing Lawhead's works. *Stephen R. Lawhead FAQ Version 2.1.5*. http://www.aracnet.com/~petercj/srl/FAQ.html. Last visited January 28, 2008.

Tanith Lee (1947–)

Biographical Sketch

Tanith Lee was born in London, England. Before writing full time, she worked at a variety of jobs, including one in a library. Highly prolific, she has written numerous novels for both adults; and children and young adults. Many of her fantasies have a dark, erotic edge. In addition to fantasy, she also writes science fiction, historical fiction, and retellings of myth and fairy tales.

I think of myself as a story-teller, and that is it. Locality is, in my case, unimportant. My mind and heart go where they wish. —(Tanith Lee, *Tabula Rasa* interview. Available online at http://www.tabula-rasa.info/Horror/TanithLee.html. Last visited January 28, 2008)

Major Works

Novels

Flat Earth series: *Night's Master* (1978), *Death's Master* (1979), *Delusion's Master* (1981), *Delirium's Mistress* (1986), *Night's Sorceries* (1987)
Secret Books of Paradys series: *The Book of the Damned* (1988), *The Book of the Beast* (1988), *The Book of the Dead* (1991) also published as *Paradys*, *The Book of the Mad*
The Blood of Roses (1990)
Secret Books of Venus series: *Faces Under Water* (1998), *Saint Fire* (1999), *A Bed of Earth* (2002), *Venus Preserved* (2003)
Lionwolf series: *Cast a Bright Shadow* (2004), *Here in Cold Hell* (2005), *No Flame But Mine* (2007)
White as Snow (2000)
Mortal Suns (2003)

Children's/Young Adult Fiction

Castle of Dark series: *The Castle of Dark* (1978), *Prince on a White Horse* (1982), *Dark Castle, White Horse* (1986)
Tanaquil series: *Black Unicorn* (1991), *Gold Unicorn* (1994), *Red Unicorn* (1997)
Claidi Journals series: *Wolf Tower* (2000) also published as *Law of the Wolf Tower*, *Wolf Star* (2000) also published as *Wolf Star Rise*, *Wolf Queen* (2001) also published as *Queen of the Wolves*, *Wolf Wing* (2002)

Short Story Collections

Red as Blood; or, Tales from the Sisters Grimmer (1983)
The Gorgon, and Other Beastly Tales (1985)
Forests of the Night (1989)
Tempting the Gods: The Selected Stories of Tanith Lee, Volume One (2007)

Research Sources

Encyclopedias and Handbooks: EF, HDF, SJGF

Biographies and Interviews

Garratt, Peter. "Unstoppable Fate: Tanith Lee Interview." *Interzone* 64 (October 1992), pp. 23–25.

"On the Lee Side." *Tabula Rasa* 4 (1994). http://www.tabula-rasa.info/Horror/TanithLee.html. Last visited January 28, 2008.

"Tanith Lee: Love & Death & Publishers." *Locus* 40(4) (April 1998), pp. 4–6, 76.

Criticism and Readers' Guides

Gordon, Joan. "Sharper Than a Serpent's Tooth: The Vampire in Search of Its Mother." *Blood Read: The Vampire as Metaphor in Contemporary Culture*. Eds., Joan Gordan and Veronica Hollinger. Philadelphia: University of Pennsylvania Press, 1997, pp. 45–55.

Haut, Mavis. *The Hidden Library of Tanith Lee: Themes and Subtexts from Dionysos to the Immortal Gene*. Jefferson, NC: McFarland, 2001.

Heldreth, Lillian M. "Tanith Lee's Werewolves Within: Reversals of Gothic Traditions." *Journal of the Fantastic in the Arts*, 2(1) (Spring 1989), pp. 15–23.

Heldreth, Lillian Marks. "Vampire Variations: Tanith Lee's Evolution of the Genre." *The Blood Is the Life: Vampires in Literature*. Eds., Leonard Heldreth and Mary Pharr. Bowling Green, OH: Popular, 1999, pp. 235–245.

Larbalestier, Justine. *Opulent Darkness: The Werewolves of Tanith Lee*. New Lambton, Australia: Nimrod Publications, 1999.

Lefanu, Sarah. "Robots and Romance: The Science Fiction and Fantasy of Tanith Lee." *Sweet Dreams: Sexuality, Gender and Popular Fiction*. London: Lawrence & Wishart, 1988, pp. 121–136.

Moran, Maureen F. "Educating Desire: Magic, Power, and Control in Tanith Lee's Unicorn Trilogy." *Utopian and Dystopian Writing for Children and Young Adults*. Eds., Carrie Hintz and Elaine Ostry. New York: Routledge, 2003, pp. 139–155.

Moran, Maureen F. "Tanith Lee." In Darren Harris-Fain, ed., *British Fantasy and Science-Fiction Writers Since 1960. (Dictionary of Literary Biography 261)*. Detroit, MI: Gale, 2002, pp. 274–292.

Pattison, Jim and Paul A. Soanes, compliers. Continued by Allison Rich. *Daughter of the Night: An Annotated Bibliography of Tanith Lee*. Available online at http://www.daughterofthenight.com. Last visited January 28, 2008.

Smith, Jeanette C. "The Heroine Within: Psychological Archetypes in Tanith Lee's *A Heroine of the World*." *Extrapolation* 39(1) (1998), pp. 52–56.

Web Sites

Tanith Lee. http://www.tanithlee.com. Last visited January 28, 2008. Author's official web site.

Ursula K. Le Guin (1929–)

Biographical Sketch

The daughter of anthropologist Alfred L. Kroeber and writer Theodora Kroeber, Ursula Le Guin grew up in Berkley, California and attended Radcliffe and

Columbia. She was awarded a Fullbright fellowship to study in France, where she met her husband Charles Le Guin. She currently resides in Portland, Oregon.

Le Guin started publishing science fiction and fantasy in the late 1960s and was part of the "New Wave" of the 1960s and 1970s. She continues to be prolific in a number of genres and forms, where she has explored a number of themes, including Jungian psychology, Taoist philosophy, and feminism. Le Guin has won a number of awards, including several Hugo and Nebula awards, the Gandalf Grand Master award in 1979 and the Science Fiction and Fantasy Writers of America Grand Master award in 2003.

> For after all, as great scientists have said and as all children know, it is above all by the imagination that we achieve perception, and compassion, and hope.—(Ursula K. LeGuin, *The Language of the Night: Essays on Fantasy and Science Fiction*)

Major Works

Novels

The Earthsea Cycle: *A Wizard of Earthsea* (1968), *The Tombs of Atuan* (1971), *The Farthest Shore* (1972), *Tehanu: The Last Book of Earthsea* (1990), *Tales from Earthsea* (2001), *The Other Wind* (2001)

Books for Children and Young Adults

Very Far from Anywhere Else (1976)
The Beginning Place (1980)
Catwings (1988)
Chronicles of the Western Shore: *Gifts* (2004), *Voices* (2006), *Powers* (2007)

Short Story Collections

Orsinian Tales (1975)
The Wind's Twelve Quarters (1975)
The Compass Rose (1982)
Unlocking the Air (1996)
The Birthday of the World and Other Stories (2002)
Changing Planes: Stories (2005)

Essay Collections

The Language of the Night: Essays on Fantasy and Science Fiction (1979, 1992)
Dancing at the Edge of the World: Thoughts on Words, Women, Places (1989, 1992)
Steering the Craft (1998)
The Wave in the Mind: Talks and Essays on the Writer, the Reader, and the Imagination (2004)

Essays and Articles

"Imaginary Friends." *New Statesman* (December 18, 2006). Available online at http: //www.newstatesman.com/200612180040. Last visited January 28, 2008.

"Thoughts on YA." *Locus* 56(5) (May 2006), p. 33.

Research Sources

Encyclopedias and Handbooks: EF, HDF, SJGF

Biographies and Interviews

Gevers, Nick. "Driven by a Different Chauffeur: An Interview with Ursula K. Le Guin." *SF Site*. November–December 2001. http://www.sfsite.com/03a/ul123.htm. Last visited January 28, 2008.

Jaggi, Maya. "The Magician." *Guardian Unlimited*. http://books.guardian.co.uk/departments/childrenandteens/story/0,6000,1669112,00.html. Last visited January 28, 2008.

Justice, Faith L. "Ursula K. Le Guin." *Salon*. January 2001. http://www.salon.com/people/bc/2001/01/23/le_guin. Last visited January 28, 2008.

"Ursula K. Le Guin." *Hour 25*. August 2003. http://www.hour25online.com/Hour25_Previous_Shows_2003–08.html#ursula-k-leguin_2003–08-17. Last visited January 28, 2008. Audio interview.

Criticism and Readers' Guides

Atwood, Margaret. "The Queen of Quinkdom." *The New York Review of Books*. September 26, 2002. http://www.nybooks.com/articles/15677. Last visited January 28, 2008.

Comoletti, Laura B. and Michael D.C. Drout. "How They do Things with Words: Language, Power, Gender, and the Priestly Wizards of Ursula K. Le Guin's Earthsea Books." *Children's Literature* 29 (2001), pp. 113–141.

Cummins, Elizabeth. *Understanding Ursula K. Le Guin*. Columbia, SC: University of South Carolina Press, 1990.

Griffin, Jan M. "Ursula Le Guin's Magical World of Earthsea." *ALAN Review*. 23(3) (Spring 1996). http://scholar.lib.vt.edu/ejournals/ALAN/spring96/griffin.html. Last visited January 28, 2008.

Reid, Suzanne Elizabeth. *Presenting Ursula K. Le Guin*. New York: Twayne Publishers, 1997.

Rochelle, Warren. *Communities of the Heart: The Rhetoric of Myth in the Fiction of Ursula K. Le Guin*. Liverpool, UK: Liverpool University Press, 2001.

Tax, Meredith. "In the Year of Harry Potter, Enter the Dragon." *The Nation*. January 28, 2002, pp. 30–36.

Walker, Catharine Zoe. "Ursula K. Le Guin." In Roger Thompson and J. Scott Bryson, eds., *Dictionary of Literary Biography*, Volume 275*: Twentieth Century American Nature Writers: Prose*. Gale Group, Detroit, Michigan, 2003, pp. 155–165.

White, Donna. *Dancing with Dragons: Ursula K. Le Guin and the Critics*. Columbia, SC: Camden House, 1999.

Web Sites

Le Guin's World. http://hem.passagen.se/peson42/lgw/. Last visited January 28, 2008.

Ursula K. Le Guin's Official Website. Author's official Web site. Last visited January 28, 2008. http://www.ursulakleguin.com/.

If you like Ursula K. Le Guin

Although Le Guin uses many "traditional" fantasy tropes such as dragons and wizards, she often critiques them and their underlying assumptions. Women and issues of gender feature strongly in her fantasies; she also brings in Eastern philosophies such as the Tao.

Then you might like

Lloyd Alexander

Based on Welsh mythology, Alexander's Prydain series focuses on Taran, an assistant pig keeper who is anxious to prove himself as a hero. The series starts with *The Book of Three*, and continues with *The Black Cauldron*, *The Castle of Llyr*, *Taran Wanderer*, and *The High King*.

Lois McMaster Bujold

Bujold's Chalion series (*The Curse of Chalion*, *Paladin of Souls*, *The Hallowed Hunt*) places likeable characters in a well-imagined world of military and religious conflict. Like Le Guin, Bujold pays close attention to issues of gender and the choices that women find themselves forced to make.

Susan Cooper

Cooper's Dark Is Rising series catches four young English children up in a mythic centuries-old battle between the forces of light and darkness. The series includes *Over Sea, Under Stone*, *The Dark Is Rising*, *Greenwitch*, *The Grey King*, and *Silver on the Tree*.

Patricia McKillip

McKillip's Riddle Master of Hed trilogy follows Morgan, Prince of Hed, as he journeys far from his home and finds himself embroiled in a war beyond his imaginings (*The Riddle-Master of Hed*, *Heir of Sea and Fire*, and *Harpist in the Wind*). Like Le Guin, McKillip features strong female characters.

Philip Pullman

Although Pullman's fantasy books are marketed for children and young adult, they are often enjoyed by adults as well. Pullman's best known series is probably "His Dark Materials" trilogy, which is set in an alternate universe (*The Golden Compass*, *The Subtle Knife*, and *The Amber Spyglass*).

Fritz Leiber (1910–1992)

Biographical Sketch

The son of an actor, Fritz Leiber appeared in two films before he began his writing career (*Camille* and *Equinox*). He worked as an assistant editor for *Science Digest* for several years.

A prolific writer, Leiber wrote horror and science fiction, in addition to fantasy. Many of his fantasy novels and stories featured the Fafhrd, a barbarian, and his companion, the Gray Mouser. These characters had originally grown out of a correspondence between Leiber and his friend Harry Fischer during the 1930's.

> They [Fafhrd and the Gray Mouser] are a projection of myself and Harry Fischer, who invented them in the first place. So it's a very direct participation on my part. Fafhrd is a projection of myself and the Mouser of Harry Fischer. It's very personal. I am Fafhrd, for better or for worse. —(Fritz Leiber, "An Interview with Fritz Leiber")

Major Works

Novels and Short Stories

Fafhrd and Gray Mouser series: "Two Sought Adventure." *Unknown* (August 1939), *Swords and Deviltry* (1970), *Swords against Death* (1970) (based on *Two Sought Adventure* (1956)), *Swords in the Mist* (1968), *Swords against Wizardry* (with Harry Fischer, 1968), *The Swords of Lankhmar* (1968), *Swords and Ice Magic* (1977), *The Knight and Knave of Swords* (1988), reprinted as *Farewell to Lankhmar* (1998)

Graphic Novels

Fafhrd & The Gray Mouser. Epic Comics (1990–1991)

Other Short Story Collections

The Ghost Light: Masterworks of Science Fiction and Fantasy (1984)
The Leiber Chronicles: Fifty Years of Fritz Leiber (1990)

Other Important Writings

Fafhrd & Me (1990)

Research Sources

Encyclopedias and Handbooks: EF, HDF, SJGF

Biographies and Interviews

Frane, Jeff. *Fritz Leiber*. Mercer Island, WA: Starmont House, 1980.

"Fritz Leiber: In Memoriam." *Locus* 29(5) (November 1992), pp. 46–49, 73–74.

Henderson, C.J. "Starlog Interview: Fritz Leiber." *Starlog* 83 (June 1984), pp. 54–58, 63.

Purviance, Jim. "Algol Interview: Fritz Leiber." *Algol: Magazine about Science Fiction* 15(3) (1978), pp. 23–28.

Schweitzer, Darrell. "An Interview with Fritz Leiber." *Marion Zimmer Bradley's Fantasy Magazine* 15 (Winter 1992) pp. 7–10.

Criticism and Readers' Guides

Adair, Gerald M.: "Illuminating the Ghost Light: Final Acts in the Theater of Fritz Leiber." *Journal of the Fantastic in the Arts* 12(4) (2002), pp. 364–381.

Barrett, Mike. "From Simorgya to Stardock: The Odyssey of the Two Greatest Heroes in Lankhmar." *Fantasy Commentator* 11(1–2) (Summer 2004), pp. 36–43.

Byfield, Bruce. "Fafhrd and Fritz." *New York Review of Science Fiction* 9(8) (April 1997), pp. 1, 8–12.

Byfield, Bruce. *Witches of the Mind: A Critical Study of Fritz Leiber*. West Warwick, RI: Necronomicon, 1991.

Leiber, Justin. "Fritz Leiber: Swordsman and Philosopher." *Fantasy Commentator* 11(1–2) (Summer 2004), pp. 26–35.

Lovett-Graff, Bennett. "Parodying the Theater of Religion in the Fantasy of Fritz Leiber." *Studies in American Humor* 3(3) (1996), pp. 66–81.

Moorcock, Michael. "Fritz Leiber." *Para-doxa* 1(3) (1995), pp. 320–324.

Reginald, Robert. "One Is One and All Alone: Fritz Leiber's Solopsistic Fantasy." In Robert Reginald, ed., *Xenograffiti: Essays in Fantastic Literature*. San Bernardino, CA: Borgo Press, 1996, pp. 51–53.

Stephensen-Payne, Phil Benson and R. Gordon Jr. *Fritz Leiber: Sardonic Swordsman, A Working Bibliography*. 2nd ed. Albuquerque, NM: Galactic Central, 1990.

Web Sites

Crawford, Gary William. "Fritz Leiber: A Database." http://www.gothicpress.com/leiber.html. Last visited January 28, 2008. Lists articles and books about Leiber and his works.

"Fritz Leiber Papers." University of Houston. *Texas Archival Resources Online.* http://www.lib.utexas.edu/taro/uhsc/00021/hsc-00021.html. Last visited January 28, 2008. Description of archival papers pertaining to Fritz Leiber held at the University of Houston. Includes a biographical note.

"Leiber, F. MSS." *Lilly Library Manuscript Collections.* Indiana University. http://www.indiana.edu/~liblilly/lilly/mss/html/leiberf.html. Last visited January 28, 2008. Description of Leiber manuscripts held at Indiana University. Includes a discussion of Leiber's life and works.

George MacDonald (1824–1905)

Biographical Sketch

George MacDonald was born in Huntly, Aberdeenshire in Scotland. He studied Moral Philosophy and Sciences at the University in Aberdeen in King's College and then trained as a Congregational minister. He was asked to resign his first ministerial post, in Arundun, because of doctrinal differences, and subsequently became a writer.

MacDonald's fantasies, which include novels and short stories written for both children and adults, were highly influential on later fantasy writers. He also published romance and realistic fiction, much of which incorporated his native "Scots" dialect.

> The imagination is that faculty which gives form to thought—not necessarily uttered form, but form capable of being uttered in shape or in sound, or in any mode upon which the senses can lay hold. It is, therefore, that faculty in man which is likest to the prime operation of the power of God, and has, therefore, been called the *creative* faculty, and its exercise *creation. Poet* means *maker.*—(George MacDonald, "The Imagination: Its Functions and its Culture." *A Dish of Orts.* Available online at http://www.gutenberg.org/etext/9393. Last visited January 28, 2008)

Major Works

Novels

Phantastes: A Faerie Romance for Men and Women (1858)
Lilith (1895)

Children's/Young Adult Fiction

At the Back of the North Wind (1871)
The Princess and the Goblin (1872)
The Princess and Curdie (1883)

Short Story Collections

Dealings with the Fairies (1867)
The Gifts of the Christ Child (1882)
The Fairy Tales of George MacDonald (1904) five volumes
'The Golden Key,' and Other Stories (1978), illustrated by Craig Yoe
'The Wise Woman,' and Other Stories (1980), illustrated by Craig Yoe
'The Gray Wolf,' and Other Stories (1980), illustrated by Craig Yoe
'The Light Princess,' and Other Stories (1980), illustrated by Craig Yoe

Research Sources

Encyclopedias and Handbooks: EF, HDF, SJGF

Biographies and Interviews

An Expression of Character: The Letters of George MacDonald. Ed., Glenn Edward Sadler. Grand Rapids, MI: Eerdmans, 1994.

Hein, Rolland, *George MacDonald: Victorian Mythmaker,* Nashville, TN: Star Song Publishing Group, 1993.

Saintsbury, Elizabeth. *George MacDonald: a Short Life*. Edinburgh, UK: Canongate, 1987.

Triggs, Kathy. *The Stars and the Stillness: A Portrait of George MacDonald.* Cambridge: Lutterworth Press, 1986.

Criticism and Readers' Guides

Aiura-Vigers, Reiko. "The Link between George MacDonald and the Grimms' Fairy Tales." *Swansea Review* (1994), pp. 113–120.

Billone, Amy. "Hovering between Irony and Innocence: George MacDonald's 'The Light Princess' and the Gravity of Childhood." *Mosaic: A Journal for the Interdisciplinary Study of Literature* 37(1) (March 2004), pp. 135–148.

Gaarden, Bonnie. "Cosmic and Psychological Redemption in George MacDonald's Lilith." *Studies in the Novel* 37(1) (Spring 2005), pp. 20–36.

The Gold Thread: Essays on George MacDonald. Ed., William Raeper. Edinburgh, UK: Edinburgh University Press, 1990.

Gray, William N. "George MacDonald, Julia Kristeva, and the Black Sun." *SEL: Studies in English Literature, 1500–1900* 36(4) (Autumn 1996), pp. 877–893.

Gunther, Adrian. "The Multiple Realms of George MacDonald's Phantastes." *Studies in Scottish Literature* 29 (1996), pp. 174–190.

Jenkins, Ruth Y. "'I am Spinning This for You, My Child': Voice and Identity Formation in George MacDonald's Princess books." *Lion and the Unicorn* 28(3) (2004), pp. 325–344.

John, Judith Gero. "Searching for Great-Great-Grandmother: Powerful Women in George MacDonald's Fantasies." *The Lion and the Unicorn* 15(2) (December 1991), pp. 27–34.

Kegler, Adelheid. "Below in the Depths: MacDonald's Symbolic Landscape." *North Wind: Journal of George MacDonald Studies* 24 (2005), pp. 29–40.
Manlove, Colin. "MacDonald's Shorter Fairy Tales: Journeys into the Mind." *Seven: An Anglo-American Literary Review* 22 (2005), pp. 11–28.
McGillis, Roderick. "'A Fairytale Is Just a Fairytale': George MacDonald and the Queering of Fairy." *Marvels & Tales: Journal of Fairy-Tale Studies* 17(1) (2003), pp. 86–99.
Pennington, John. "Solar Mythology in George MacDonald's 'Little Daylight' and 'The Day Boy and the Night Girl'." *Journal of the Fantastic in the Arts* 10(3) (1999), pp. 308–320.
Rutledge, Amelia A. "George MacDonald." In Darren Harris-Fain, ed., *British Fantasy and Science-Fiction Writers Before World War I (Dictionary of Literary Biography 178)*. Detroit, MI: Gale, 1997, pp. 163–173.
Shaberman, R.B. "George MacDonald: A Bibliographical Study." Winchester, UK: St. Paul's Bibliographies, 1990.
Sheley, Erin: "From Eden to Eternity: The Timescales of Genesis in George MacDonald's 'The Golden Key' and 'Lilith.'" *Children's Literature Association Quarterly* 29(4) (Winter 2004), pp. 329–344.

Web Sites

"George MacDonald: An Overview." *The Victorian Web*. Last visited January 28, 2008. http://www.macdonaldsociety.org. Includes articles on various aspects of MacDonald's life and works.
"MacDonald, George, 1824–1905." *Project Gutenberg*. http://www.gutenberg.org/browse/authors/m#a127. Last visited January 28, 2008. Online texts for several of MacDonald's works.
The Golden Key. http://www.george-macdonald.com. Last visited January 29, 2008. Includes online texts for several of MacDonald's works. *The George MacDonald Society*. http://www.macdonaldsociety.org. Last visited January 28, 2008.

If you like George MacDonald

Victorian writer George MacDonald wrote numerous books for both children and adults, many of which reflected his deeply held Christian faith. He is best known for such fantasies as *The Princess and Curdie* and *Lilith.*

Then you might like

Lloyd Alexander

Based on Welsh mythology, Alexander's "Prydain" series focuses on Taran, an assistant pig keeper who is anxious to prove himself as a hero. The series starts with *The Book of Three*, and continues with *The Black Cauldron*, *The Castle of Llyr*, *Taran Wanderer*, and *The High King*.

Susan Cooper

Cooper's Dark Is Rising series catches four young English children up in a mythic centuries-old battle between the forces of light and darkness. The series includes *Over Sea, Under Stone, The Dark Is Rising, Greenwitch, The Grey King*, and *Silver on the Tree.*

Stephen Lawhead

Lawhead's fantasies tend to be deeply embedded in English history and myth. He is probably best known for his the Pendragon Cycle (*Taliesin, Merlin, Arthur, Pendragon*, and *Grail*).

C.S. Lewis

The Lion and the Witch, and the Wardrobe takes place in Narnia, a land where it is always winter, yet never Christmas. Four English children stumble into it through a wardrobe and have numerous adventures. Lewis wrote six additional books in the Narnia series, chronicling its rise, history, and fall.

John Ronald Reuel Tolkien (J.R.R. Tolkien)

Tolkien's Middle Earth fantasies reflect his scholarly interests in languages and myth. Beginning with prequel *The Hobbit*, they continue with *The Fellowship of the Ring, The Two Towers*, and *The Return of the King.*

Jane Yolen

Yolen has written numerous books of fantasy for children and adults that feature myth and fable. Among them are her Books of the Great Alta (*Sister Light, Sister Dark, White Jenna*, and *The One Armed Queen*).

Gregory Maguire (1954–)

Biographical Sketch

Gregory Maguire wrote his first story at the age of five and published his first novel (*Lights on the Lake*) as a college student. He did a PhD in English and American Literature at Tufts University, and has taught children's literature at Simmons College. As a fantasy writer, Maguire is perhaps best known for his revisionist retellings of fairy tales and other classic stories. His novel *Wicked*, a novel set in Oz from the viewpoint of the Wicked Witch of the East proved to be a hit, and inspired a similarly successful Broadway musical. He has also written several children's and young adult novels.

> I'm not a writer because I want to make money. I'm a writer because I'm a very slow thinker but I do care about thinking, and the only way I know how to think with any kind of finesse is by telling stories.—(Gregory Maguire, "Gregory Maguire Steps Out from Behind the Curtain," available online at http://www.powells.com/authors/maguire.html. Last visited January 28, 2008)

Major Works

Novels

Wicked: The Life and Times of the Wicked Witch of the West (1995)
Confessions of an Ugly Stepsister (1999)
Lost (2001)
Mirror, Mirror (2003)
Son of a Witch (2005)

Children's/Young Adult Fiction

The Lightening Time (1978)
The Daughter of the Moon (1980)
Lights on the Lake (1981)
The Dream Stealer (1983)

Short Story Collections

Leaping Beauty and Other Animal Fairy Tales (2004, illustrated by Chris Demarest)

Research Sources

Encyclopedias and Handbooks: HDF

Biographies and Interviews

Barrett, Mary Brigid. "Gregory Maguire: An Interview." *The National Children's Book and Literacy Alliance*. http://thencbla.org/boardinterviews/maguireinterview.html. Last visited January 28, 2008.

Fraser, Stephen: "Wicked with Words" *Writing* 28(5) (February/March 2006), pp. 8–11.

Kerr, Euan. "Gregory Maguire and his 'Son of a Witch.' " *Minnesota Public Radio*. http://news.minnesota.publicradio.org/features/2005/11/15_kerre_maguire. Last visited January 28, 2008.

Minzesheimer, Bob. "'Wicked' Author Gregory Maguire Casts His Spell." *USA Today.com*, October 12, 2005. http://www.usatoday.com/life/books/news/2005-10-12-gregory-maguire-interview_x.htm. Last visited January 28, 2008.

Weich, Dave. "Gregory Maguire Steps Out from Behind the Curtain." *Powells.com*, February 27, 2004. http://www.powells.com/authors/maguire.html. Last visited January 28, 2008.

Web Sites

Welcome to the World of Gregory Maguire. Publisher's official Web site. http://www.gregorymaguire.com. Last visited January 28, 2008.

If you like Gregory Maguire

As a writer, Maguire is perhaps best known for his revisionist retellings of fairy tales and other classic stories. His versions, often set in specific historical milieus, comment on and deepen the original tales.

Then you might like

Lyman Frank Baum (L. Frank Baum)

Baum's *Wizard of Oz*, which inspired Maguire's *Wicked*, is the first of many Oz books. Published in the early twentieth century, it features a mixture of magic and folksy "common sense."

Angela Carter

Carter's work is dark, bizarre, baroquely written, and disturbing. Her influences ranged from Shakespeare to de Sade to fairy tales. Carter's *Bloody Chamber* is a collection of revisionist fairy tales, many of which are written from a feminist point of view.

Philip José Farmer

In *A Barnstomer in Oz*, Farmer takes Dorothy Gale's son back to Oz. Farmer's Oz is strange, yet surreally familiar.

Robin McKinley

McKinley retells classic fairy tales in *Beauty: A Re-Telling of the Story of Beauty and the Beast* and *Deerskin*. Both of these novels feature strong female heroines and reflect McKinley's interest in gender issues.

Linda Medley

Medley's *Castle Waiting* graphic-novel series presents fairy tale settings with a twist. Its characters pop off the page, ranging from Sleeping Beauty's ladies-in-waiting to a stork-headed chamberlain to a bearded-lady nun, brim-full of personality and humor.

Sherri Tepper

Tepper's *Beauty* takes Beauty up to and beyond the modern era, along with other fairy tales such as "Snow White" and "Cinderella."

Jane Yolen

Yolen has written numerous collections of fairy tales and fables, including *The Fish Prince: and Other Stories* and *The Hundredth Dove: And Other Tales*, while her *Briar Rose* sets the "Sleeping Beauty" story against the background of the Holocaust.

George R.R. Martin (1948–)

Biographical Sketch

George Raymond Richard Martin received a BS and an MA in journalism from Northwest University. His MA came in 1971, the same year that he sold his first story. As a conscientous objector during the Vietnam Conflict, he did alternative service with VISTA.

Martin has written science fiction and horror in addition to fantasy. During the 1980s, he took a break from writing fiction to work in Hollywood as a writer and producer (his credits include work on the *The Twilight Zone* and *Beauty and the Beast*). He currently lives in New Mexico.

> I'm attracted to 'gray' characters, characters who are not what they seem, characters who change. I think that's the most interesting part of fiction, and a lot of fantasy doesn't have that. —(George R.R. Martin, "George R. R. Martin: The Grey Lords." *Locus* interview, available online at http://www.locusmag.com/2005/Issues/11Martin.html. Last visited January 28, 2008)

Major Works

Novels

Song of Ice and Fire series: *A Game of Thrones* (1996), *A Clash of Kings* (1999), *A Storm of Swords* (2000), *A Feast for Crows* (2005), *A Dance with Dragons* (2007)

Graphic Novels

The Hedge Knight (2004)

Children's/Young Adult Fiction

The Ice Dragon (1980)

Short Story Collections

A Song for Lya: And Other Stories (1976)
Portraits of His Children (1987)
GRRM: A RRetrospective (2003) also published as *Dreamsongs*

Research Sources

Encyclopedias and Handbooks: EF, HDF

Biographies and Interviews

"George R.R. Martin." *Fast Forward.* November 2005. http://www.fast-forward.tv/audio/audio184.m3u. Last visited January 28, 2008.

"George R.R. Martin: The Grey Lords." *Locus* 55(5) (November 2005), pp. 6–7, 69–70.

"George R.R. Martin: Necessary Lies." *Locus* 45(6) (December 2000), pp. 6–7, 80.

Gevers, Nick. "Sunsets of High Renown: An Interview with George R.R. Martin." *Infinity Plus: SF, Fantasy, Horror.* 2001. http://www.users.zetnet.co.uk/iplus/nonfiction/intgrrm.htm. Last visited January 28, 2008.

MacLaurin, Wayne. "A Conversation with George R.R. Martin." *The SF Site.* November 2000. http://www.sfsite.com/01a/gm95.htm. Last visited January 28, 2008.

Richards, Linda. "January Interview: George R.R. Martin." *January Magazine.* January 2001. http://www.januarymagazine.com/profiles/grrmartin.html. Last visited January 28, 2008.

Robinson, Tasha. "Interview: George R.R. Martin Continues to Sing a Magical Tale of Ice and Fire." *Science Fiction Weekly.* http://www.scifi.com/sfw/issue190/interview.html. Last visited January 28, 2008.

St. Denis, Patrick. "Interview with George R.R. Martin." *ssfworld.com.* May 17, 2005. http://www.sffworld.com/interview/186p0.html. Last visited January 28, 2008.

Web Sites

Brotherhood Without Banners: An Official George R.R. Martin Fan. http://www.bwbfanclub.com. Last visited January 28, 2008.

"George R.R. Martin: Book Fest 05."*The Library of Congress Webcasts.* http://www.loc.gov/today/cyberlc/feature_wdesc.php?rec=3749. Last visited January 28, 2008.

The George R.R. Martin Podcast. http://feeds.feedburner.com/TheGeorgeRRMartinPodcast. Last visited January 28, 2008.

GRRM. http://www.georgerrmartin.com. Last visited January 28, 2008. Author's official Web site.

Not a Blog. http://grrm.livejournal.com. Last visited January 28, 2008. Author's personal journal.

Anne McCaffrey (1926–)

Biographical Sketch

Anne McCaffrey was born on April 1 in Cambridge, Massachussets, and attended Radcliffe College. She studied voice and opera for several years. She currently lives in Ireland in a house called "Dragonhold-Underhill" that she designed. She used to ride horseback, and still runs a private livery stable.

Many of Anne McCaffrey's novels could be described as science fiction/fantasy. Although the Dragonriders of Pern books, possibly her most popular series, take place on an alien planet, the society and culture have a strong medieval flavor. Many of her novels include strong female characters as well as a touch of romance and adventure.

> I have always used emotion as a writing tool. That goes back to me being on the stage. The thing is, emotion—if it's visibly felt by the writer—will go through all the processes it takes to publish a story and still hit the reader right in the gut. But you have to really mean it. —(Anne McCaffrey, "Heirs to Pern." *Locus* interview, 2004)

Major Works

Novels

Dragonriders of Pern trilogy: *Dragonflight* (1968), *Dragonquest* (1971), *The White Dragon* (1978)
Harper Hall trilogy: *Dragonsong* (1976), *Dragonsinger* (1977), *Dragondrums* (1979)
Moreta: Dragonlady of Pern (1983)
Nerilka's Story: A Pern Adventure (1986)
Dragonsdawn (1988)
The Renegades of Pern (1989)
All the Weyrs of Pern (1991)
Chronicles of Pern: First Fall (1993)
The Dolphins of Pern (1994)
Dragonseye (1997) also published as *Red Star Rising*
The Masterharper of Pern (1998)
The Skies of Pern (2001)
Dragon's Kin (2003, with Todd McCaffrey)

Short Story Collections

Get off the Unicorn (1977)
The Girl Who Heard Dragons (1994)
A Gift of Dragons (2002), illustrated by Tom Kidd

Other Important Writings

The Atlas of Pern (1984, with Karen W. Fonstad)
The People of Pern (1988) with Robin Wood
The Masterharper of Pern Songbook (1995) with Tania Opland and Mike Freeman
The Masterharper of Pern CD (1998) recorded music, with Tania Opland and Mike Freeman

Dragonholder: The Life and Dreams (So Far) of Anne McCaffrey (1999) with Todd McCaffrey

Research Sources

Encyclopedias and Handbooks: EF, HDF

Biographies and Interviews

McCaffrey, Anne. "Heirs to Pern." *Locus* 53(5) (November 2004), pp. 6–7, 75–76.

"Anne McCaffrey: Life With Dragons." *Locus* 30(3) (March 1993), pp. 5, 74.

"Interview with Anne McCaffrey." *SFF.World.* May 8, 2005. http://www.sffworld.com/interview/49p0.html. Last visited January 28, 2008.

Jamneck, Lynne. "An Interview With Anne McCaffrey." *Writing-World.com,* 2004. http://www.writing-world.com/sf/mccaffrey.shtml. Last visited January 28, 2008.

Swaim, Don. "Audio Interview with Anne McCaffrey." *Wired for Books.* (CBS Radio) 1988. http://wiredforbooks.org/swaim/AnneMcCaffrey.ram. Last visited January 28, 2008.

Criticism and Readers' Guides

Arbur, Rosemarie. *Leigh Brackett, Marion Zimmer Bradley, Anne McCaffrey: A Primary and Secondary Bibliography.* Boston, MA: G. K. Hall, 1981.

Barr, Marleen. "Science Fiction and the Fact of Women's Repressed Creativity: Anne McCaffrey Portrays a Female Artist." *Extrapolation: A Journal of Science Fiction and Fantasy* 23(1) (Spring 1982), pp. 70–76.

Hargreaves, Mathew D. *Anne Inez McCaffrey: Forty Years of Publishing, An International Bibliography.* Seattle, WA: Mathew Hargreaves, 1992.

Harkins, Patricia. "Myth in Action: The Trials and Transformation of Menolly." Ed., C.W. Sullivan. *Science Fiction for Young Readers. Contributions to the Study of Science Fiction and Fantasy,* Volume 56. Westport, CT: Greenwood, 1993, pp. 157–166.

Nye Jody Lynn and Bill Fawcett, Eds. *The Dragonlover's Guide to Pern,* 2nd ed. New York: Del Rey. 1997.

Roberts, Robin. *Anne McCaffrey: A Critical Companion.* Westport, CT; London: Greenwood Press, 1996.

Vandergrift, Kay E. "Meaning-Making and the Dragons of Pern." *Children's Literature Association Quarterly.* 15(1) (Spring 1990), pp. 27–32.

Wytenbroek, J. R. "The Child as Creator in McCaffrey's Dragonsong and Dragonsinger." *The Lion and the Unicorn* 16(2) (December 1992), pp. 210–214.

Web Sites

The Worlds of Anne McCaffrey. http://annemccaffrey.net/index.php. Last visited January 28, 2008. Author's official Web site.

Patricia McKillip (1948–)

Biographical Sketch

Patricia McKillip was born in Salem, Oregon, on Leap Year Day (February 29, 1948). She went to the College of Notre Dame, Belmont, and San Jose University where she earned a BA in English. She then earned an MA at San Jose State University.

McKillip started writing early, and wrote her first book, *The House on Parchment Street*, as a teenager. She has written numerous fantasy, science fiction, and young adult novels. Her novels range from high fantasy (such as *The Riddle Master of Hed*) to fairy tale retellings. McKillip currently lives in Oregon.

> I went through decades of writing fantasy and telling myself "this has nothing to do with me—it's just fantasy." Then damned if that book doesn't catch you somewhere, and you realize suddenly that all these things are crowding into your head from your life, and you're sitting there writing what you think is fantasy—and it just makes a jigsaw puzzle.—(Patricia McKillip, "Patricia A. McKillip: Springing Surprises." *Locus* interview, 1996)

Major Works

Novels

The Throme of the Earl of Sherril (1973)
The Forgotten Beasts of Eld (1974)
Quest of the Riddle-Master trilogy: *The Riddle-Master of Hed* (1976), *Heir of Sea and Fire* (1977), *Harpist in the Wind* (1979)
The Changeling Sea (1988)
Cygnet series: *The Sorceress and the Cygnet* (1991), *The Cygnet and the Firebird* (1993)
The Book of Atrix Wolfe (1995)
Winter Rose (1996)
Song for the Basilisk (1998)
The Tower at Stony Wood (2000)
Ombria in Shadow (2002)
In the Forests of Serre (2003)
Alphabet of Thorn (2004)
Od Magic (2005)
Solstice Wood (2006)

Children's/Young Adult Fiction

The House on Parchment Street (1973)

Short Story Collections

Harrowing the Dragon (2005)

Other Important Writings

McKillip, Patricia: "Motive, Magic and Mundanity: Why Do We Write?" *Extrapolation* 46(1) (Spring 2005), pp. 17–22.

Research Sources

Encyclopedias and Handbooks: EF, HDF

Biographies and Interviews

"Patricia A. McKillip: Moving Forward." *Locus* 28(2) (August 1992), pp. 4, 69. Available online at http://www.patriciamckillip.com/Bio/MovingForward.htm. Last visited January 28, 2008.

"Patricia A. McKillip: Springing Surprises." *Locus* 37(1) (July 1996), pp. 6–7.

Criticism and Readers' Guides

Greenlee, Jessica. "No Longer Divided: Wholeness in *Winter Rose*." *Extrapolation* 42(1) (2001), pp. 75–86.

Kelso, Sylvia. "The King and the Enchanter: Gender, Power and Authority in Patricia McKillip's Fantasy Novels." *New York Review of Science Fiction* 18(6) (February 2006), pp. 1, 8–12.

Mains, Christine. "Having It All: The Female Hero's Quest for Love and Power in Patricia McKillip's Riddle-Master Trilogy." *Extrapolation* 46(1) (Spring 2005), pp. 23–35.

Mains, Christine. "The Use, Misues, and Abuse of Power: The Wizards of Patricia A. McKillip." *Fantastic Odysseys: Selected Essays from the Twenty-Second International Conference on the Fantastic in the Arts*. Ed., Mary Pharr. Westport, CT: Praeger, 2003, pp. 59–64.

Pilinovsky, Helen. "The Mother of All Witches: Baba Yaga and Brume in Patricia McKillip's *In the Forests of Serre*." *Extrapolation* 46(1) (Spring 2005), pp. 36–49.

Web Sites

Patricia A. McKillip. http://www.patriciamckillip.com. Last visited January 28, 2008. Fan site.

Robin McKinley (1952–)

Biographical Sketch

Robin McKinley was born in Ohio, but moved to England after marrying Peter Dickinson, a British writers. She grew up in a military family that moved around a lot. She is currently taking fencing and learning English change ringing, and grows roses.

McKinley's fantasy novels, many of which are marketed to young adult readers, are known for their strong female protagonists. One notable example is the Damar series, which feature a young female warrior. McKinley has also written novels based on fairy tales, many of which question the original fairy tale conventions.

> I have no idea where I get my ideas. It's how I'm built. I have an imagination that gets sparked off by things, and produces stories. Everything that interests me feeds my imagination, and so I am in the extremely pleasant position of *needing* to follow my interests so I can do what I do, which is write stories.—(Robin McKinley, http://www.robinmckinley.com/Interviews/20Hundred.html. Last visited January 28, 2008

Major Works

Novels

Folktales series: *Beauty: A Re-Telling of the Story of Beauty and the Beast* (1978), *Rose Daughter* (1997), *Spindle's End* (2000)
Deerskin (1993)
The Stone Fey (1998), illustrated by John Clapp
Sunshine (2003)

Children's/Young Adult Fiction

Damar series: *The Blue Sword* (1982), *The Door in the Hedge* (1981), *The Hero and the Crown* (1984)
The Outlaws of Sherwood (1988)

Short Story Collections

A Knot in the Grain and Other Stories (1994)
Water: Tales of Elemental Spirits (2002) with Peter Dickinson

Research Sources

Encyclopedias and Handbooks: HDF, SJGF

Biographies and Interviews

Brunsdale, Mitzi. "PW Talks with Robin McKinley—Sunshine and Dark, Dark Shadows." *Publishers Weekly* 250(39) (September 29, 2003), p. 48.
Wright, Allen W. "Interviews in Sherwood: Robin McKinley." *Robin Hood Bold Outlaw of Barnsdale and Sherwood.* http://www.boldoutlaw.com/robint/mckinley1.html. Last visited January 28, 2008.

Criticism and Readers' Guides

Marchant, Jennifer. "'An Advocate, a Defender, an Intimate': Kristeva's Imaginary Father in Fictional Girl-Animal Relationships." *Children's Literature Association Quarterly* 30(1) (Spring 2005), pp. 3–15.

Paxton, Tamara. "McKinley Deerskin: From Passive Princess to Independent Heroine." *The Image of the Hero in Literature, Media, and Society*. Ed., Will Wright and Steven Kaplan. Pueblo: Colorado State University, 2004, pp. 150–156.

Perry, Evelyn. "Real-izing Fantasy: The Double Sided Mirror of Magical Realism and The Other Side of Reality in Robin McKinley's *Spindle's End*, Part 1" *The Looking Glass* 8(3) (September 2, 2004). Available online at http://www.the-looking-glass.net/rabbit/v8i3/curious.html. Last visited January 28, 2008.

Rutledge, Amelia A. "Robin McKinley's Deerskin: Challenging Narcissisms." *Marvels & Tales: Journal of Fairy-Tale Studies* 15(2) (2001), pp. 168–182.

Sanders, Lynn M. "Girls Who Do Things: The Protagonists of Robin McKinley's Fantasy Fiction." *ALAN Review* 24(1) (Fall 1996), pp. 38–42.

Woolsey, Daniel P. "The Realm of the Fairy Story: J. R. R. Tolkien and Robin McKinley's Beauty." *Children's Literature in Education* 22(2) (June 1991), pp. 129–136.

Web Sites

Robin McKinley. http://www.robinmckinley.com/index.html. Last visited January 28, 2008. Author's official web site.

Linda Medley (1964–)

Biographical Sketch

Born in Stockton, CA, Linda Medley did a Bachelor of Fine Arts degree in Illustration at the Academy of Art College in San Francisco, CA. She has written and drawn comics for a number of publishers, as well as other aspects of the process (such as cover paintings and penciling). Linda Medley began her *Castle Waiting* graphic-novel series as a self published venture in. She is currently working with Fantagraphic Books to continue the series.

Medley's *Castle Waiting* has drawn praise for its reinvention of fairy tales. Set in an isolated castle, many of its characters are linked to fairy tales, but didn't play leading roles. Medley also illustrates books, and currently lives in Portland, Oregon.

> *Castle Waiting* is a complete story, with a definite beginning, middle and end, chronicling the history of a community. On a deeper level the whole saga is really an allegory of death and rebirth, although you don't need to be aware of that to understand or appreciate the story. —(Linda Medley, "On Books and Waiting: Linda Medley." *Sequential Tart* interview, 1999. Available at http://www.sequentialtart.com/archive/nov99/medley.shtml. Last visited January 28, 2008)

Major Works

Graphic Novels

Castle Waiting (1997–present)
The Collected Castle Waiting, Volume 1 (2006)

Research Sources

Biographies and Interviews

Atchison, Lee. "On Books and Waiting: Linda Medley." *Sequential Tart*, November 1999. http://www.sequentialtart.com/archive/nov99/medley.shtml. Last visited January 28, 2008.

Furey, Emmett. "CCI XTRA: Spotlight on Linda Medley." *The Comic Wire*, July 25, 2006. http://www.comicbookresources.com/news/newsitem.cgi?id=7962. Last visited January 28, 2008.

"Trilogy Tour Heroes Con Interview July 5, 1998." http://www.geocities.com/Heartland/Plains/9205/trilogytour/tritour98/hconinterview.html. Last visited January 28, 2008.

Criticism and Readers' Guides

Web Sites

Medleyography: A Linda Medley Bibliography. http://www.shiningsilence.com/medley. Last visited January 28, 2008.

Studiolio: Featuring the Art of Linda Medley. http://www.studiolio.com. Last visited January 28, 2008. Author's official web site.

China Miéville (1972–)

Biographical Sketch

China Miéville was raised in London. He has also lived in Egypt, where he taught English. He did a BA in social anthropology at Cambridge University and an MA and a PhD at the London School of Economics. He considers himself a Socialist, and is politically active.

Miéville's writing is often described as "urban fantasy" or "new weird." Many of his novels and stories are set in dark, forboding, urban areas, crossing the genres of fantasy, science fiction, and horror. He currently lives in London.

> I am conscious of writing in a tradition that blurs the boundaries between three fantastic genres: supernatural horror, fantasy and science fiction. I have always been of the opinion that you can't make firm distinctions between those three. —(China Miéville, *Strange Horizons* interview, 2001. Available online at

http://www.strangehorizons.com/2001/20011001/china.shtml. Last visited January 28, 2008)

Major Works

Novels

New Crobuzon series: *Perdido Street Station* (2000), *The Scar* (2001), *Iron Council* (2004)
King Rat (1998)
Un Lun Dun (2007)

Short Story Collections

Looking for Jake (2005)

Other Important Writings

"Fifty Fantasy & Science Fiction Works that Socialists Should Read." *Fantastic Metropolis*, January 23, 2002. http://www.fantasticmetropolis.com/i/50socialist/full. Last visited January 28, 2008.
Between Equal Rights: A Marxist Theory of International Law (2005)

Research Sources

Encyclopedias and Handbooks: HDF

Biographies and Interviews

Anders, Lou. "China Miéville [SCIENCE-FICTION AUTHOR]." (Illustrated by Charles Burns) *The Believer*, April 2005. http://www.believermag.com/issues/200504/?read=interview_mieville. Last visited January 28, 2008.
"China Miéville." *Fast Forward*. September, 2004. http://www.fast-forward.tv/audio/audio170.m3u. Last visited January 28, 2008.
"China Miéville: Messing with Fantasy." *Locus* 48(3) (March, 2002), pp. 4–5, 75–76.
Gordon, Joan. "Reveling in Genre: An Interview with China Miéville." *Science Fiction Studies*, 30(3) (November, 2003), pp. 355–373. Available online at http://www.depauw.edu/sfs/interviews/mievilleinterview.htm. Last visited January 28, 2008.
Morgan, Cheryl. "Interview: China Miéville." *Strange Horizons* (October 1, 2001) http://www.strangehorizons.com/2001/20011001/china.shtml. Last visited January 28, 2008.
Newsinger, John. "Fantasy and Revolution: An Interview with China Miéville." *International Socialism Journal* 88 (Autumn 2000). Available online at http://pubs.socialistreviewindex.org.uk/isj88/newsinger.htm. Last visited January 28, 2008

"The Road to Perdido: An Interview with China Mieville." *3:AM Magazine*. http://www.3ammagazine.com/litarchives/2003/feb/interview_china_mieville.html. Last visited January 28, 2008.

Templeton, Tom. "This Much I Know." *The Observer*. November 28, 2004. http://books.guardian.co.uk/departments/sciencefiction/story/0,6000,1362833,00.html. Last visited Janaury 28, 2008.

Criticism and Readers' Guides

Aichele, George. "Dark Conceptions, or, the Birth of a Messiah in King Rat and the Gospel of Luke." *Foundation* 34(9) (Autumn 2005), pp. 62–70.

Farrell, Henry. "Fantasy Remade: China Mieville's New Crobuzon novels" *n* + 1. http://www.nplusonemag.com/mieville.html. Last visited January 28, 2008.

Freedman, Carl. "To the Perdido Street Station: The Representation of Revolution in China Miéville's Iron Council." *Extrapolation* 46(2) (Summer 2005), pp. 235–248.

Freedman, Carl. "Towards a Marxist Urban Sublime: Reading China Miéville's King Rat." *Extrapolation* 44(4) (Winter 2003), pp. 395–408.

Gordon, Joan. "Hybridity, Heterotopia, and Mateship in China Miéville's Perdido Street Station." *Science Fiction Studies* 30(3) (November 2003), pp. 456–476.

Mills, Alice. "Inspiration and Astonishment: Peake's Influence on Perdido Street Station." *Peake Studies*, 7(4) (April 2002), pp. 19–24.

Web Sites

Black, G. *Runagate Rampant: The Unofficial Home Page of China Miéville, Weird Fiction Author*. http://runagate-rampant.netfirms.com. Last visited January 28, 2008.

Elizabeth Moon (1945–)

Biographical Sketch

Elizabeth Moon earned an undergraduate history degree at Rice University and another in Biology at the University of Texas at Austin. She also spent three years in the Marine Corps. She is active in land management.

Perhaps not surprisingly, Moon is known for her military themes and strong women. She also writes science fiction, and currently lives in Texas.

> [I]n fantasy, you can make a complete break, and you can put people in a situation where they are confronted with things that they would not confront in the real world. That they would avoid confronting. They may never have considered the cost of courage, for instance, which is something you can make explicit in fantasy. —(Elizabeth Moon, "A Conversation with Elizabeth Moon." *SF Site*

interview. 1999. Available online at http://www.sfsite.com/02a/em74.htm. Last visited January 28, 2008)

Major Works

Novels

Deed of Paksenarrion series: *The Sheepfarmer's Daughter* (1988), *Divided Allegiance* (1988), *Oath of Gold* (1989)
Legacy of Gird series: *Surrender None* (1990), *Liar's Oath* (1992)

Research Sources

Encyclopedias and Handbooks: EF, SJGF

Biographies and Interviews

Blaschke, Jayme Lynn. "A Conversation with Elizabeth Moon." *The SF Site*. November 1999. http://www.sfsite.com/02a/em74.htm. Last visited January 28, 2008.
Dow, Christopher. "Making Contact: Elizabeth Moon's Path to the Stars." *Rice University Sallyport* (Summer 2006). http://www.rice.edu/sallyport/2006/summer/features/moon.html. Last visited January 28, 2008
"Elizabeth Moon: Explorations." *Locus* 52(3) (March 2004), pp. 76–78.
"Elizabeth Moon: Question Assumptions." *Locus* 34(3) (March 1995), pp. 4–5, 80–81.
"Interviews: Elizabeth Moon." *Adventures in Crime and Space*. http://www.crimeandspace.com/Interviews/MoonInt.htm. Last visited January 28, 2008.
Rand, Ken. "Because She Has To: A Conversation with Elizabeth Moon." *The Broadsheet*. May 26, 2004. http://broaduniverse.org/broadsheet/archive/0405kr.html. Last visited January 28, 2008.

Web Sites

MoonScape. http://www.elizabethmoon.com. Last visited January 28, 2008.
Author's official Web site.

Michael Moorcock (1939–)

Biographical Sketch

Michael Moorcock was born in England, and has worked with editing and publishing. Moorcock wrote a number of comic strips in the early 1960s. He has also worked with bands such as "Hawkwind" and "Blue Oyster Cult," including writing song lyrics. He is currently a member of "Michael Moorcock and the Deep Fix."

Among fantasy readers, Moorcock is probably best known for his character "Elric of Melniboné," an antiheroic figure who has appeared in a number of novels as well as role playing games and comic books. Moorcock has also written adventure, suspense, nonfiction, mainstream, and science fiction books. Many of Moorcock's fantasy and science-fiction novels are linked through a "Multiverse." He currently lives in Texas.

> And for a writer, particularly a writer of imaginative work, there's always a tendency to put yourself in an ivory tower and write about things as they should be rather than things as they are. I prefer to write versions of things as they are.—(Michael Moorcock, *SF Site* interview. Available online at http://www.sfsite.com/05b/samm200.htm. Last visited January 28, 2008)

Major Works

Novels and Related Short Story Collections

Elric Saga: *The Stealer of Souls, and Other Stories* (1961), *The Singing Citadel* (1970), *The Sailor on the Seas of Fate* (1976), *The Weird of the White Wolf* (1977), *The Sleeping Sorceress* (1970) also published as *The Vanishing Tower*, *Elric of Melnibone* (1972) previously published as *The Dreaming City*, *The Jade Man's Eyes* (1973), *The Return to Melnibone* (with Philippe Druillet, 1973), *The Sailor on the Seas of Fate* (1976), *The Bane of the Black Sword* (1977), *Stormbringer* (1963), *Elric at the End of Time* (1985), *The Fortress of the Pearl* (1989), *The Revenge of the Rose* (1991), *The Dreamthief's Daughter: A Tale of the Albino* (2001), *The Skrayling Tree: The Albino in America* (2003), *The White Wolf's Son: The Albino Underground* (2005)

Gloriana (1978) also published as *Gloriana, or the Unfufill'd Queen*

Von Bek Family series: *The Warhound and the World's Pain* (1981), *The Brothel in Rosenstrasse* (1982), *The City in the Autumn Stars* (1986) *Lunching with the Antichrist: A Family History: 1925–2015* (1994), *Von Bek* (1995)

Second Ether series: *Blood* (1994), *Fabulous Harbors* (1995), *The War Amongst the Angels (1996)*

Graphic Novels

Michael Moorcock's Multiverse, 1–12 (1997–)

Children's/Young Adult Fiction

Sojan (1977)

Short Story Collections

The Prince with the Silver Hand (1993)

Other Important Writings

Wizardry and Wild Romance: A Study of Epic Fantasy (1987)

"Epic Pooh." *Revolution SF* (2002). http://www.revolutionsf.com/article.html?id=953. Last visited January 28, 2008.

"The Bayley-Moorcock Letters: An Old Farts' Fireside Chat" (with Barrington J. Bayley). *Fantastic Metropolis*. January 31, 2002. http://www.fantasticmetropolis.com/i/bayley. Last visited January 28, 2008.

Research Sources

Encyclopedias and Handbooks: EF, HDF, SJGF

Biographies and Interviews

Auden, Sandy. 'Chaotic Lives: An Interview with Michael Moorcock.' *SF Site*. 2005. http://www.sfsite.com/05b/samm200.htm. Last visited January 28, 2008.

Klaw, Rick. "Michael Moorcock Serves Up Sword and Sorcery with a New Elric Adventure." *Science Fiction Weekly*. http://www.scifi.com/sfw/issue206/interview.html. Last visited January 28, 2008.

"Michael Moorcock: King of the Cats." *Locus* 39(5) (November 1997), pp. 5, 77.

"Michael Moorcock: Movements and Myths." *Locus* 50(3) (March 2003), pp. 6–7, 71–73.

Mondschein, Ken. "The Corporate MOFO Interview: Michael Moorcock on Politics, Punk, Tolkien, and Everything Else." *Corporate MOFO* (2004). http://www.corporatemofo.com/stories/Moorcock1.htm. Last visited January 28, 2008.

Criticism and Readers' Guides

Collins, William J. "Michael Moorcock." In Darren Harris-Fain, ed., *British Fantasy and Science-Fiction Writers Since 1960. (Dictionary of Literary Biography 261).* Detroit, MI: Gale, 2002, pp. 293–311.

Dorton, Harold. "Michael Moorcock, Postmodernism, and (Not) Fantasy: A Primer." *Studies in Fantasy Literature* 1 (2004), pp. 38–50.

Glover, David. "Utopia and Fantasy in the Late 1960's: Burroughs, Moorcock, Tolkien." In Christopher Pawling, ed., *Popular Fiction and Social Change*. New York: St Martin's, 1984, pp. 185–211

Kaplan, Carter. "Fractal Fantasies of Transformation: William Blake, Michael Moorcock, and the Utilities of Mythographic Shamanism." *Extrapolation* 45(4) (Winter 2004), pp. 419–436.

Web Sites

Moorcock's Miscellany. http://www.multiverse.org. Last visited January 28, 2008. Author's official Web site.

Catherine Lucille Moore (C.L. Moore) (1911–1987)

Biographical Sketch

C.L. Moore was born in Indianapolis, Indiana. She was a sickly child, and semi-invalid. Encouraged by her mother, she read widely. She attended Indiana University, but had to leave school to get a job in a bank because of the Great Depression. Moore started publishing short stories in the so-called pulp science-fiction/fantasy magazines. Worried that she might lose her job if the bank found out, she published under a pen name. After meeting and marrying Henry Kuttner, she frequently collaborated with him under the pen name "Lewis Padgett." She stopped writing fiction after Kuttner's death in 1958.

Moore is probably best known for her short story "Shambleau," which retold the Greek myth of Medusa on Mars. It was widely admired for its evocative style. Moore wrote several other short stories alone and with Kuttner, many of which blended science fiction and fantasy. Moore was awarded the World Fantasy Lifetime Achievement Award in 1981. She also has a star named for her in the constellation of Cepheus.

> I was *never* a formula writer, certainly not in the sense that the term is commonly understood. That would have been much too boring for me. I don't think I could have written that way for any period of time. I tried to vary my approach from story to story simply to keep from going crazy. —C.L. Moore, "C. L. Moore: Poet of Far-Distant Futures," 1983)

Major Works

Short Stories and Short Story Collections

"Shambleau." *Weird Tales.* November 1933

A Gnome There Was, and Other Tales of Science Fiction and Fantasy (1950) with Henry Kuttner, under the joint pseudonym "Lewis Padgett"

Judgment Night: A Collection of Science Fiction (1952)

Shambleau and Others (1953)

No Boundaries (1955) with Henry Kuttner

Jirel of Joiry (1969) later published as *Black Gods*

The Best of C. L. Moore (1975)

Two-Handed Engine: The Selected Short Fiction of Henry Kuttner & C.L. Moore (2005)

Research Sources

Encyclopedias and Handbooks: EF, HDF, SJGF

Biographies and Interviews

Elliot, Jeffrey M. "C. L. Moore: Poet of Far-Distant Futures." *Pulp Voices or Science Fiction Voices #6: Interviews with Pulp Magazine Writers and Editors*. San Bernardino, CA: Borgo Press, 1983, pp. 45–51.

Criticism and Readers' Guides

Benson, Gordon R. Jr. and Virgil S. Utter. *C. L. Moore & Henry Kuttner: A Marriage of Souls and Talent, A Working Bibliography*, 3rd ed. Albuquerque, NM: Galactic Central, 1989.

Bleiler, E.F. "Fantasy, Horror... and Sex: The Early Stories of C.L. Moore." *The Scream Factory* 13 (Spring 1994), pp. 41–47.

Bredehoft, Thomas A. "Origin Stories: Feminist Science Fiction and C. L. Moore's 'Shambleau'," *Science Fiction Studies* 24(3) (November 1997), pp. 369–386.

Gamble, Sarah. "'Shambleau... and Others': The Role of the Female in the Fiction of C. L. Moore." *Where No Man Has Gone Before: Women and Science Fiction.* Ed., Lucie Armitt. New York: Routledge, 1991, pp. 29–49.

Gubar, Susan. "C. L. Moore and the Conventions of Women's Science Fiction." *Science-Fiction Studies* 7(1) (March 1980), pp. 16–27.

Pat Murphy (1955–)

Biographical Sketch

Pat Murphy was born in Spokane, Washington. She earned a BA in biology and general sciences from the University of California, Santa Cruz, where she also took classes in the Science Writing Program. She has been publishing science articles in magazines and newspapers since 1976. She currently works for the Exploratorium, a museum in San Francisco, and has written a number of nonfiction science books for them.

Murphy writes both fantasy and science-fiction novels. Together with Karen Joy Fowler, Murphy cofounded the Tiptree Award in 1991. Her favorite color is ultraviolet.

> One of my friends has accused me of having an office like Frankenstein's workshop with extra bits and pieces of things lying around. Because the way work tends to come together for me is I have an idea and it kicks around for a long, long time before they come together. I'll have an idea, a character and a setting and things are lying around. —(Pat Murphy, *Science Fiction Chronicle* interview, 2001)

Major Works

Novels

The Shadow Hunter (1982)
The Falling Woman (1986)
The City, Not Long After (1989)
Nadya (1996)
The Wild Angel (2000)

Short Story Collections

Letters From Home (with Pat Cadigan and Karen Joy Fowler, 1989)
Points of Departure (1990)

Other Important Writings

Murphy, Pat. "Adventures in Writing with Max Merriwell." *The Broadsheet*. March 6, 2003. http://broaduniverse.org/broadsheet/archive/0303pm.html. Last visited January 28, 2008.

Murphy, Pat. "Adventures in Writing with Max Merriwell: Facing Your Monsters." *The Broadsheet*. November 5, 2003. http://broaduniverse.org/broadsheet/archive/0308pm.html. Last visited January 28, 2008.

Research Sources

Encyclopedias and Handbooks: EF, SJGF

Biographies and Interviews

Brandenburg, Sandra and Debora Hill. "Interview with Pat Murphy." *Marion Zimmer Bradley's Fantasy Magazine* 13 (Summer 1991), pp. 47–49.

Morehouse, Lyda. "SFC Interview: Pat Murphy." *Science Fiction Chronicle* 22(4) (April, 2001), pp. 16–20.

"Pat Murphy: Magnificent Obsessions." *Locus* 21(10) (October 1988), pp. 7, 81.

"Pat Murphy: Playing with Reality." *Locus* (43)(1) July 1999, pp. 6, 76–77.

Wohleber, Carl. "Interview: Pat Murphy Goes Wild in *Wild Angel*." *Science Fiction Weekly*. http://www.scifi.com/sfw/issue175/interview.html. Last visited January 28, 2008.

Web Sites

"Pat Murphy." *The Brazen Hussies*. http://www.brazenhussies.net/murphy. Last visited January 28, 2008. Author's official Web site.

Edith Nesbit (E. Nesbit) (1858–1924)

Biographical Sketch

Edith Nesbit started writing for children largely as a way to earn money and support her large family (her husband suffered from ill health). In addition to children's books, she published poetry, plays, and novels and short stories for adults. She also edited some collections of essays, poetry, and stories. She was an active Socialist, and was a founding member of the Fabian Society.

Nesbit's books portrayed children far more realistically than had previous American and English books for children. Her children were not perfect and often got into trouble. She also used a lot of humor. Her fantasy books influenced a number of later writers and continue to be reissued.

> It is wonderful how quickly you get used to things, even the most astonishing. —(E. Nesbit, *Five Children and It*, 1902. Available online at http://www.gutenberg.org/dirs/etext97/fivit10.txt. Last visited January 28, 2008)

Major Works

Children's/Young Adult Fiction

Psammead series: *Five Children and It* (1902), *The Phoenix and the Carpet* (1904), *The Story of the Amulet* (1906)

The Enchanted Castle (1907)

House of Arden series: *The House of Arden* (1908), *Harding's Luck* (1909)

Short Story Collections

The Book of Dragons (1900)

Research Sources

Encyclopedias and Handbooks: EF, HDF, SJGF

Biographies and Interviews

Briggs, Julia. *A Woman of Passion: The Life of E. Nesbit.* New York: New Amsterdam Books, 1987.

Moore, Doris Langley. *E. Nesbit: A Biography*. Philadelphia, PA: Chilton Books, 1966 (originally published in 1933).

Criticism and Readers' Guides

Bar-Yosef, Eitan. "E. Nesbit and the Fantasy of Reverse Colonization: How Many Miles to Modern Babylon?" *English Literature in Transition* 46(1) (2003), pp. 5–28.

Bavidge, Jenny. "Treasure Seekers in the City: London in the Novels of E. Nesbit." In Lawrence Phillips, ed., *The Swarming Streets: Twentieth-Century Literary Representations of London*. Atlanta, GA: Rodopi, 2004, pp. 45–59.

Frank, Cathrine. "Tinklers and Time Machines: Time Travel in the Social Fantasy of E. Nesbit and H. G. Wells." *Utopian and Dystopian Writing for Children and Young Adults*. Eds., Carrie Hintz and Elaine Ostry. New York: Routledge, 2003, pp, 72–88.

Fromm, Gloria G. "E. Nesbit and the Happy Moralist." *Journal of Modern Literature* 11(1) (March 1984), pp. 45–65.

Rutledge, Amelia A. "E. Nesbit." In Darren Harris-Fain, ed., *British Fantasy and Science-Fiction Writers Before World War I (Dictionary of Literary Biography 178)*. Detroit, MI: Gale, 1997, pp. 200–213.

Sircar, Sanjay. "The Generic Decorum of the Burlesque *Kunstmärchen*: E. Nesbit's *The Magician's Heart*." *Folklore* 110 (1999), pp. 75–91.

Vidal, Gore. "The Writing of E. Nesbit." *The New York Book Review of Books* 3(8) (December 3, 1964). Available online at http://www.nybooks.com/articles/13132. Last visited January 28, 2008.

Web Sites

"Nesbit, E. (Edith), 1858–1924." *Project Gutenberg*. http://www.gutenberg.org/browse/authors/n#a407. Last visited January 28, 2008. Online texts for several of Nesbit's novels.

"Online Books by E. Nesbit." *The Online Books Page*. http://onlinebooks.library.upenn.edu/webbin/book/search?amode=start&author=Nesbit%2c%20E%2e%20. Last visited January 28, 2008. Lists links to various online versions of texts by E. Nesbit, many of which are scanned from printed books (and thus include illustrations).

Garth Nix (1963–)

Biographical Sketch

A native Australian, Garth Nix has long loved fantasy. In fact, his mother was reading Tolkien's books while pregnant with him. Nix did a BA degree in professional writing at the University of Canberra. He served in the Australian Army Reserves, and has worked at a variety of jobs in the publishing industry. He has been writing full time since 2002.

Most of Nix's fantasy books have been marketed in the young adult and/or children's area, but are enjoyed by readers of all ages. He is probably best known for his Old Kingdom trilogy. He currently lives in Sydney, Australia.

> I think in Western culture we have this big reservoir of myth and legend and fairytales which is inside us, and we respond to that and there's some connection in a fantasy novel to that myth and legend. I never consciously set out to write a metaphorical story or to communicate any sort of message. At the same time if I've done my job well there will be more to it, people will find metaphors and find things that speak to them just beyond their enjoyment of the story. —(Garth Nix, *Jubilee Books Magazine* interview, 2002. Available online at http://www.jubileebooks.co.uk/jubilee/magazine/authors/garth_nix/garth_nix_interview.asp. Last visited January 28, 2008)

Major Works

Children's/Young Adult Fiction

Old Kingdom series: *Sabriel* (1995), *Lirael: Daughter of the Clayr* (2001), *Abhorsen* (2003)
Seventh Tower series: *The Fall* (2000), *Castle* (2000), *Aenir* (2000), *Above the Veil* (2000), *Into Battle* (2001), *The Violet Keystone* (2001)
Keys to the Kingdom series: *Mister Monday* (2003), *Grim Tuesday* (2004), *Drowned Wednesday* (2005), *Sir Thursday* (2006), *Lady Friday* (2007)
The Ragwitch (1990)

Short Story Collections

Across the Wall: Tales of the Old Kingdom and Beyond (2005)
The Creature in the Case (2005)

Other Important Writing

"Which Shelf Do I Put this Book On?" *Locus* 56(5) (May 2006), p. 38.

Research Sources

Encyclopedias and Handbooks: HDF

Biographies and Interviews

"Garth Nix." *Fast Forward.* December 2003. http://www.fast-forward.tv/audio/audio161.m3u. Last visited January 30, 2008.
"Garth Nix: Digging into Fantasy." *Locus* 50(1) (January 2003), pp. 76–78.
"Garth Nix: The Midden and the River." *Locus* 38(4) (April 1997), pp. 6–7, 63, 66.
Pike, Joseph. "Author Interview: Garth Nix." *Jubilee Books Magazine* (September 2002). http://www.jubileebooks.co.uk/jubilee/magazine/authors/garth_nix/garth_nix_interview.asp. Last visited January 28, 2008.
White, E. Claire. "A Conversation with Garth Nix." The Internet Writing Journal (July–August 2000) http://www.writerswrite.com/journal/jul00/nix.htm. Last visited January 28, 2008.

Web Sites

The Almost Current Garth Nix Website. http://www.garthnix.com. Last visited January 28, 2008. Author's site. Includes biographical material and articles on writing.
"Excerpt: 'Sabriel' by Garth Nix." *NPR.org*. June 8, 2005. http://www.npr.org/templates/story/story.php?storyId=4695407. Last visited January 28, 2008. Includes an excerpt from the first chapter of *Sabriel*, and an audio excerpt from *Sabriel*.

Andre Norton (1912–2005)

Biographical Sketch

One of the first major female fantasy writers, Andre Norton was born "Alice Mary Norton," but subsequently changed her legal name to "Andre Alice Norton" because masculine-sounding author names sold better. She was a children's librarian for several years, while continuing to write and publish books. She wrote in a large number of genres including science fiction, fantasy, young adult, children's, historical, romance, mystery, and even westerns.

Norton is probably best known for her "Witch World" books, a sprawling set of series, novels, and short stories that she wrote on and off for much of her career. Highly influential in the field, Norton collaborated with several authors and edited numerous anthologies. She was the first woman to receive the Gandalf Grand Master Award from the World Science Fiction Society in 1977, and won numerous other awards during her career.

> There's no writer that doesn't make mistakes, or no writer who can say that they've reached the top, because you never do. No writer is ever entirely pleased with a finished product. It isn't the exact same thing that was in their mind.—(Andre Norton, *Tangent Magazine* interview, 1996. Available online at http://www.sff.net/people/dtruesdale/hh1.htp. Last visited January 28, 2008)

Major Works

Novels and Related Short Stories

Witch World, Estcarp Cycle: *Witch World* (1963), *Web of the Witch World* (1964), *Three Against the Witch World* (1965), *Warlock of the Witch World* (1967), *Sorceress of the Witch World* (1968), *Trey of Swords* (1977), *'Ware Hawk* (1983), *The Gate of the Cat* (1987)

Witch World, High Halleck Cycle: *Year of the Unicorn* (1965), *The Crystal Gryphon* (1972), *Spell of the Witch World* (1972), *The Jargoon Pard* (1974), *Zarsthor's Bane* (1978) *Gryphon in Glory* (1981), *Horn Crown* (1981)

Witch World, short stories: *Trey of Swords* (1977), *Lore of the Witch World* (1980)

Here Abide Monsters (1973)

Quag Keep (1978)

Mirror of Destiny (1995)

Three Hands for Scorpio (2005)

Return to Quag Keep (2006)

Children's/Young Adult Fiction

Magic Books series: *Steel Magic* (1965, also published as *Gray Magic*), *Octagon Magic* (1967), *Dragon Magic* (1967), *Fur Magic* (1968), *Lavender-Green Magic* (1974), *Red Hart Magic* (1976)

Short Story Collections

High Sorcery (1970)
Moon Mirror (1988)

Research Sources

Encyclopedias and Handbooks: EF, HDF, SJGF

Biographies and Interviews

"Andre Norton (1912–2005)." *Locus* (April 2005), pp. 5, 63.

"Andre Norton (1912–2005)." *SF/F & Publishing News*. http://sfwa.org/news/anorton.htm. Last visited January 28, 2008. Obituary from Science Fiction and Fantasy Writers of America. Includes tributes from science fiction and fantasy authors.

Coker, John L. III. "Days of Wonder: A Conversation with Andre Norton." *Tangent Magazine* (1996). Available online at http://www.sff.net/people/dtruesdale/hh1.htp. Last visited January 28, 2008.

Holland, Steve. "Obituary: Andre Norton." *The Guardian*. March 29, 2005. Available online at *Guardian Unlimited*. http://www.guardian.co.uk/obituaries/story/0,,1447052,00.html. Last visited January 28, 2008.

Shwartz, Susan. "Interview with Andre Norton." *Marion Zimmer Bradley's Fantasy Magazine* 12 (Spring 1991), pp. 35–37.

Thompson, Robert. "Interview with Andre Norton." March 23, 1991. *Interviews with Authors of Modern Arthurian Literature* (part of the University of Rochester's *Camelot Project*). http://www.lib.rochester.edu/camelot/intrvws/norton.htm. Last visited January 28, 2008.

Criticism and Readers' Guides

Dressel, Janice H. and Francis J. "Octagon Magic: Andre Norton and Revitalizing the Girls' Book." *Children's Literature in Education* 27(4) (December 1996), pp. 209–218.

Schlobin, Roger C. and Irene R. Harrison. *Andre Norton, a Primary and Secondary Bibliography*. Rev. ed. Framingham, MA: NESFA Press, 1994.

Schlobin, Roger C. "The Formulaic and Rites of Transformation in Andre Norton's Magic Series." In C.W. Sullivan, ed., *Science Fiction for Young Readers. Contributions to the Study of Science Fiction and Fantasy 56*. Westport, CT: Greenwood, 1993, pp. 37–45.

Yoke, Carl B. "Slaying the Dragon within: Andre Norton's Female Heroes." *Journal of the Fantastic in the Arts* 4(3) (1991), pp. 79–92.

Web Sites

andre-norton.org. http://www.andre-norton.org. Last visited January 28, 2008. Fan site.

Diana L. Paxson (1943–)

Biographical Sketch

Diana Paxson graduated from Mills College and then did an MA in Comparative Literature at the University of California, Berkeley. Her continuing interest in medieval culture and literature has informed much of her life and writing. Paxson helped to found the Society for Creative Anachronism and continued to design and sew period costumes. She also plays and composes music for the folk harp, and is an active Neo-Pagan.

Paxson started writing seriously in 1971, and her first novel was published in 1981. Many of her her novels are fantasy and/or historical fiction. She is best known for the long-running Westria series, fantasies that are set in a very future California landscape. Paxson currently lives in Berkeley, CA.

> The more complex a culture becomes, the more it needs to reinterpret the legends that everybody knows in order to draw new meanings from them and to play with them.—(Diana Paxson, Thompson interview, 1989. Available online at http://www.lib.rochester.edu/camelot/intrvws/paxson.htm. Last visited January 28, 2008)

Major Works

Novels

Westria series: *Lady of Light* (1982), *Lady of Darkness* (1983), *Silverhair the Wanderer* (1986), *The Earthstone* (1987), *The Sea Star* (1988), *The Wind Crystal* (1990), *The Jewel of Fire* (1992), *The Golden Hills of Westria* (2006)

Brisingamen (1984)

White Mare, Red Stallion (1986)

The Paradise Tree (1987)

The White Raven (1988)

The Serpent's Tooth (1991)

Wodan's Children series: *The Wolf and the Raven* (1993), *The Dragon of the Rhine* (1995), *The Lord of Horses* (1996)

Avalon series (with Marion Zimmer Bradley): *The Forest House* (1994, uncredited), *The Lady of Avalon* (1997, uncredited), *The Priestess of Avalon* (2000), *The Ancestors of Avalon* (2004)

Hallowed Isle series: *The Book of the Sword* (1999), *The Book of the Spear* (1999), *The Book of the Cauldron* (1999), *The Book of the Stone* (2000), *The Hallowed Isle* (2000)

Other Important Writings

Taking Up the Runes: A Complete Guide to Using Runes in Spells, Rituals, Divination, and Magic (2005)

Essential Asatru: Walking the Path of Norse Paganism (2007)

Research Sources

Encyclopedias and Handbooks: EF, HDF, SJGF

Biographies and Interviews

Bradley, Marion Z. "An Interview with Diana Paxson." *Marion Zimmer Bradley's Fantasy Magazine* 10 (Autumn 1990), pp. 41–42.

Thompson, Robert. "Interview with Diana Paxson." July 29, 1989. *Interviews with Authors of Modern Arthurian Literature* (part of the University of Rochester's *Camelot Project*). http://www.lib.rochester.edu/camelot/intrvws/paxson.htm. Last visited January 28, 2008.

Web Sites

Diana Paxson. http://home.pon.net/rhinoceroslodge/paxson.htm. Last visited January 28, 2008. Author's web site. Includes a primary bibliography.

Westria. http://www.westria.org. Last visited January 28, 2008. Author's web site. Includes biographical material.

Mervyn Peake (1911–1968)

Biographical Sketch

Mervyn Peake was born in China, where his parents were medical missionaries. After the family returned to England, he studied art, and became a painter and illustrator. He applied to be a war artist during World War II, but was turned down, and suffered a subsequent nervous breakdown. He began writing the Gormenghast books during the 1940s. As his health deteriorated (Peake suffered from Parkinson's disease), he struggled to finish them. The last of the trilogy, *Titus Alone*, was published near the end of his life.

Peake's *Gormenghast* books proved very popular and continue to be critically acclaimed for their dark surreal vision. Peake also wrote several nonsense verse books and plays and illustrated several books.

> All things are questionable. —(Mervyn Peake, *Writings and Drawings*)

Major Works

Novels

Gormenghast series: *Titus Groan* (1946), *Gormenghast* (1950), *Titus Alone* (1959)

Children's/Young Adult Fiction

Captain Slaughterboard (1939)
Letters from a Lost Uncle (from Polar Region) (1948)

Other Important Writings

A Book of Nonsense (1972)
Selected Poems (1972)
Mervyn Peake: Writings and Drawings (1974)
Peake's Progress: Selected Writings and Drawings of Mervyn Peake (1978)

Research Sources

Encyclopedias and Handbooks: EF, HDF, SJGF

Biographies and Interviews

Batchelor, John. *Mervyn Peake: A Biographical and Critical Exploration*. London: Duckworth, 1974.

Gardiner-Scott, Tanya J. *Mervyn Peake: The Evolution of a Dark Romantic*. New York: Peter Lang, 1989.

Gilmore, Maeve. *A World Away: Memoir of Mervyn Peake*. London: Gollancz, 1970.

Smith, Gordon. *Mervyn Peake: A Personal Memoir*. London: Gollancz, 1984.

Winnington, G. Peter. *Vast Alchemies: The Life and Work of Mervyn Peake*. London: P. Owen, 2000.

Yorke, Malcolm. *Mervyn Peake: My Eyes Mint Gold*. London: Murray, 2000.

Criticism and Readers' Guides

Bratman, David. "Mervyn Peake, the Gormenghast Diptych, and Titus Alone." *New York Review of Science Fiction* 8(9) (May 1996), pp. 1, 4–6.

Gardiner-Scott, Tanya. "Mervyn Peake." In Darren Harris-Bain, ed., *British Fantasy and Science-Fiction Writers, 1918–1960 (Dictionary of Literary Biography 255)*. Detroit, MI: Gale, 2002, pp. 174–187.

Gardiner-Scott, Tanya J. "Mervyn Peake: The Relativity of Perception." *Journal of the Fantastic in the Arts* 1(2) (1988), pp. 13–24.

Gardiner-Scott, Tanya. "Through the Maze: Textual Problems in Mervyn Peake's Titus Alone." *Extrapolation* 30(1) (Spring 1989), pp. 70–83.

Hughes, Jamie A. "'I Have My Battleground No Less than Nations': Peake's Daydream of Gormenghast." *Journal of Evolutionary Psychology* 25(1–2) (March 2004), pp. 24–31.

Manlove, Colin. "Rebel without a Cause: The Cultural Matrix of the Titus Books." *Peake Studies* 7(4) (April 2002), pp. 7–18.

Moorcock, Michael. "An Excellence of Peake." *Fantastic Metropolis*. October 15, 2001. http://www.fantasticmetropolis.com/show.html?ey,peake,1. Last visited January 28, 2008.

Sanders, J.L. "Passions in the Clay: Mervyn Peake's Titus Stories." In Thomas D. Clareson, ed., *Voices for the Future,* Vol. 3. Bowling Green, OH: Popular Press, 1984, pp. 75–105.

Web Sites

The Official Website of Mervyn Peake, author of Gormenghast. http://www.mervynpeake.org. Last visited January 28, 2008.

Peake Studies. http://www.peakestudies.com. Last visited January 28, 2008. Web site for *Peake Studies*, "a periodical dedicated to the life and work of Mervyn Peake."

Wendy Pini (1951–) and Richard Pini (1950–)

Biographical Sketch

Wendy and Richard Pini met via the Letters Column in the *Silver Surfer* comic book series. After a lengthy correspondence, they met in person and subsequently married and began producing the *Elf Quest* comic books together. Although they both developed the story, Wendy did the art, while Richard did editing and took care of the business aspects. Unhappy with their original publisher, the Pinis decided to self-publish and formed the company WaRP Graphics.

Published starting in 1978, the original *Elf Quest* series was one of the first fantasy comic book series, and features elves descended from cosmic travelers. *Elf Quest* was also notable for its popularity with female readers. The Pinis have published numerous subsequent series, and also wrote novels based on the characters; roleplaying and board games were even developed.

> Reader identification is very important to the acceptance of any story, and that the *Elfquest* elves are human in general form, as well as appealing aesthetically and sensually, gives readers easy access to that identification. From the beginning, we've gotten feedback that's just about unanimous about how beautiful readers perceive the elves to be, and how much they—the readers—would like to be elves or be like the elves. —(Richard Pini, "Elfquestions." *Sequential Tart*. http://www.sequentialtart.com/archive/june01/pini.shtml. Last visited January 28, 2008)

> It's my firm belief, based on years of fan feedback, that anyone willing to fully explore the epic-sized world of Elfquest will find their views of modern society mirrored, their prejudices challenged and their understanding of relationships—of all kinds—forever changed. —(Wendy Pini, "Elfquestions – Part Two." *Sequential Tart*. http://www.sequentialtart.com/archive/june01/pini_2.shtml. Last visited January 28, 2008)

Major Works

Novels

Elfquest the Novel: Journey to Sorrow's End (1982)
The Quest Begins (1996)
Captives of Blue Mountain (1998)

Graphic Novels

Elfquest: Original Series. Issues #1–21. 1978–1984. Black and white. Originally published by WarP Graphics, and later reissued by Marvel and then DC Comics.
Reader's Collection #1—Fire and Flight (issues #1–5) color
Reader's Collection #2—The Forbidden Grove (issues #6–10) color
Reader's Collection #3—Captives of Blue Mountain (issues #11–15) color
Reader's Collection #4—Quest's End (issues #16–20) color
Elfquest: Siege at Blue Mountain. Issues #1–8 (1986–1988) black and white
Reader's Collection #5—Siege at Blue Mountain (issues #1–4) color
Reader's Collection #6—The Secret of Two-Edge (issues #5–8) color
Elfquest: Kings of the Broken Wheel. Issues #1–9 (1988–1990) black and white
Reader's Collection #7—The Cry From Beyond (issues #1–4) color
Reader's Collection #8—Kings of the Broken Wheel (issues #5–9) color
Elfquest: The Searcher and the Sword (2004) color graphic novel

Children's/Young Adult Fiction

A Gift of Her Own: An Elfquest Story (1995) (Wendy Pini)

Research Sources

Encyclopedias and Handbooks: EF

Biographies and Interviews

Fletcher, Dani. "Elfquestions." *Sequential Tart*. http://www.sequentialtart.com/archive/june01/pini.shtml. Last visited January 28, 2008.
Fletcher, Dani. "Elfquestions—Part Two." *Sequential Tart*. http://www.sequentialtart.com/archive/june01/pini_2.shtml. Last visited January 28, 2008.
James, Warren W. "Loscon 2004." *Hodel's Hour 25*. November 27, 2004. http://www.hour25online.com/hr25_2004-11-27_show.m3u. Last visited January 28, 2008. Includes an audio interview with Wendy Pini.
Mitleid, Corbie. "The Metaphysics of Elfquest." Broadcast on the Crystal Palace radio show on Web radio WXBH on November 10, 2002. Transcript available at http://www.elfquest.com/edits/CrysPal.html. Last visited January 28, 2008.
Whitt, Tony. "The Pinis: Mightier Than the Sword (Part One)." *Mania*. August 18, 2004. http://www.mania.com/42341.html. Last visited January 28, 2008.
Whitt, Tony. "The Pinis: Mightier Than the Sword (Part Two)." *Mania*. August 25, 2004. http://www.mania.com/42375.html. Last visited January 28, 2008.

Criticism and Readers' Guides

Robeson, Theresa, Joellyn Auklandus, and Richard Pini. *The Wolfrider's Guide to the World of Elfquest*. Poughkeepsie, NY: Wolfrider Books, 1997.
Wilkerson, Cherie and Richard Pini. *The Big Elfquest Gatherum*. Poughkeepsie, NY: Father Tree Press, 1994.

Web Sites

Elfquest.com. http://www.elfquest.com. Last visited January 28, 2008. Official Web site.

Shara's Guide to All ElfQuest Publications. http://eqpubguide.miravisu.net. Last visited January 28, 2008.

Tim Powers (1952–)

Biographical Sketch

Born on Leap Year Day (February 29), Tim Powers grew up with books and began writing early. He received his first rejection slip when he was thirteen years old. He attended California State University at Fullerton, where he met James T. Blaylock. He and Blaylock invented the fictional poet William Ashbless, who has appeared in some form in several, if not all, of Powers' books.

As a writer, Powers, along with Blaylock, considers himself to be "steampunk." Many of his novels are set in historical settings and have a blend of science fiction and fantasy elements. He first received critical acclaim with the publication of *The Anubis Gate*, and has continued to be popular among readers. He currently lives in California.

> I want the magic to seem to be really happening—I want the readers to be as vicariously disoriented by the appearance of the supernatural in the story as they would actually be if it happened to them in real life. (Easy to say!) —(Tim Powers, *Strange Horizons* interview, 2005)

Major Works

Novels

The Drawing of the Dark (1979)
The Anubis Gates (1983)
On Stranger Tides (1987)
The Stress of Her Regard (1989)
Last Call series: *Last Call* (1992), *Expiration Date* (1996), *Earthquake Weather* (1997), *Declare* (2000)
Three Days to Never (2006)

Short Story Collections

Night Moves, and Other Stories (2000)
The Devil in the Details (2003) with James P. Blaylock
Strange Itineraries (2004)

Research Sources

Encyclopedias and Handbooks: EF, HDF, SJGF

Biographies and Interviews

Fawcett, Kim. "A Conversation with Tim Powers." *The SF Site*. July 1999. http://www.sfsite.com/09a/9tp.htm. Last visited January 28, 2008.

Kelleghan, Fiona. "Interview with Tim Powers." *Science Fiction Studies* 25(1) (March 1998), pp. 7–28. Available online at http://www.depauw.edu/sfs/interviews/powers74interview.htm. Last visited January 28, 2008.

Morehouse, Lyda. "Interview: Tim Powers." *Strange Horizons* (February 7, 2005). http://www.strangehorizons.com/2005/20050207/powers-int-a.shtml. Last visited January 28, 2008.

Shirley, John. "An Existentially Poignant, Angst-Ridden, Grimly Realistic Yet Surreal Interview With Tim Powers." *Emerald City: Science Fiction and Fantasy Book Reviews* 130 (June 2006). http://www.emcit.com/emcit130.php?a=2. Last visited January 28, 2008.

Szumskyj, Benjamin. "A Conversation with Tim Powers." *Studies in Fantasy Literature* 3 (2005), pp. 29–35.

"Tim Powers, Part 1." *TV Bookshelf*. October 1, 2004. http://tvbookshelf.ws/Tim1.mov. Last visited January 30, 2008.

"Tim Powers, Part 2." *TV Bookshelf*. October 1, 2004. http://tvbookshelf.ws/tim2.mov. Last visited January 30, 2008.

"Tim Powers: In Praise of Paranoia." *Locus* 40(1) (March 1998), pp. 4–5, 75–76.

"Tim Powers: The Physics of Fantasy." *Locus* 48(2) (February 2002), pp. 4–5, 92.

Criticism and Readers' Guides

Dembo, Arinn. "Impassion'd Clay: On Tim Powers' The Stress of Her Regard." *New York Review of Science Fiction* 37 (September 1991), pp. 1, 3–7.

Hantke, Steffen. "Difference Engines and Other Infernal Devices: History According to Steampunk." *Extrapolation* 40(3) (1999), pp. 244–254.

Kelleghan, Fiona. "Getting a Life: Haunted Spaces in Two Novels of Tim Powers." *New York Review of Science Fiction* 115 (March 1998), pp. 13–17.

Stein, Altara. "Fictionalized Romantics: Byron, Shelley, and Keats as Characters in Contemporary Genre Fiction." *Journal of the Fantastic in the Arts* 13(4) (2003), pp. 379–388.

Webb, Janeen. "Simmons and Powers: Postmodernism to Postromanticism." *Visions of the Fantastic: Selected Essays from the Fifteenth International Conference on the Fantastic in the Arts*. Ed., Allienne R. Becker. Westport, CT: Greenwood, 1996, pp. 139–148.

Web Sites

The Works of Tim Powers. http://www.theworksoftimpowers.com. Last visited January 28, 2008.

If you like Tim Powers

Part of the so-called steampunk movement, Powers sets many of his novels in historical milieus with a blend of science fiction and fantasy elements.

Then you might like

James Blaylock

Another steampunk writer and sometime collaborator with Powers, Blaylock mixes fantastical elements with historical settings and strong, often autobiographical characters. An example is his Christian trilogy: *The Last Coin*, *The Paper Grail*, and *All the Bells on Earth.*

Susanna Clarke

Written in the most byzantinely elegant Victorian prose imaginable and heavily footnoted, Clarke's *Jonathan Strange and Mr. Norrell* evokes an England that feels both unbearably familiar and unbearably bizarre.

Neil Gaiman

Like Powers, Gaiman often mixes the fantastic with elements of horror. He is perhaps best known for his *Sandman* graphic-novel series, but has written a number of novels, including the recent *Anansi Boys*.

China Miéville

Many of Miéville's novels and stories are set in dark, forboding, urban areas, crossing the genres of fantasy, science fiction, and horror. He is probably best known for his New Crobuzon series (*Perdido Street Station*, *The Scar*, and *Iron Council*).

Terry Pratchett (1948–)

Biographical Sketch

Terry Pratchett sold his first story when he was 13, and used the money to buy a second-hand typewriter. He continued to write in his spare time for some years while working as a press officer and journalist. He became a full-time writer in 1987.

Pratchett is best known for his humorous light fantasy "Discworld" series, of which there are now at least 30. Although Discworld exists in its own universe (and on the backs of four elephants standing on the back of a giant turtle), much of his books contain satires of contemporary society. He was named an Officer of the

British Empire "for services to literature" in 1998 and presently lives in England with his family.

> The genres have, to a large extent, become *tendencies*. Romance, western, fantasy, science fiction, are now flavors rather than substances. I've always said that I consider science fiction to be fantasy with nuts and bolts on the inside. The hardness of science fiction is often the hardness of the crust on the meringue.—Terry Pratchett, *Locus* interview, 1999)

Major Works

Novels

Discworld series: *The Colour of Magic* (1983), *The Light Fantastic* (1986), *Equal Rites* (1987), *Mort* (1987), *Sourcery* (1988), *Wyrd Sisters* (1988), *Pyramids* (1989), *Guards! Guards!* (1989), *Eric* (1990), *Moving Pictures* (1990), *Reaper Man* (1991), *Witches Abroad* (1991), *Small Gods* (1992), *Lords and Ladies* (1993), *Men at Arms* (1993), *Soul Music* (1994), *Interesting Times* (1994), *Maskerade* (1995), *Feet of Clay* (1996), *Hogfather* (1996), *Jingo* (1997), *The Last Continent* (1998), *Carpe Jugulum* (1998), *The Fifth Elephant* (1999), *The Truth* (2000), *The Last Hero* (2001) illustrated by Paul Kidby, *Thief of Time* (2001), *Night Watch* (2002), *Monstrous Regiment* (2003), *Going Postal* (2004), *Thud!* (2005)

Good Omens: The Nice and Accurate Predictions of Agnes Nutter, Witch (1990) with Neil Gaiman

Graphic Novels

Mort: A Discworld Big Comic (1994, illustrated by Graham Higgins)

Guards! Guards!: A Discworld Graphic Novel (2000), illustrated by Graham Higgins

Children's/Young Adult Fiction

The Carpet People (1971)

Bromeliad trilogy: *Truckers* (1989), *Diggers* (1990), *Wings* (1990)

Discworld children's series: *Amazing Maurice and His Educated Rodents* (2001), *The Wee Free Men* (2003), *A Hat Full of Sky* (2004), *Wintersmith* (2006)

Where's My Cow? (2005)

Other Important Writings

Pratchett, Terry. "Imaginary Worlds, Real Stories." *Folklore* 111(2) (October 2000), pp. 159–168.

Research Sources

Encyclopedias and Handbooks: EF, HDF, SJGF

Biographies and Interviews

James, Warren W. "Terry Pratchett." *Hodel's Hour 25.* February 29, 2004. http://www.hour25online.com/hr25_2004-02-29_show.m3u. Last visited January 28, 2008. Audio interview.

Richards, Linda L. "Terry Pratchett: January Interview." *January Magazine* (August 2002). http://www.januarymagazine.com/profiles/tpratchett2002.html. Last visited January 28, 2008.

Robinson, Tasha. "Interview: On the Business—or Busyness—of being Terry Pratchett." *Science Fiction Weekly.* http://www.scifi.com/sfw/issue156/interview.html. Last visited January 28, 2008.

Silver, Steven H. "A Conversation with Terry Pratchett." *The SF Site.* April 2000. http://www.sfsite.com/04b/tp79.htm. Last visited January 28, 2008.

"Terry Pratchett." *Fast Forward.* October 2005. http://www.fast-forward.tv/audio/audio183.m3u. Last visited January 28, 2008.

"Terry Pratchett: Discworld & Beyond." *Locus* 43(6) (December 1999), pp. 4, 73–76.

"Terry Pratchett, Part 1." *TV Bookshelf.* March 26, 2005. http://tvbookshelf.ws/terrryp1.mov. Last visited January 30, 2008.

"Terry Pratchett, Part 2." *TV Bookshelf.* March 26, 2005. http://tvbookshelf.ws/terryp2.mov. Last visited January 30, 2008.

"Terry Pratchett: 21 Years of Discworld." *Locus* 51(5) (May 2004), pp. 9, 58–59.

Criticism and Readers' Guides

Brown, Martin. "Imaginary Places, Real Monuments: Field Monuments of Lancre, Terry Pratchett's Discworld." In Miles Russell, ed., *Digging Holes in Popular Culture: Archaeology and Science Fiction.* Oxford, UK: Oxbow Books, 2002, pp. 67–76.

Butler, Andrew M. "Terry Pratchett and the Comedic Bildungsroman." *Foundation: The Review of Science Fiction* 67 (Summer 1996), pp. 56–62.

Butler, Andrew M., Edward James, and Farah Mendlesohn, eds. *Terry Pratchett: Guilty of Literature.* Baltimore, MD: Old Earth Books, 2004.

Holloway, John. "Terry Pratchett and Douglas Adams: A Consideration of the Similarities in Their Style and Technique and Their Common Interest in Science." *Textures* 8 (1994), pp. 7–17.

Pratchett, Terry and Stephen Briggs. *The Discworld Companion.* London: Gollancz, 1995.

Pratchett, Terry, Ian Stewart, and Jack S. Cohen. *The Science of Discworld.* London: Ebury Press, 1999.

Sawyer, Andy. "Narrativium and Lies-to-Children: 'Palatable Instruction' in The Science of Discworld." *Journal of the Fantastic in the Arts* 13(1) (2002), pp. 62–81.

Web Sites

The Annotated Pratchett File, v9.0. http://www.sfsite.com/04b/tp79.htm. Last visited January 28, 2008.

Terry Pratchett Books.com. http://www.terrypratchettbooks.com/. Last visited January 28, 2008. Author's Web site.

If you like Terry Pratchett

Best known for his sprawling Discworld series set in the remarkable city of Ankh-Morpork, Pratchett combines sharp observation of human nature with satire and memorable characterizations. Although all of the Discworld books are self-contained and can be read by themselves, *The Color of Magic* is the very first.

Then you might like

Piers Anthony

Anthony's "Xanth" books are generally lighthearted romps through the pun-heavy, character-driven, almost cartoonish peninsular realm of Xanth. Initial titles include *A Spell for Chameleon*, *The Source of Magic*, and *Castle Roogna.*

Robert Asprin

Asprin's Myth Adventures series concerns an inept would-be magician named Skeeve and the motley crew of allies, enemies, pets, and hangers-on he acquires during various adventures on his home world and in a motley multiverse. Initial titles include *Another Fine Myth*, *Myth Conceptions*, *Myth Directions*, and *Myth-Ing Persons*.

Esther Friesner

Friesner's comic fantasies are high paced, with plenty of pointed commentary on the way. An especially good example is her "Demons" series (*Here Be Demons*, *Demon Blues*, *Hooray for Hellywood*).

Fritz Leiber

Leiber's humorous "Fafhrd and the Gray Mouser" stories are modern classics. *Two Sought Adventure* is the first of many collections (you may also see it under the title *Swords Against Death*).

John Moore

Moore has written a number of humorous, often satiric fantasies including *A Fate Worse Than Dragons*, *Bad Prince Charlie*, and *The Unhandsome Prince*.

Jeff Smith

Smith's *Bone* graphic-novel series includes a princess, a hero, a quest, and dragons, yet to unexpected (and humorous) results.

Philip Pullman (1946–)

Biographical Sketch

Philip Pullman attended Oxford University and then worked as a middle school teacher for several years. He had enjoyed making stories since childhood but honed his skills by telling stories from the *Odysessy* and other works to his students.

Pullman has published a number of children's and young adult books, many of which have historical and/or fantasy settings. He is probably most well known for the His Dark Materials trilogy, which combines magic with travel between universes. Although Dark Materials was originally marketed as a young adult book, it has also been popular with adults. Pullman has also written several plays.

> I can't believe that everyone isn't having ideas all the time. I think they are, actually, and they just don't recognise them as potential stories. Because the important thing is not just having the idea; it's writing the book. That's the difficult thing, the thing that takes the time and the energy and the discipline.—(Philip Pullman, "About the Writing." Available at http://www.philip-pullman.com/about_the_writing.asp. Last visited January 29, 2008)

Major Works

Novels

Galatea (1978)

Children's/Young Adult Fiction

His Dark Materials trilogy: *The Golden Compass* (1995) also published as *Northern Lights*, *The Subtle Knife* (1997), *The Amber Spyglass* (2000)
The Firework-Maker's Daughter (1995)
Clockwork, or All Wound Up (1996)
I Was a Rat!, or The Scarlet Slippers (1999)
Puss in Boots: or The Ogre, the Ghouls and the Windmill (2000)
Lyra's Oxford (2003)
The Scarecrow And His Servant (2004)

Other Important Writings

Frankenstein (1990)
Sherlock Holmes and the Limehouse Horror (1993)

"The Dark Side of Narnia." *The Guardian*. October 1, 1998. Available online at http://www.crlamppost.org/darkside.htm. Last visited January 28, 2008.

"The Science of Fiction." *The Guardian*. August 26, 2004. Available online at *The Guardian Unlimited*. http://www.guardian.co.uk/life/lastword/story/0,13228,1290618,00.html. Last visited January 28, 2008.

"The Making and Faking of Lyra's Oxford." *Lion and the Unicorn* 29(1) (2005), pp. 6–8.

Research Sources

Encyclopedias and Handbooks: EF, HDF

Biographies and Interviews

Cornwell, John. "Some Enchanted Author." *The Sunday Times*. October 24, 2004. Available online via *Timesonline*. http://www.timesonline.co.uk/article/0,2099-1311328,00.html. Last visited January 28, 2008.

Lane, Harriet. "Pullman's Progress." *The Observer*. October 10, 2003. Available online via *The Guardian Unlimited*. http://books.guardian.co.uk/departments/childrenandteens/story/0,,1323626,00.html. Last visited January 28, 2008.

Parsons, Wendy and Catriona Nicholson. "Talking to Philip Pullman: An Interview." *Lion and the Unicorn* 23(1) (January 1999), pp. 116–134.

"Philip Pullman: Storming Heaven." *Locus* 45(6) (December 2000), pp. 8, 80–82.

Renton, Jennie. "Philip Pullman Interview." *Textualities* (2005). http://www.textualities.net/writers/features-n-z/pullmanp01.php. Last visited January 28, 2008.

Roberts, Susan. "A Dark Agenda?" *surefish.co.uk*. November 2002. http://www.surefish.co.uk/culture/features/pullman_interview.htm. Last visited January 28, 2008.

Weich, Dave. "Philip Pullman Reaches the Garden." *Powells.com*. August 31, 2000. http://www.powells.com/authors/pullman.html. Last visited January 28, 2008.

Criticism and Readers' Guides

Bird, Anne-Marie. "Without Contraries Is No Progression: Dust As an All-Inclusive, Multifunction Metaphor in Philip Pullman's His Dark Materials." *Children's Literature in Education* 32(2) (June 2001), pp. 111–123.

Bobby, Susan R. "What Makes a Classic? Daemons and Dual Audience in Philip Pullman's *His Dark Materials*." *The Looking Glass* 8(1) (January 2, 2004). http://www.the-looking-glass.net/rabbit/v8i1/academy1.html. Last visited January 28, 2008.

Colás, Santiago. "Telling True Stories; or, The Immanent Ethics of Material Spirit (and Spiritual Matter) in Philip Pullman's *His Dark Materials*." *Discourse* 27(1) (2005), pp. 34–66.

Gooderham, David. "Fantasizing It As It Is: Religious Language in Philip Pullman's Trilogy *His Dark Materials*." *Children's Literature* 31 (2003), pp. 155–175.

King, Shelley. "All Wound Up: Pullman's Marvelous/Uncanny Clockwork." *Children's Literature* 33 (2005), pp. 66–93.

Lenz, Millicent and Carole Scott. *His Dark Materials Illuminated: Critical Essays on Philip Pullman's Trilogy*. Detroit, MI: Wayne State University Press, 2005.

Lenz, Millicent. "Story As a Bridge to the Transformation: The Way Beyond Death in Philip Pullman's The Amber Spyglass." *Children's Literature in Education* 34(1) (September 2003), pp. 47–55.

Squires, Claire. *Philip Pullman's "His Dark Materials" Trilogy: A Reader's Guide*. New York: Continuum, 2003.

Tilton, Lois. "His Norse Materials." *The Internet Review of Science Fiction* 2(10) (November 2005). http://www.irosf.com/q/zine/article/10205. Last visited January 28, 2008.

Wood, Naomi. "Paradise Lost and Found: Obedience, Disobedience, and Storytelling in C. S. Lewis and Philip Pullman." *Children's Literature in Education* 32(4) (December 2001), pp. 237–259.

Yeffeth, Glenn, ed. *Navigating the Golden Compass: Religion, Science, and Demonology in His Dark Materials*. Dallas, TX: BenBella, 2005.

Web Sites

Bridge to the Stars.net. http://www.bridgetothestars.net. Last visited January 28, 2008.

His Dark Materials.org http://www.hisdarkmaterials.org. Last visited January 28, 2008.

Philip Pullman http://www.philip-pullman.com. Last visited January 28, 2008. Author's Web site.

Joanne Kathleen Rowling (J.K. Rowling) (1965–)

Biographical Sketch

J.K. Rowling attended the University of Exeter, where she majored in French. After university, she worked various jobs in London, the longest of which was for Amnesty International. She has also lived and worked in Portugal and currently lives in Scotland.

Rowling started telling stories to her sister as a child and had early ambitions to be a writer. The idea for the Harry Potter series came to her on a crowded train between London and Manchester. Although she conceived Harry's character and many important plot elements on that train ride, it took some five years to write the first book of the series, *Harry Potter and the Philospher's Stone*. Her Harry Potter books have been immensely popular both with children and adults.

> When I write the books, I really do write them for me. Very often I get asked, 'Who do you have in mind when you write? Is it your daughter or is it the children you've met?' No. It's for me. Just for me. I'm very selfish: I just write for me.

So the humor in the books is really what I find funny. —(J.K. Rowling, *January Magazine* interview, 2000. Available online at http://www.januarymagazine.com/profiles/jkrowling.html. Last visited January 29, 2008)

Major Works

Novels

Harry Potter series: *Harry Potter and the Sorcerer's Stone* (1997, also published as *Harry Potter and the Philosopher's Stone), Harry Potter and the Chamber of Secrets* (1998), *Harry Potter and the Prisoner of Azkaban* (1999), *Harry Potter and the Goblet of Fire* (2000), *Harry Potter and the Order of the Phoenix* (2003), *Harry Potter and the Half-Blood Prince* (2005), *Harry Potter and the Deathly Hallows* (2007)

Other Important Writings

Fantastic Beasts and Where to Find Them (2001) writing as "Newt Scamander"
Quidditch Through the Ages (2001) writing as "Kennilworthy Whisp"

Research Sources

Encyclopedias and Handbooks: HDF

Biographies and Interviews

Fraser, Lindsey. *Conversations with J.K. Rowling*. New York: Scholastic, 2001.

Grossman, Lev. "J.K. Rowling Hogwarts and All." *TIME.com* (July 17, 2005). http://www.time.com/time/magazine/article/0,9171,1083935,00.html. Last visited January 28, 2008.

Kirk, Connie Ann. *J. K. Rowling: A Biography*. Westport, CT: Greenwood Press, 2003.

Paxman, Jeremy. "JK Rowling Interview in Full." *BBC News*. June 19, 2003. http://news.bbc.co.uk/1/hi/entertainment/arts/3004456.stm. Last visited January 28, 2008.

Richards, Linda L. "January Profile: J.K. Rowling." *January Magazine* (October 2000). http://www.januarymagazine.com/profiles/jkrowling.html. Last visited January 28, 2008.

Smith, Sean. *J. K. Rowling: A Biography*. Revised and Expanded Edition. London, UK: Michael O'Mara, 2003.

Weir, Margaret. "Of Magic and Single Motherhood." *Salon*. March 31, 1999. http://www.salon.com/mwt/feature/1999/03/cov_31featureb.html. Last visited January 28, 2008.

Criticism and Readers' Guides

Anatol, Giselle Liza. *Reading Harry Potter: Critical Essays*. Westport, CT: Praeger, 2003.

Beahm, George. *Muggles and Magic: J. K. Rowling and the Harry Potter Phenomenon*. Charlottesville, VA: Hampton Roads, 2004.

Behr, Kate. "'Same-as-Difference': Narrative Transformations and Intersecting Cultures in Harry Potter." *Journal of Narrative Theory* 35(1) (2005), pp. 112–132.

Billone, Amy. "The Boy Who Lived: From Carroll's Alice and Barrie's Peter Pan to Rowling's Harry Potter." *Children's Literature* 32 (2004), pp. 178–202.

Chevalier, Noel. "The Liberty Tree and the Whomping Willow: Political Justice, Magical Science, and Harry Potter." *Lion and the Unicorn* 29(3) (2005), pp. 397–415.

Chihara, Michelle. "Harry Potter and the Great Big Hoopla." *Alternet*. June 16, 2003. http://www.alternet.org/story/16174. Last visited January 28, 2008.

Gibbs, Nancy. "The Real Magic of Harry Potter." *Time* 161(25) (June 23, 2003), pp. 60–67. Available online at http://www.time.com/time/magazine/article/0,9171,1101030623-458732,00.html. Last visited January 28, 2008.

Greven, David. "The Fantastic Powers of the Other Sex: Male Mothers in Fantastic Fiction." *Journal of the Fantastic in the Arts* 14(3) 2003, pp. 301–317.

Heilman, Elizabeth E., ed. *Harry Potter's World: Multidisciplinary Critical Perspectives*. New York: RoutledgeFalmer, 2003.

Jentsch, Nancy K. "Harry Potter Speaks in Tongues: Translating J. K. Rowling's Magical World." *Kentucky Philological Review* 16 (2001), pp. 54–60.

Katz, Maureen. "Prisoners of Azkaban: Understanding Intergenerational Transmission of Trauma Due to War and State Terror (with Help from Harry Potter)." *Journal for the Psychoanalysis of Culture and Society* 8(2) 2003, pp. 200–207.

Kirk, Connie Ann. *The J. K. Rowling Encyclopedia*. Westport, CT: Greenwood Press, 2006.

Lackey, Mercedes and Leah Wilson, eds. *Mapping the World of Harry Potter: Science Fiction and Fantasy Writers Explore the Bestselling Fantasy Series of all Time*. Dallas, TX: BenBella Books, 2005.

Lathey, Gillian. "The Travels of Harry: International Marketing and the Translation of J. K. Rowling's Harry Potter Books." *Lion and the Unicorn* 29(2) 2005, pp. 141–151.

Mayes-Elma, Ruthann. *Females and Harry Potter: Not all that Empowering*. Lanham, MD: Rowman & Littlefield, 2006.

Mendlesohn, Farah. "Crowning the King: Harry Potter and the Construction of Authority." *Journal of the Fantastic in the Arts* 12(3) 2001, pp. 287–308.

Natov, Roni. "Harry Potter and the Extraordinariness of the Ordinary." *Lion and the Unicorn* 25(2) 2001, pp. 310–327.

Nel, Philip. "Is There a Text in this Advertising Campaign? Literature, Marketing, and Harry Potter." *Lion and the Unicorn* 29(2) 2005, pp. 236–267.

Nel, Philip. *J. K. Rowling's Harry Potter Novels: A Reader's Guide*. New York: Continuum, 2001.

Pennington, John. "From Elfland to Hogwarts, or, the Aesthetic Trouble with Harry Potter." *Lion and the Unicorn* 26(1) (January 2002), pp. 78–97.

Stephenson, Sarah Kate. "The Real Magic of Harry Potter." *The Looking Glass* 4(2) (August 2, 2000). http://www.the-looking-glass.net/rabbit/4.2/content.html. Last visited January 28, 2008.

Taylor, Charles. "A.S. Byatt and the Goblet of Vile." *Salon*. July 2003. http://dir.salon.com/story/books/feature/2003/07/08/byatt_rowling/index.html. Last visited January 28, 2008.

Wannamaker, Annette. "Men in Cloaks and High-Heeled Boots, Men Wielding Pink Umbrellas: Witchy Masculinities in the *Harry Potter* Novels." *Looking Glass* 10(1) (January 2, 2006). http://www.the-looking-glass.net/rabbit/v10i1/alice4.html. Last visited January 28, 2008.

Whited, Lana. "1492, 1942, 1992: The Theme of Race in the Harry Potter Series." *The Looking Glass* 10(1) (January 2, 2006). http://www.the-looking-glass.net/rabbit/v10i1/alice5.html. Last visited January 28, 2008.

Whited, Lana A., ed. *The Ivory Tower and Harry Potter: Perspectives on a Literary Phenomenon*. Columbia: Missouri University Press, 2002.

Willson-Metzger, Alicia. "But is He Really Smart? Gardner's Multiple Intelligences Theory in the world of Harry Potter." *Popular Culture Review* 14(2) 2003, pp. 55–61.

Web Sites

J. K. Rowling Official Site. http://www.jkrowling.com. Last visited January 28, 2008. Author's Web site.

MuggleNet. http://www.mugglenet.com/jkrinterview.shtml. Last visited January 28, 2008.

If You Like Joanne Kathleen Rowling (J.K. Rowling)

Rowling's best-selling Harry Potter books tell the story of an orphan magician and his magical boarding school. Starting with *Harry Potter and the Sorcerer's Stone*, the series extends for seven volumes, one each for his school years.

Then you might like

Lloyd Alexander

Based on Welsh mythology, Alexander's "Prydain" series focuses on Taran, an assistant pig keeper who is anxious to prove himself as a hero. The series starts with *The Book of Three*, and continues with *The Black Cauldron*, *The Castle of Llyr*, *Taran Wanderer*, and *The High King*.

Susan Cooper

Cooper's Dark Is Rising series catches four young English children up in a centuries-old battle between the forces of light and darkness. The series includes *Over Sea, Under Stone*, *The Dark Is Rising*, *Greenwitch*, *The Grey King*, and *Silver on the Tree*.

Diana Wynne Jones

Jones' books are full of magic and sly humor. She is probably best known for the so-called Chrestomanci books including *Charmed Life* and *The Lives of Christopher Chant*, but has written numerous other books, one of which, *Year of the Griffin* (sequel to *Dark Lord of Derkholm*) is especially recommended for Potter fans.

C.S. Lewis

The Lion and the Witch, and the Wardrobe takes place in Narnia, a land where it is always winter, yet never Christmas. Four English children stumble into it through a wardrobe and have numerous adventures. Lewis wrote six additional books in the Narnia series, chronicling its history, rise, and fall.

Edith Nesbit (E. Nesbit)

Victorian children's writer Nesbit published several fantasy books, including *Five Children and It*, *The Phoenix and the Carpet*, and *The Enchanted Castle*.

Philip Pullman

Although Pullman's fantasy books are marketed for children and young adult, they are often enjoyed by adults as well. Pullman's best known series is probably His Dark Materials trilogy, which is set in an alternate universe (*The Golden Compass*, *The Subtle Knife*, and *The Amber Spyglass*).

Fred Saberhagen (1930–)

Biographical Sketch

Fred Saberhagen served in the Air Force as an electrical technician. Afterward, he worked for a time as an assistant editor of the *Encyclopedia Britannica*, where he wrote and edited science and technology articles. He currently lives and works in Albuquerque, New Mexico.

In addition to fantasy, Saberhagen has written within the science fiction, horror, and gothic genres. As a fantasy writer, he is probably best known for his Book of Swords series. He has also edited anthologies.

> I don't set out to teach moral lessons or anything like that. I like to entertain people, I like to have stories where you wonder what's going to happen next, and you can't wait to find out. This to me is a real achievement. If you have people turning the page and they just want to see what happens next.—(Fred Saberhagen, "Simply Fred Saberhagen." http://www.berserkerfan.org/randinterview.htm#interview. Last visited January 28, 2008)

Major Works

Novels

The Empire of the East series: *The Broken Lands* (1968), *The Black Mountains* (1971), *Changeling Earth* (1973) also published as *Ardneh's World*

Book of Swords series: *The First Book of Swords* (1983), *The Second Book of Swords* (1983), *The Third Book of Swords* (1984)

Book of the Lost Swords series: *The First Book of Lost Swords: Woundhealer's Story* (1986), *The Second Book of Lost Swords: Sightblinder's Story* (1987), *The Third Book of Lost Swords: Stonecutter's Story* (1988), *The Fourth Book of Lost Swords: Farslayer's Story* (1989), *The Fifth Book of Lost Swords: Coinspinner's Story* (1989), *The Sixth Book of Lost Swords: Mindsword's Story* (1990), *The Seventh Book of Lost Swords: Wayfinder's Story* (1992), *The Last Book of Lost Swords: Shieldbreaker's Story* (1994)

Book of the Gods series: *The Face of Apollo* (1998), *Ariadne's Web* (2000), *The Arms of Hercules* (2000), *God of the Golden Fleece* (2001), *Gods of Fire and Thunder* (2002)

Dancing Bears (1995)

Merlin's Bones (1995)

Ardneh's Sword (2006)

Research Sources

Encyclopedias and Handbooks: EF, HDF, SJGF

Biographies and Interviews

James, Warren W. "Live 'on-disc' from LosCon 2003." *Hodel's Hour 25*. November 28, 2005. http://www.hour25online.com/hr25_2003-11-28_show.m3u. Last visited January 28, 2008.

Rand, Ken. "Simply Fred Saberhagen." *The Taj: Official Fan Site of Fred Saberhagen's Beserker © Universe*. http://www.berserkerfan.org/randinterview.htm#interview. Last visited January 28, 2008.

Web Sites

Saberhagen's Worlds of SF and Fantasy. http://www.berserker.com. Last visited January 28, 2008. Author's Web site.

Robert Anthony Salvatore (R.A. Salvatore) (1959–)

Biographical Sketch

Although he was a heavy reader as a child, Robert Anthony Salvatore lost interest in books as an adolescent. He rediscovered his love of fantasy and literature when his sister introduced him to Tolkien in college. That in turn led to him becoming an English major, and ultimately, an author. He started writing seriously in 1982 and held a variety of jobs prior to writing full time beginning in 1990. He lives in Massachusetts.

Many of Salvatore's novels are set in a world that is used in the Advanced Dungeons and Dragons role playing game, many of which feature Drizzt Do'Urden, a drow elf. Salvatore is very popular with young adult fantasy readers and has spoken at a number of American Libraries Association conferences. He has also written for computer games.

> I value my job not just for the art, but as my work. The fantasy genre, in particular, I believe, has a cyclical, often temporary, hold on its fan base. People find fantasy at different times in their lives. Some will stay forever and ever, but others will move on to other things in a few years. A writer who isn't on the shelves regularly will have a very hard time in building and maintaining an audience in this genre.—(R.A. Salvatore, *sfreader.com* interview. Available online at http://www.sfreader.com/interview022.asp. Last visited January 28, 2008)

Major Works

Novels

The Icewind Dale Trilogy: *The Crystal Shard* (1988), *Streams of Silver* (1989), *The Halfling's Gem* (1990)

The Dark Elf Trilogy: *Homeland* (1990), *Exile* (1990), *Sojourn* (1991)

The Cleric Quintet: *Canticle* (1991), *In Sylvan Shadows* (1992), *Night Masks* (1992), *The Fallen Fortress* (1993), *The Chaos Curse* (1994)

Legacy of the Drow series: *The Legacy* (1992), *Starless Night* (1993), *Siege of Darkness* (1994), *Passage to Dawn* (1996)

Crimson Shadow series: *The Sword of Bedwyr* (1995), *Luthien's Gamble* (1996), *The Dragon King* (1996)

Paths of Darkness series: *The Silent Blade* (1998), *The Spine of the World* (1999, with Philip Athans), *Servant of the Shard* (2000), *Sea of Swords* (2001), *Paths of Darkness* (2004)

The Sellswords series: *Servant of the Shard* (2000), *Promise of the Witchking* (2005), *Road of the Patriarch* (2006)

Spearwielder's Tale trilogy: *The Woods Out Back* (1993), *The Dragon's Dagger* (1994), *Dragonslayer's Return* (1995)

The Hunter's Blades Trilogy: *The Thousand Orcs* (2002), *The Lone Drow* (2003), *The Two Swords* (2004)

Research Sources

Encyclopedias and Handbooks: EF, HDF, SJGF

Biographies and Interviews

Blackston, Dan. "An Interview with R.A. Salvatore." *SFReader.com*. November 14, 2004. http://www.sfreader.com/interview022.asp. Last visited January 28, 2008.

"Lavender Eyes Interviews R.A. Salvatore." *Lavender Eyes*. October 13, 2006. http://lavendereyes.rivkashome.com/index.php?name=News&file=article&sid=283. Last visited January 28, 2008.

Noonan, David and Mike Mearls. "D&D Podcast December 2006, Part 2." *Dungeons & Dragons Roleplaying Game Official Home Page*. December 15, 2006. http://www.wizards.com/default.asp?x=dnd/pod/20061215a. Last visited January 28, 2008.

Web Sites

Lavender Eyes. http://lavendereyes.rivkashome.com/index.php. Last visited January 28, 2008. A site devoted to Salvatore's drow elf character Drizzt Do'urden.

N. Y. Times Bestselling Author R. A. Salvatore. http://www.rasalvatore.com. Last visited January 28, 2008. Author's Web site. Includes a biographical piece and podcast interviews with the author.

If you like Robert Anthony Salvatore (R.A. Salvatore)

Set in the world of Advanced Dungeons and Dragons, Salvatore's fantasies are epic in scope with numerous characters and quests. He is probably best known for his character Drizzt Do'Urden, a drow elf who has chosen to go against the ways of his people.

Then you might like

David and Leigh Eddings

The Eddings' Belgariad series tells the story of young Garion as he slowly realizes his long prophesied destiny. They include *Pawn of Prophecy*, *Queen of Sorcery*, *Magician's Gambit*, *Castle of Wizardry*, and *Enchanters' End Game*.

Kate Elliott

Elliott's epic fantasies are based on a densely thought out alternate world reminiscent of European myth. Her interest in religious and political conflict is evident in her Crown of Stars series (*King's Dragon*, *Prince of Dogs*, *The Burning Stone*, *Child of Flame*, *The Gathering Storm*, *In the Ruins*, and *The Crown of Stars*).

Tracy Hickman

Hickman's Dragonlance books, written with Margaret Weis, are also set in a fantasy role playing game universe. A good place to start is their Dragonlance Chronicles (*Dragons of Autumn Twilight*, *Dragons of Winter Night*, *Dragons of Spring Dawning*, *Dragons of Summer Flame*, *The Annotated Chronicles*).

George R.R. Martin

Martin's epic Song of Ice and Fire series encompasses a broad tapestry of characters and kingdoms. So far, it includes *A Game of Thrones*, *A Clash of Kings*, *A Storm of Swords*, *A Feast for Crows*, and *A Dance with Dragons*.

John Ronald Reuel Tolkien (J.R.R. Tolkien)

Tolkien's Middle Earth fantasies reflect his scholarly interests in languages and myth. Beginning with prequel *The Hobbit*, they continue with *The Fellowship of the Ring*, *The Two Towers*, and *The Return of the King*.

Margaret Weis

Weis' Dragonlance books, written with Tracy Hickman, are also set in a fantasy role playing game universe. A good place to start is their Dragonlance Chronicles (*Dragons of Autumn Twilight*, *Dragons of Winter Night*, *Dragons of Spring Dawning*, *Dragons of Summer Flame*, *The Annotated Chronicles*).

Elizabeth Ann Scarborough (1947–)

Biographical Sketch

Elizabeth Ann Scarbrough attended the University of Alaska at Fairbanks. She served as a military nurse during the Vietnam Conflict, an experience which informed her Nebula winning novel *The Healer's War*. She has lived in Alaska and currently lives in a cabin in the Pacific Northwest. In addition to writing, she designs beadwork.

Scarbrough has written a number of fantasy novels, many of which have a lot of humor and reflect her love of folk music. She has also edited several anthologies.

> I tend to do things a little backwards. Other people were becoming artists and hippies when I was busy nursing in the army, so now that other people have settled down to work real jobs, or (ahem, considering my age) retiring from them, I'm going through my artistic phase. Long may it last!—(Elizabeth Ann Scarborough, *Beadtime Stories*. http://www.eascarborough.com/books/mybio.htm. Last visited January 28, 2008)

Major Works

Novels

Songs from the Seashell Archives: *Song of Sorcery* (1982), *The Unicorn Creed* (1983), *Bronwyn's Bane* (1984), *The Christening Quest* (1986)

The Harem of Aman Akbar (1985)

The Drastic Dragon of Draco, Texas (1986)
The Goldcamp Vampire (1987)
The Healer's War (1989)
Nothing Sacred (1990)
Last Refuge (1991)
The Songkiller Saga: *Phantom Banjo* (1991), *Picking the Ballad's Bones* (1992), *Strum Again?* (1993)
Godmother series: *The Godmother* (1994), *The Godmother's Apprentice* (1995), *The Godmother's Web* (1998)
Carol for Another Christmas (1996)
The Lady in the Loch (1998)

Short Story Collections

Scarborough Fair and Other Stories (2003)

Other Important Writings

Beadtime Stories (1988), book of beading patterns based on fairy tales.

Research Sources

Encyclopedias and Handbooks: EF, HDF, SJGF

Biographies and Interviews

Holmen, Rachel E. "With Elizabeth Ann Scarborough." *Marion Zimmer Bradley's Fantasy Magazine* 21 (Fall 1993), pp. 42–47.

Web Sites

Beadtime Stories. http://www.eascarborough.com/index.htm. Last visited January 28, 2008.
Author's home page.

Susan Shwartz (1949–)

Biographical Sketch

Susan Shwartz completed a PhD in medieval literature at Harvard University prior to beginning her writing career. Her PhD work has informed her writing in a number of ways, perhaps most obviously in terms of the research that goes into her historical fantasy novels. Shwartz' writing is also influenced by her day job as a stock broker. Because of time contraints, she is forced to be discplined in her writing.

Shwartz is known for her strong female characters and historical settings. She has also edited anthologies.

> I personally feel very strongly about the fact that science fiction and fantasy get relatively short shrift from the academic world. I don't feel this is justified. I think that, at the very least, as part of literary history they deserve more emphasis.—(Susan Shwartz, Thompson interview. Available online at http://www.lib.rochester.edu/camelot/intrvws/shwartz.htm. Last visited January 28, 2008)

Major Works

Novels

Heirs to Byzantium series: *Byzantium's Crown* (1987), *The Woman of Flowers* (1987), *Queensblade* (1988)
Shards of Empire series: *Shards of Empire* (1996), *Cross and Crescent* (1997)
Silk Roads and Shadows (1988)
Imperial Lady: A Fantasy of Han China (1989, with Andre Norton)
The Grail of Hearts (1992)
Empire of the Eagle (1993) with Andre Norton

Short Story Collections

Suppose They Gave a Peace, and Other Stories (2002)

Research Sources

Encyclopedias and Handbooks: EF, HDF, SJGF

Biographies and Interviews

McBain, Lesley. "Interview: Susan Shwartz." *Strange Horizons* (November 8, 2004). http://www.strangehorizons.com/2004/20041108/0shwartz.shtml. Last visited January 28, 2008.

Thompson, Robert. "Interview with Susan Shwartz." August 27, 1988. *Interviews with Authors of Modern Arthurian Literature* (part of the University of Rochester's *Camelot Project*). http://www.lib.rochester.edu/camelot/intrvws/shwartz.htm. Last visited January 28, 2008.

Web Sites

Susan Shwartz. http://www.sff.net/people/SusanShwartz. Last visited January 28, 2008. Author's personal Web site.

Robert Silverberg (1935–)

Biographical Sketch

Robert Silverberg started writing and publishing while still a student at Columbia University. He literally has never held a traditional "desk" job, but has been a writer and editor for most of his adult life.

Despite a couple of "retirements" from writing fiction in the early 1950s and late 1970s, Silverberg is extremely prolific. His early work was within the "pulp" tradition of science fiction; after his first retirement, he emerged as a New Wave writer. His second retirement heralded a shift to works more in the vein of fantasy such as the Lord Valentine's Castle series. However, even his fantasy has a certain science element to it. In addition to writing fiction, he has written several nonfiction books and articles as well as children's books. He has also edited numerous anthologies and has won numerous Hebula and Hugo awards. He won the Damon Knight Grand Master Award for 2004.

> Fantasy is the dominant commercial artform of our genre now, though you couldn't *give* fantasy books away in the '30s, '40's, '50s, and early '60s. The artistic freedom I see in fantasy (and of course I'm not talking now about writing formula Tolkienesque trilogies) lies in the ability to get away from the *Star Wars/Star Trek/Blade Runner* straightjacket and use my imagination, use my knowledge of history, of archaeology, of the past.—(Robert Silverberg, *Locus* interview, 1996)

Major Works

Novels

Lord Valentine series: *Lord Valentine's Castle* (1980), *Majipoor Chronicles* (1982), *Valentine Pontifex* (1983)
Lord Prestimion series: *Sorcerers of Majipoor* (1996), *Lord Prestimion* (1999), *The King of Dreams* (2001)
To the Land of the Living (1989)
The Mountains of Majipoor (1995)

Research Sources

Encyclopedias and Handbooks: EF, HDF

Biographies and Interviews

Horwich, David. "Interview: Robert Silverberg." *Strange Horizons* (December 11, 2000). http://www.strangehorizons.com/2000/20001211/silverberg.shtml. Last visited January 30, 2008.

Huddleston, Kathie. "Interview: Robert Silverberg Has Had an Amazing, Astounding, and Thrilling SF journey." *Science Fiction Weekly* 276. http://www.scifi.com/sfw/issue276/interview.html. Last visited January 29, 2008.

"Robert Silverberg: Farewell to the Future." *Locus* 37(5) (November 1996), pp. 6–7, 76–77.
"Robert Silverberg: One Word at a Time." *Locus* (March 2004), pp. 7, 64–67.
Shindler, Dorman T. "Interview: Newly Minted Grand Master Robert Silverberg Reflects on a Lifetime Spent in Science Fiction." *Science Fiction Weekly* 375. http://www.scifi.com/sfw/issue375/interview.html. Last visited January 29, 2008.

Criticism and Readers' Guides

Clareson, Thomas D. "Whose Castle? Speculations as to the Parameters of Science Fiction." *Essays in Arts and Sciences* 9 (1980), pp. 139–143.
Flodstrom, John H. "Personal Identity in Majipoor Trilogy, To Live Again, and Downward to Earth." In Charles Elkins, Martin Harry Greenberg, eds., *Robert Silverberg's Many Trapdoors: Critical Essays on His Science Fiction. Contributions to the Study of Science Fiction and Fantasy 53*. Westport, CT: Greenwood, 1992, pp. 73–94.

Web Sites

Davis, Jon. *The Quasi-Official Robert Silverberg Web Site*. http://www.majipoor.com. Last visited January 29, 2008. Although independent of Silverberg, Silverberg regards this as the closest to an "official" site and has given assistance to Davis. Includes bibliographies, a biographical piece, a section on the Majipoor books, and links to other sites.
The Worlds of Robert Silverberg. http://groups.yahoo.com/group/theworldsofrobert silverberg. Last visited January 30, 2008. Yahoo Groups discussion board that Silverberg has been known to post on.

Jeff Smith (1958–)

Biographical Sketch

Jeff Smith has long loved comics and cartoons and learned to read largely because of comics such as *Peanuts* and *Pogo*. He started drawing the characters that would eventually be in his *Bone* series at the age of five. *Bone*, Smith's epic work, is the story of the three cartoonesque Bone brothers who stumble into a valley full of magic, danger, and dragons. Smith finished *Bone* in 1994, but various collected editions are still available. One of the first comics self-publishers, Smith founded Cartoon Books in 1991.

> [T]hat's what storytelling is—it's tapping into wherever dreams come from. You tap into that source, and it just takes off. In other words, there's software inside your hardware—or whatever that metaphor should be—*[laughs]* that's inside

you, and you can tap into that.—(Jeff Smith, *Ain't It Cool News* interview. Available online at http://www.aintitcool.com/?q=node/15612. Last visited January 29, 2008)

Major Works

Graphic Novels

Bone: Original Series Issues #1–50

Bone Collected Volumes: *Out from Boneville* (1996), *The Great Cow Race* (1996), *Eyes of the Storm* (1996), *The Dragonslayer* (1997), *Master of the Eastern Border* (1998), *Old Man's Cave* (1999), *Ghost Circles* (2001), *Treasure Hunters* (2002), *Crown of Horns* (2004)

Thorn: Tales from the Lantern (1983)

Stupid, Stupid Rat Tails (2000, written by Tom Sniegoski, illustrated by Jeff Smith)

Rose (2002), illustrated by Charles Vess

Other Important Writings

Bone Reader (1996)

Research Sources

Biographies and Interviews

DuPont, Alexandra. "Jeff Smith: The Ain't It Cool Interview." *Ain't It Cool News*. July 4, 2003. http://www.aintitcool.com/display.cgi?id=15592. Last visited January 29, 2008.

Kerr, Euan. "Telling Fone Bone's Epic Story." *Minnesota Public Radio*. March 16, 2005. http://news.minnesota.publicradio.org/features/2005/03/16_kerre_bone. Last visited January 29, 2008.

Oeming, Michael Avon. "OEMED!—Jeff Smith." *PopCultureShock.com*. February 10, 2006. http://popcultureshock.com/features.php?id=1291. Last visited January 29, 2008.

Robinson, Tasha. "Interview: Jeff Smith." *The Onion*. May 31, 2000. http://www.avclub.com/content/node/22860. Last visited January 29, 2008.

Russell, Mike and Jeff Smith. "The Jeff Smith Interview." *CulturePulp 50*. April 21, 2006. http://homepage.mac.com/merussell/iblog/B835531044/C1162162177/E20060421152419/index.html. Last visited January 29, 2008.

"Spotlight on Jeff Smith." *DC Podcast* (March 9, 2007). http://www.dccomics.com/media/podcasts/DCComics_2007–03-09_Spotlight_On_Jeff_Smith_New_York_Comic_Con_2007.mp3. Last visited January 29, 2008.

Spurgeon, Tom. "A Short Interview with Jeff Smith." *The Comics Reporter*. December 31, 1999. Available online at http://www.comicsreporter.com/index.php/resources/interviews/2257.Last visited January 29, 2008.

Criticism and Readers' Guides

Holman, Curt. "Heavenly Creatures." *Salon.com.* June 14, 2004. http://dir.salon.com/story/books/feature/2004/06/14/bone_cerebus/index2.html?pn=1. Last visited January 29, 2008.

Web Sites

Boneville http://www.boneville.com. Last visited January 29, 2008. Author's Web site. Includes a blog, biographical information, a primary bibliography, and articles by Smith.

Midori Snyder (1954–)

Biographical Sketch

Midori Snyder studied African language and literature at the University of Wisconsin, eventually receiving an MA in English Literature and Literary Theory. She teaches secondary English, and lives in Milwaukee, Wisconsin, with her husband and two children.

Snyder has published several fantasy novels as well as short stories and children's fiction. Her writing often combines mythic and folkloric elements; she has also published essays on myth and folklore. She is an associate editor at the *Journal of Mythic Arts* and part of the so-called Interstitial Arts movement.

> The interesting thing about writing is that it has an almost oxymoronic life—when we write we are locked in the "present" moment of the book, yet the whole thing is a process that takes place over time. Our current experiences keep threading in emotional details to the work and the novel keeps ordering them out of their chaos into the form of the work.—(Midori Snyder, "Into the Labyrinth: A Writer's Journey. Available online at http://www.endicott-studio.com/rdrm/formslt4.html. Last visited January 29, 2008)

Major Works

Novels

The Oran Trilogy: *New Moon* (1989), *Sadar's Keep* (1990), *Beldan's Fire* (1993), *Soulstring* (1987)
The Flight of Michael McBride (1994)
The Innamorati (1998)

Children's/Young Adult Fiction

Hatchling (1995) set in Jim Guerney's *Dinotopia* world
Hannah's Garden (2002)

Other Important Writings

"Into the Labyrinth: A Writer's Journey." 2000. http://www.endicott-studio.com/rdrm/formslt1.html. Last visited January 29, 2008.

Research Sources

Encyclopedias and Handbooks: EF, HDF, SJGF

Biographies and Interviews

"Midori Snyder—A Brief Biography." http://www.endicott-studio.com/bios/biomidori.html. Last visited January 29, 2008.

Nancy Springer (1948–)

Biographical Sketch

Nancy Springer spent much of her adolescence near Gettysburg, PA, where her parents had bought a hotel. After graduating from Gettysburg College, she became a minister's wife, and raised several children. She began writing partly in order to gain her own selfhood.

Springer has written a number of young adult books, young adult fantasy, general fantasy, and suspense books. She was one of two winners of the 1994 James Tiptree, Jr. Award for *Larque on a Wing* (the other winner was Ursula K. Le Guin). Springer has taught creative writing at a number of colleges and universities, and has visited numerous K-12 schools.

> 'Conform, go crazy, or become an artist.' I have a rubber stamp declaring those words, and they pretty much delineate my life.—(Nancy Springer, "Nancy Springer." Available online at http://www.stlf.org/ntc/11/nsbio.htm. Last visited January 29, 2008)

Major Works

Novels

Book of the Isle: *The White Hart* (1979), *The Silver Sun* (1980), *The Sable Moon* (1981), *The Black Beast* (1982), *The Golden Swan* (1983)
Wings of Flame (1985)
Chains of Gold (1986)
Sea King series: *Madbond* (1987), *Mindbond* (1987), *Godbond* (1988)
The Hex Witch of Sheldon (1988)
Tales of Camelot: *I am Mordred* (1988), *I Am Morgan le Fay* (2001)
Apocalypse (1989)
Larque on the Wing (1994)

Metal Angel (1994)
Fair Peril (1996)
Plumage (1999)

Children's/Young Adult Fiction

Red Wizard (1990)
The Friendship Song (1992)

Short Story Collections

Chance and Other Gestures of the Hand of Fate (1987)

Other Important Writings

Stardark Songs (1993)

Research Sources

Encyclopedias and Handbooks: EF, HDF, SJGF

Biographies and Interviews

Knapp, Tom. "Nancy Springer: Writing What she Wants to Read." *Rambles: A Cultural Arts Magazine* (1989) http://www.rambles.net/nancy_springer.html. Last visited January 29, 2008.

"Nancy Springer: Looking Under Rocks." *Locus* 34(6) (June 1995), pp. 4, 72–73.

Web Sites

Nancy Springer—Writer/Organic Word Farmer. April 2006. http://www.nancyspringer.net. Last visited January 29, 2008. Author's Web site.

"Nancy Springer Info Sheet." http://www.stlf.org/ntc/11/nsinfo.htm. Last visited January 29, 2008. Includes a short autobiographical profile.

Caroline Stevermer (1955–)

Biographical Sketch

Caroline Stevermer grew up on a dairy farm in Minnesota and graduated with a BA in art history from Bryn Mawr College. She started writing stories when she was eight years old.

Stevermer has written a number of fantasies. Many of her fantasies take place in a historical setting similar to the original, only with magic. One example are the Cecelia and Kate books that she co-wrote with Patricia Wrede, and are set in the

Regency period. The first, *Sorcery and Cecelia*, was the outcome of a letters game with Wrede (in a letters game, players write letters to each other's characters).

> I've always been interested in things that would permit me to escape from wherever I was, mentally, so the urge to write fantasy is probably a reaction. It's probably related to the reason why I don't write about what I know. As we're always told we should.—(Caroline Stevermer, "Between Planets," 2004. Availble online at http://citypages.com/databank/25/1225/article12152.asp. Last visited January 29, 2008)

Major Works

Novels

The Serpent's Egg (1988)
Scholarly Magics series: *A College of Magics* (1994), *A Scholar of Magics* (2004)
When the King Comes Home (2000)

Children's/Young Adult Fiction

Cecelia and Kate series (with Patricia Wrede): *Sorcery and Cecelia: or The Enchanted Chocolate Pot* (1988).
The Grand Tour: or The Purloined Coronation Regalia: Being a Revelation of Matters of High Confidentiality and Greatest Importance, Including Extracts from the Intimate Diary of a Noblewoman and the Sworn Testimony of a Lady of Quality (2004).
The Mislaid Magician: or Ten Years After (2006)

Research Sources

Encyclopedias and Handbooks: EF, HDF, SJGF

Biographies and Interviews

"Caroline Stevermer." *TV Bookshelf*. September 4, 2004. http://tvbookshelf.ws/Caroline.mov. Last visited January 29, 2008.
Sutton, Teri. "Between Planets." *City Pages*. May 26, 2004. http://citypages.com/databank/25/1225/article12152.asp. Last visited January 29, 2008.

Web Sites

"Caroline Stevermer." http://members.authorsguild.net/carolinestev. Last visited January 29, 2008. Brief profile and primary bibliography.
Lenander, David. *The Enchanted Chocolate Pot: A Page for Caroline Stevermer/C.J. Stevermer and for Patricia C. Wrede*. http://www.tc.umn.edu/~d-lena/Stevermer%20page.html. Last visited January 29, 2008.

Mary Stewart (1916–)

Biographical Sketch

Mary Stewart was born in Durnham, England. The daughter of a Church of England clergyman, she attended the University of Durnham, graduating with a BA and an MA. She served in the Royal Observer Corps during World War II and married Sir Frederick Henry Stewart in 1945. Prior to becoming a writer full time, she taught as a lecturer at the University of Durnham.

Stewart began writing as a child. Prior to the 1970s, she published several romance/suspense novels. However, she had long wanted to write a historical novel, and having decided on Roman Britain, soon found herself attracted to the Arthurian material, especially the character of Merlin. Her publisher wasn't anxious to publish *The Crystal Cave* because of the change in genre, but once published, it turned out to be a best seller. Stewart followed it up with two more Arthurian novels, as well as other writings with a historical and/or mystic bent.

> I've never written for a market. In fact, if I'd ever thought about markets, I would never have written *The Crystal Cave* because it was such a big change. It was the historical book I'd always wanted to write.—(Mary Stewart, Thompson interview. Available online at http://www.lib.rochester.edu/camelot/intrvws/stewart.htm. Last visited January 29, 2008)

Major Works

Novels

Arthurian Saga: *The Crystal Cave* (1970), *The Hollow Hills* (1973), *The Last Enchantment* (1979), *The Wicked Day* (1983)

A Walk in Wolf Wood (1980)

Thornyhold (1988)

The Prince and the Pilgrim (1995)

Children's/Young Adult Fiction

The Little Broomstick (1971)

Ludo and the Star Horse (1974)

Short Story Collections

Selected Works (1978)

Other Important Writings

Frost on the Window: Poems (1990)

Research Sources

Encyclopedias and Handbooks: EF, HDF, SJGF

Biographies and Interviews

Thompson, Raymond H. "Interview with Mary Stewart." April 14, 1989. *Interviews with Authors of Modern Arthurian Literature* (part of the University of Rochester's *Camelot Project*). http://www.lib.rochester.edu/camelot/intrvws/stewart.htm. Last visited January 29, 2008.

Criticism and Readers' Guides

Friedman, Lenemaja. *Mary Stewart*. Boston, MA: Twayne, 1990.

Fries, Maureen. "The Rationalization of the Arthurian 'Matter' in T. H. White and Mary Stewart." *Philological Quarterly* 56 (1977), pp. 258–265.

Jurich, Marilyn. "Mithraic Aspects of Merlin in Mary Stewart's *The Crystal Cave*." In Donald E. Morse, ed., *The Celebration of the Fantastic*. Westport, CT: Greenwood, 1992, pp. 91–101.

Nelson, Marie. "King Arthur and the Massacre of the May Day Babies: A Story Told by Sir Thomas Malory, Later Retold by John Steinbeck, Mary Stewart, and T. H. White." *Journal of the Fantastic in the Arts* 11(3) (2000), pp. 266–281.

Watson, Jeanie.: "Mary Stewart's Merlin: Word of Power." In Jeanie Watson and Maureen Fries, eds., *The Figure of Merlin in the Nineteenth and Twentieth Centuries*. Lewiston, NY: Edwin Mellen Press, 1989, pp. 155–174.

If you like Mary Stewart

Set in Roman Britain, Stewart's Arthurian novels have proven immensely popular and influential. Although much of her material is mythic, she bases it in solid historical research.

Then you might like

Marion Zimmer Bradley

Like Stewart, Bradley tells the story of Arthur, but from a feminist perspective in her *The Mists of Avalon* (the Avalon series was later continued by Diana Paxson).

Susan Cooper

The much-loved "Dark Is Rising" series catches four young English children up in a centuries-old battle between the forces of light and darkness, in an England that remembers King Arthur and Wayland Smith, Stonehenge and the Holy Grail.

Stephen Lawhead

Like Stewart, Lawhead imbeds his Arthurian fantasies in careful historical research. His Pendragon Cycle includes *Taliesin*, *Merlin*, *Arthur*, *Pendragon*, and *Grail*.

Susan Shwartz

Like Stewart, Shwartz blends fantasy with historical fiction. One example is her Heirs to Byzantium series (*Byzantium's Crown*, *The Woman of Flowers*, and *Queensblade*).

Nancy Springer

Springer's Tales of Camelot fantasies retell the familiar Arthurian saga from alternate points of view (*I am Mordred* and I *am Morgan le Fay*).

T.H. White

White's much loved Once and Future King series encompasses the story of Arthur and his round table (*The Sword in the Stone*, *The Queen of Air and Darkness*, *The Ill-Made Knight*, and *The Candle in the Wind*).

Judith Tarr (1955–)

Biographical Sketch

Judith Tarr did a BA in Latin and English at Mount Holyoke, and then an MA in Classics at Cambridge, and a PhD in Medieval Studies from Yale. She first started writing historical fantasy during graduate school, often picking overlapping topics for her novels and academic papers. She currently lives in Arizona, where she breeds and raises Lipizzan horses at Dancing Horse Farm.

Tarr has written a number of historical books, historical fantasies, and "high" fantasies as well as many that could be classified and marketed under more than one "genre." Many of her books are set in Medieval Europe and the Middle East. She has also published under the pen names of "Caitlin Brennan" and "Kathleen Bryan."

> People seem to think that I'm a 'character' writer; they always comment on the characters. That's nice. What I concentrate on depends on the book. Plot, characters, research are all such a continuum that I can't really tell you, in a general sense, what dominates.—(Judith Tarr, *Science Fiction Chonicle* interview, 1993)

Major Works

Novels

Hound and the Falcon series: *Isle of Glass* (1985), *The Golden Horn* (1985), *The Hounds of God* (1986)

Alamut series: *Alamut* (1989), *The Dagger and the Cross* (1991)

Avaryan Chronicles: *The Hall of the Mountain King* (1986), *The Lady of Han-Gilen* (1987), *A Fall of Princes* (1988), *Arrows of the Sun* (1993), *Spear of Heaven* (1994), *Tides of Darkness* (2002)

Devil's Bargain series: *Devil's Bargain* (2002), *House of War* (2003)

William the Conqueror series: *Rite of Conquest* (2004), *King's Blood* (2005)

White Magic series (writing as "Caitlin Brennan"): *The Mountain's Call* (2004), *Song of Unmaking* (2005), *Shattered Dance* (2006)

The War of the Rose series (writing as "Kathleen Bryan"): *The Serpent and the Rose* (2007)

Ars Magica (1989)

A Wind in Cairo (1989)

Household Gods (1999) with Harry Turtledove

Kingdom of the Grail (2000)

Pride of Kings (2001)

Children's/Young Adult Fiction

His Majesty's Elephant (1993)

Other Important Writings

"Beyond the Looking Glass: How to Write Meaningful Description." *Reflection's Edge*. http://www.reflectionsedge.com/archives/july2005/blg_jt.html. Last visited January 29, 2008.

Research Sources

Encyclopedias and Handbooks: EF, HDF, SJGF

Biographies and Interviews

King, T. Jackson. "SFC Interview: Judith Tarr." *Science Fiction Chronicle* 14(7) (April 1993), pp. 5, 27–29.

Web Sites

Caitlin Brennan. http://www.sff.net/people/cait-brennan. Last visited January 29, 2008. Author's web site (as "Caitlin Brennan").

Judith Tarr's Brand-New Shiny Home Page. http://www.sff.net/people/judith-tarr. Last visited January 29, 2008. Author's Web site.

Life Among the Lipizzans. http://dancinghorse.livejournal.com. Last visited January 29, 2008. Author's blog.

Sheri S. Tepper (1929–)

Biographical Sketch

Sheri S. Tepper was born near Littleton, Colorado. She spent several years working for Rocky Mountain Planned Parenthood as well as other organizations such as CARE, an international relief agency. She currently runs a guest ranch in Santa Fe, New Mexico, with her husband, Gene Tepper.

Tepper had written a few poems and children's stories in the mid-sixties, but stopped writing seriously until the early 1980s. After retiring in 1986, she began writing full time. Most of her fantasy comes from the earlier part of her career; she currently writes more science fiction. She has also written mystery and horror novels under various pseudonyms (A.J. Orde, E.E. Horlak, and B.J. Oliphant). Tepper is known for her strong female characters and feminist and ecological themes.

> I can't use an outline. I tried, and it's utterly impossible. I let the character or the vision or the picture or the drama develop itself. Then the task, the real task, is to knit this whole thing together.—Sheri S. Tepper, Science Fiction Chronicle Interview, 1998)

Major Works

Novels

Land of the True Game: Peter: *King's Blood Four* (1983), *Necromancer Nine* (1983), *Wizard's Eleven* (1984)

The Revenants (1984)

Land of the True Game: Mavin: *The Song of Mavin Manyshaped* (1985), *The Flight of Mavin Manyshaped* (1985), *The Search of Mavin Manyshaped* (1985)

Land of the True Game: Jinian: *Jinian Footseer* (1985), *Dervish Daughter* (1986), *Jinian Star-Eye* (1986)

Marianne trilogy: *Marianne, the Magus, and the Manticore* (1985), *Marianne, the Madame, and the Momentary Gods* (1988), *Marianne, the Matchbox, and the Malachite Mouse* (1989)

Beauty (1991)

Singer from the Sea (1999)

Other Important Writings

Tepper, Sheri. "The Power of Art." *sffworld.com*. 2002. http://www.sffworld.com/authors/t/tepper_sheri/articles/powerofart.html. Last visited January 29, 2008.

Research Sources

Encyclopedias and Handbooks: EF, HDF, SJGF

Biographies and Interviews

Morehouse, Lyda. "SFC Interview: Sheri S. Tepper." *Science Fiction Chronicle*. 20(3) (December 1988/January 1999), pp. 8, 38–39.

"Science Fiction Writer Sheri S. Tepper" *Fresh Air*. (National Public Radio). http://www.npr.org/templates/story/story.php?storyId=1142218. Last visited January 29, 2008.

"Sheri S. Tepper: Fiction, Farming, and Other Rare Breeds." *Locus* (331) (July 1994), pp. 4, 80–81.

"Sheri S. Tepper: Speaking to the Universe." *Locus* 4(3) (September 1998), pp. 4–5, 84, 86.

Criticism and Readers' Guides

Attebery, Brian. "Gender, Fantasy, and the Authority of Tradition." *Journal of the Fantastic in the Arts* 7(1) (1996), pp. 51–60.

Collins, Robert A. "Tepper's 'Chinanga': A Parable of Deconstruction." *Journal of the Fantastic in the Arts* 8(4) (1997), pp. 464–471.

Reid, Robin A. "Momutes: Momentary Utopias in Tepper's Trilogies." In Martha Bartter, ed., *The Utopian Fantastic: Selected Essays from the Twentieth International Conference on the Fantastic in the Arts*. Westport, CT: Praeger, 2004, pp. 101–108.

Wagner-Lawlor, Jennifer A. "The Play of Irony: Theatricality and Utopian Transformation in Contemporary Women's Speculative Fiction." *Utopian Studies* 13(1) (2002), pp. 114–134.

Web Sites

Sheri S. Tepper. http://www.sheri-s-tepper.com. Last visited January 29, 2008. Author's Web site.

John Ronald Reuel Tolkien (J.R.R. Tolkien) (1892–1973)

Biographical Sketch

J.R.R. Tolkien was born in South Africa and spent his early childhood there. After his father died, his mother moved the family back to England. She also converted to Catholicism, a faith and identity that was central to Tolkien's life and writing. Tolkien developed an early love for learning and inventing languages, a passion that continued throughout his life and career.

Tolkien attended university at Oxford and then served in the British army during World War I. He was wounded and spent much of his convelesence writing stories that would eventually become the mythos of his *Lord of the Rings* novels. He continued to rework these stories throughout his life. Tolkien also created a language for his mythos. Some years later, when he was teaching at the University of Leeds, he found himself writing *The Hobbit*. Written largely with the intent of being read aloud, *The Hobbit's* tone is lighter than the subsequent *Lord of the Rings*, which Tolkien finished during World War II.

Tolkien's works, especially *Lord of the Rings* have had a tremendous influence on modern fantasy books, games, and movies. There has also been a recent explosion of scholarship on Tolkien and his works.

> The realm of fairy-story is wide and deep and high and filled with many things: all manner of beasts and birds are found there; shoreless seas and stars uncounted, beauty that is an enchantment, and an everpresent peril; both joy and sorrow as sharp as swords.—(J.R.R. Tolkien, "On Fairy-Stories")

Major Works

Novels and Related Writings

The Hobbit: or, There and Back Again (1937)
The Lord of the Rings trilogy: *The Fellowship of the Ring* (1954), *The Two Towers* (1954), *The Return of the King* (1955)
The Simarillion (1977), edited by Christopher Tolkien
Unfinished Tales of Numenor and of Middle-Earth (1980), edited by Christopher Tolkien
The Book of Lost Tales (1983), edited by Christopher Tolkien
The Book of Lost Tales. Part II (1984), edited by Christopher Tolkien
History of Middle-Earth: The Lays of Beleriand (1985), edited by Christopher Tolkien
The Lost Road and Other Writings: Language and Legend Before 'The Lord of the Rings,' (1987), edited by Christopher Tolkien
The History of The Lord of the Rings series (edited by Christopher Tolkien): *The Return of the Shadow* (1988), *The Treason of Isengard* (1989), *The War of the Ring* (1990), *Sauron Defeated* (1992)
Morgoth's Ring: The Legends of Aman (1993), edited by Christopher Tolkien
The War of the Jewels: The Legends of Beleriand (1994), edited by Christopher Tolkien
The Children of Hurin (2007), edited by Christopher Tolkien

Other Important Writings

A Middle English Vocabulary (1922)
Beowulf: The Monsters and the Critics (1937)
Chaucer As a Philologist (1943)
Tree and Leaf (1945)

The Adventures of Tom Bombadil (1962)
The Road Goes Ever On: A Song Cycle (1967), lyrics by J.R.R. Tolkien, music by Donald Swann
Farmer Giles of Ham / The Adventures of Tom Bombadil (1975)
The Father Christmas Letters (1976)
The Letters of J.R.R. Tolkien (1981)
The Monsters and the Critics: The Essays of J.R.R. Tolkien (1983)
Poems by J.R.R. Tolkien (1993)
Roverandom (1998)

Research Sources

Encyclopedias and Handbooks: EF, HDF, SJGF

Biographies and Interviews

Bramlett, Perry C. and Joe R. Christopher. *I am in Fact a Hobbit: An Introduction to the Life and Works of J. R. R. Tolkien*. Macon, GA: Mercer UP, 2003.
Carpenter, Humphrey. *The Inklings: C.S. Lewis, J.R.R. Tolkien, Charles Williams and Their Friends*. Boston, MA: Houghton Mifflin, 1979.
Carpenter, Humphrey. *J.R.R. Tolkien, a Biography*. Boston, MA: Houghton Mifflin, 1977.
Tolkien, John, and Priscilla Tolkien. *The Tolkien Family Album*. New York: HarperCollins, 1992.

Criticism and Readers' Guides

Battis, Jes. "Gazing upon Sauron: Hobbits, Elves, and the Queering of the Postcolonial Optic." *Modern Fiction Studies* 50(4) (2004), pp. 908–926.
Beahm, George. *The Essential J. R. R. Tolkien Sourcebook: A Fan's Guide to Middle-Earth and Beyond*. Franklin Lakes, NJ: New Page, 2004.
Carter, Lin. *Tolkien: A Look Behind the Lord of the Rings*. New York: Ballantine Books, 1969.
Chance, Jane., ed. *Tolkien and the Invention of Myth: a Reader*. Lexington: Kentucky UP, 2004.
Clark, George and Daniel Timmons, eds. *J. R. R. Tolkien and His Literary Resources. Contributions to the Study of Science Fiction and Fantasy, 89*. Westport, CT: Greenwood Press, 2000.
Croft, Janet Brennan. *War and the Works of J. R. R. Tolkien. Contributions to the study of Science Fiction and Fantasy, 106*. Westport, CT: Greenwood, 2004.
Drout, Michael D.C. and Hilary Wynne. "Tom Shippey's *J. R. R. Tolkien: Author of the Century* and a Look Back at Tolkien Criticism Since 1982." *Envoi* 9(2) (2000), pp. 101–167. Available online at http://members.aol.com/JamesIMcNelis/9_2/Drout_9_2.pdf. Last visited January 29, 2008.
Flieger, Verlyn. *Splintered Light: Logos and Language in Tolkien's World*. Grand Rapids, MI: Eerdmans, 1983.

Flieger, Verlyn. *A Question of Time: J. R. R. Tolkien's Road to Faërie*. Kent, OH: Kent State UP, 1997.

Fonstad, Karen Wynn. *The Atlas of Middle-Earth*. Boston, MA: Houghton Mifflin, 1981.

Garth, John. *Tolkien and the Great War: the Threshold of Middle-Earth*. Boston, MA: Houghton Mifflin, 2003.

George, Michael W. "J.R.R. Tolkien." In Darren Harris-Bain, ed., *British Fantasy and Science-Fiction Writers, 1918–1960 (Dictionary of Literary Biography 255)*. Detroit, MI: Gale, 2002, pp. 237–250.

Green, William H. "King Thorin's Mines: *The Hobbit* as Victorian Adventure Novel." *Extrapolation* 42(1) (2001), pp. 53–64.

Hammond, Wayne G, and Christina Scull. *J. R. R. Tolkien: Artist and Illustrator*. Boston, MA: Houghton Mifflin, 1995.

Hiley, Margaret. "Stolen Language, Cosmic Models: Myth and Mythology in Tolkien." *Modern Fiction Studies* 50(4) (2004), pp. 838–860.

Johnson, Judith A., *J. R. R. Tolkien: Six Decades of Criticism*. Westport, CT: Greenwood Press, 1986.

Kim, Sue. "Beyond Black and White: Race and Postmodernism in *The Lord of the Rings* Films." *Modern Fiction Studies* 50(4) (2004), pp. 875–907.

Kocher, Paul H. *Master of Middle-earth: The Fiction of J.R.R. Tolkien*. Boston, MA: Houghton Mifflin, 1972.

Nelson, Charles W. "From Gollum to Gandalf: The Guide Figures in J. R. R. Tolkien's *Lord of the Rings*." *Journal of the Fantastic in the Arts* 13(1) (2002), pp. 47–61.

Northrup, Clyde B. "The Qualities of a Tolkienian Fairy-Story." *Modern Fiction Studies* 50(4) (2004), pp. 814–837.

Raiche, Donald. "Making the Darkness Conscious: J. R. R. Tolkien's *The Lord of the Rings*."*Parabola* 29(3) (2005), pp. 95–101.

Rearick, Anderson, III. "Why Is the Only Good Orc a Dead Orc? The Dark Face of Racism Examined in Tolkien's World." *Modern Fiction Studies* 50(4) (2004), pp. 861–874.

Ripp, Joseph. "Middle America Meets Middle-Earth: American Discussion and Readership of J. R. R. Tolkien's *The Lord of the Rings*, 11 1965–1969." *Book History* 8 (2005), pp. 245–286.

Shippey, T.A. *J. R. R. Tolkien: Author of the Century*. Boston, MA: Houghton Mifflin, 2001.

Shippey, T.A. *The Road to Middle-Earth*. London: Allen and Unwin, 1982.

Sibley, Brian and John Howe. *The Maps of Tolkien's Middle-Earth*. Boston, MA: Houghton Mifflin, 2003.

Smol, Anna. "'Oh . . . oh . . . Frodo!': Readings of Male Intimacy in *The Lord of the Rings*." *Modern Fiction Studies* 50(4) (2004), pp. 949–979.

Timmons, Daniel. "J. R. R. Tolkien: The 'Monstrous' in the Mirror." *Journal of the Fantastic in the Arts* 9(3) (1998), pp. 229–246.

Werber, Niels. "Geo—and Biopolitics of Middle-Earth: A German Reading of Tolkien's *The Lord of the Rings*." *New Literary History* 36(2) (2005), pp. 227–246.

West, Richard C. "A Tolkien Checklist: Selected Criticism 1981–2004." *Modern Fiction Studies* 50(4) (Winter 2004), pp. 1015–1028.

West, Richard C. *Tolkien Criticism: An Annotated Checklist.* Kent, OH: Kent State University Press, 1981.

Web Sites

The Tolkien Society. http://www.tolkiensociety.org. Last visited January 29, 2008.
The Tolkien Library. http://www.tolkienlibrary.com. Last visited January 29, 2008.

If you like John Ronald Reuel Tolkien (J.R.R. Tolkien)

Tolkien's "Middle Earth" fantasies reflect his scholarly interests in languages and myth. Beginning with prequel *The Hobbit*, they continue with *The Fellowship of the Ring*, *The Two Towers*, and *The Return of the King*. Tolkien has been widely influential on later fantasy writers, inspiring the so-called sword and sorcery subgenre.

Then you might like

Susan Cooper

Cooper's Dark Is Rising series catches four young English children up in a mythic centuries-old battle between the forces of light and darkness. The series includes *Over Sea, Under Stone*, *The Dark Is Rising*, *Greenwitch*, *The Grey King*, and *Silver on the Tree*. Other Cooper fantasies include *Seaward* and *The Boggart*.

David and Leigh Eddings

The Eddings' Belgariad series tells the story of young Garion as he slowly realizes his long prophesied destiny. They include *Pawn of Prophecy*, *Queen of Sorcery*, *Magician's Gambit*, *Castle of Wizardry*, and *Enchanters' End Game*.

Ursula K. Le Guin

Although Le Guin uses many "traditional" fantasy tropes such as dragons and wizards, she brings a fresh and different perspective to them. One long standing example is her Earthsea series (*A Wizard of Earthsea*, *Tombs of Atuan*, *The Farthest Shore*, *Tehanu*, *The Other Wind*, and *Tales of Earthsea*).

Patricia McKillip

McKillip's Riddle Master of Hed trilogy follows Morgan, Prince of Hed, as he journeys far from his home and finds himself embroiled in a war beyond his imaginings (*The Riddle-Master of Hed*, *Heir of Sea and Fire*, and *Harpist in the Wind*).

Martha Wells

Wells' fantasy novels are set in carefully detailed alternate worlds and cultures that reflect her interest in anthropology. A recent example is the "Fall of Ile-Rien" series (*The Wizard Hunters*, *The Ships of Air*, and *The Gate of Gods*).

Jack Vance (1916–)

Biographical Sketch

Jack Vance began writing for the so-called pulp magazines in the 1940s. He published *The Dying Earth* in 1950, a novel set in a far future where the laws of physics have changed, and allow for what could be considered "magic." Because of that, *The Dying Earth* can be considered a "science fiction/fantasy" in much the same way as Robert Silverberg's *Lord Valentine's Castle*. Vance continued to publish *Dying Earth* novels and stories throughout his career, as well as more sharply "defined" science fiction and fantasy novels. He is well known for his detailed world building, and his *Dying Earth* books have influenced numerous authors.

> [I]t's hard to tell where science fiction leaves off and fantasy starts.—(Jack Vance, *Locus* interview, 1984)

Major Works

Novels

Dying Earth series: *The Dying Earth* (1950), *The Eyes of the Overworld* (1966), *Cugel's Saga* (1966), *Rhialto the Marvellous* (1984)
Lyonesse series: *Suldrun's Garden* (1983) also published as *Lyonesse*, *The Green Pearl* (1985), *Madouc* (1990)

Short Story Collections

Fantasms and Magics (1978)
Green Magic (1979)
The Jack Vance Treasury (2007)

Research Sources

Encyclopedias and Handbooks: EF, HDF, SJGF

Biographies and Interviews

Bee, Robert. "An Individualist and a World Creator: The Career of Jack Vance." *Internet Review of Science Fiction* 1(2) (December 2004). http://www.irosf.com/q/zine/article/10107. Last visited January 30, 2008.
"Jack Vance: Return to the Elder Isles." *Locus* 17(11) (November 1984), pp. 1, 54.

Criticism and Readers' Guides

Andre-Driussi, Michael. "'Asi Achih': The Future History of Jack Vance." *New York Review of Science Fiction* 113 (January 1998), pp. 1, 8–11.

Cunningham, A.E., ed. *Jack Vance: Critical Appreciations and a Bibliography*. Boston Spa: British Library, 2000.

Gevers, Nick. "Jack Vance: Lord of Language, Emperor of Dreams." *Infinity Plus*. April 15, 2000. http://www.infinityplus.co.uk/nonfiction/jvprofile.htm. Last visited January 29, 2008.

Shreve, Gregory M. "Not With a Bang But With a Whimper: Anticatastrophic Elements in Vance's Dying Earth." In Carl B. Yoke, ed., *Phoenix from the Ashes*. Westport, CT: Greenwood, 1987, pp. 125–132.

Silverberg, Robert. "Jack Vance: The Eyes of the Overworld and The Dying Earth." *Reflections and Refractions: Thoughts on Science Fiction, Science, and Other Matters*. Grass Valley, CA: Underwood Books, 1997, pp. 309–319.

Temianka, Dan, ed. *The Jack Vance Lexicon: From Ahulph to Zipangote: The Coined Words of Jack Vance*. Novato, CA: Underwood-Miller, 1992.

Tillman, Peter D. "Jack Vance in the 25th Century—and Beyond." *Infinity Plus: SF, Fantasy, Horror*. August 11, 2001. http://www.infinityplus.co.uk/nonfiction/lyonesse.htm. Last visited January 29, 2008.

Web Sites

Foreverness: The VIE Resource Site. http://www.integralarchive.org. Last visited January 29, 2008. "The Vance Integral Edition project, successfully concluded in 2006, gathered and restored the work of Jack Vance in a 44 volume edition." Includes a number of resources, including full text of first chapters of several of Vance's works, bibliographies, a vocabulary search tool, and online full text issues of *Extant*, the VIE newsletter.

The Jack Vance Archive. http://www.jackvance.com. Last visited January 29, 2008.

The Jack Vance Information Page. http://www.massmedia.com/~mikeb/jvm. Last visited January 29, 2008.

Jack Vance Message Board. http://server2.ezboard.com/bjackvance. Last visited January 29, 2008.

Evangeline Walton (1907–1996)

Biographical Sketch

Evangeline Walton was chronically ill as a child and privately tutored. She spent much of her time reading, developing an early and enduring love for mythology. Walton was treated for her many illnesses in part with treatments that contained silver nitrate that eventually turned her skin a bluish grey color.

Walton was an early interpreter of mythology and folklore, most notably, the Mabinogi, which she recast as series of books in the 1930's and 1940's. One, *The*

Virgin and the Swine, was published in 1936, but the rest were not published until the early 1970's. She also wrote a trilogy based on the Greek myth of Theseus, the first book of which, *The Sword is Forged*, was published in 1983. Walton was awarded the Lifetime Achievement Award by the World Fantasy Convention in 1989.

> I don't like to contradict anything positively stated in myth. If there are alternate versions I feel free to choose the one I like best. I also feel free to make any additions that don't contradict the original material.—(Evangeline Walton, Marion Zimmer Bradley's Fantasy Magazine interview, 1990)

Major Works

Novels

Mabinogi series: *The Prince of Annwn* (1974), *The Children of Llyr* (1971), *The Song of Rhiannon* (1972), *The Virgin and the Swine: The Fourth Branch of the Mabinogi* (1936) later published as *The Island of the Mighty*
Witch House (1945)
The Sword is Forged (1983)

Research Sources

Encyclopedias and Handbooks: EF, HDF, SJGF

Biographies and Interviews

"Evangeline Walton Obituary." *Locus* 36(4) (April 1996), p. 65
Lenander, David. "Evangeline Walton, Remembered." *Wood Between the Worlds: Webs Between Writers*. http://www.tc.umn.edu/~d-lena/WaltonRemembered.html. Last visited January 29, 2008.
Schweitzer, Darrell. "Evangeline Walton: Interview." *Marion Zimmer Bradley's Fantasy Magazine* 7 (1990), pp. 36–37.

Criticism and Readers' Guides

Evans, W.D. Emrys. "The Welsh Mabinogion: Tellings and Retellings." *Children's Literature in Education* 9(1) (March 1978), pp. 17–33.
Herman, John. "Recommended: Evangeline Walton." *English Journal* 74(4) (April 1985), pp. 75–76.
Spivack, Charlotte. "Evangeline Walton." *Merlin's Daughters: Contemporary Women Writers of Fantasy*. Westport, CT: Greenwood, 1987, pp. 67–86.
Zahorski, Kenneth J. and Robert H. Boyer. *Lloyd Alexander, Evangeline Walton Ensley, Kenneth Morris: A Primary and Secondary Bibliography*. Boston, MA: Hall, 1981.

Web Sites

"Papers of Evangeline Ensley Walton, 1936–1984." *University of Arizona Library Special Collections.* http://aao.lib.asu.edu/ViewRecordFrame.jsp?record=0000000900. Last visited January 29, 2008. Description of University of Arizona holdings. Includes short biographical note.

Margaret Weis (1948–)

Biographical Sketch

Margaret Weis grew up in Independence, Missouri. She did a BA at the University of Missouri, and then worked in publishing for several years. She began writing the "DragonLance" books with Tracy Hickman when she was an editor in the books division of TSR, a company that produced roleplaying games. TSR had contracted with professional writers to write tie in novels for Hickman's *Dragonlance* game modules, but none of them quite seemed to get it. Frustrated, Hickman and Weis started writing their own. The books were a huge hit, even among non roleplayers. They continue to collaborate on a number of *Dragonlance* series, as other fantasy novels and series.

Weis has also published a number of other books on her own and in collaboration with other authors. She currently lives in southeast Wisconsin.

> We deliberately tried to make the characters [in Dragonlance] not so much larger-than-life but ordinary people dealing with larger-than-life situations and trying to cope not only with saving the world but with their own inner turmoil, and resolving those issues. So people can see themselves in these characters.—(Margaret Weis, "Dragon Lady Keeps Flying," 2004)

Major Works

Dragonlance Novels

Dragonlance Chronicles series, with Tracy Hickman: *Dragons of Autumn Twilight* (1984), *Dragons of Winter Night* (1985), *Dragons of Spring Dawning* (1985), *Dragons of Summer Flame* (1995), *The Annotated Chronicles* (1999)

Dragonlance Legends series, with Tracy Hickman: *Test of the Twins* (1986), *War of the Twins* (1986), *Time of the Twins* (1986), *The Annotated Legends* (2003)

Dragonlance War of Souls series, with Tracy Hickman: *Dragons of a Fallen Sun* (2000), *Dragons of a Lost Star* (2001), *Dragons of a Vanished Moon* (2002)

Dragonlance Dark Chronicles series, with Tracy Hickman: *Dragons of the Dwarven Depths* (2006), *Dragons of the Highlord Skies* (2007)

Other Novels and Series

Endless Catacombs (1984)

Darksword series, with Tracy Hickman: *Forging the Darksword* (1987), *Darksword Adventures* (1988), *Doom of the Darksword* (1988), *Triumph of the Darksword* (1988), *Legacy of the Darksword* (1997)

Rose of the Prophet series, with Tracy Hickman: *The Will of the Wanderer* (1988), *The Paladin of the Night* (1989), *The Prophet of Akharan* (1989)

Star of the Guardians: *The Lost King* (1990), *King's Test* (1991), *King's Sacrifice* (1991), *Ghost Legion* (1993)

Death Gate series, with Tracy Hickman: *Dragon Wing* (1990), *Elven Star* (1990), *Fire Sea* (1991), *The Serpent Mage* (1992), *The Hand of Chaos* (1993), *Into the Labyrinth* (1993), *The Seventh Gate* (1994)

Sovereign Stone series, with Tracy Hickman: *Well of Darkness* (2000), *Guardians of the Lost* (2001), *Journey into the Void* (2003)

Dragonvarld: *Mistress of Dragons* (2003), *The Dragon's Son* (2004), *Master of Dragons* (2005), *Dragonvarld Adventures* (2007)

Kingdoms of Ivory and Jade: Nimrans and Nimoreans (2004)

Warrior Angel (2007) with Lizz Weis

Children's/Young Adult Fiction

Dragonlance: Young Adult Chronicles, with Tracy Hickman: *Night of the Dragons* (2003), *A Rumor of Dragons* (2003), *The Nightmare Lands* (2003), *To the Gates of Palanthas* (2003), *Hope's Flame* (2004), *A Dawn of Dragons* (2004)

Other Important Writings

Dragonlance Adventures (1987) with Tracy Hickman

Research Sources

Encyclopedias and Handbooks: EF, HDF, SJGF

Biographies and Interviews

Hall, Melissa Mia. "Dragon Lady Keeps Flying." *Publishers Weekly* 251(23) (June 7, 2004), pp. 23–24, 26.

Hunt, Stephen. "Dragon' On." *SF Crowsnest.com.* http://www.sfcrowsnest.com/sfnews/newsd0102.htm. Last visited January 29, 2008. Joint interview with Weis and Hickman.

"Margaret Weis." *Fast Forward.* August 2003. http://www.fast-forward.tv/audio/audio161.m3u. Last visited January 29, 2008. Audio file.

"Margaret Weis, Margaret Weis Productions, and the Serenity Roleplaying Game." *Pulp Gamer: The Paper Game Podshow.* http://www.pulpgamer.com/2005/12/

18/pulp-gamer-14-margaret-weis-margaret-weis-productions-and-the-serenity-roleplaying-game. Last visited January 29, 2008.

Ward, Jean Marie. "Fantasy Writer Margaret Weis Soars on the Wings of Dragons." *SciFi.com*. http://www.scifi.com/sfw/issue290/interview.html. Last visited January 29, 2008.

Criticism and Readers' Guides

Weis, Margaret and Tracy Hickman, eds. *Leaves from the Inn of the Last Home: The Complete Krynn Source Book*. Lake Geneva, WI: TSR, 1987.

Weis, Margaret and Tracy Hickman, eds. *Realms of Dragons: The Worlds of Weis and Hickman*. New York: HarperPrism, 1999.

Web Sites

The Dragonlance Nexus. http://www.dlnexus.com. Last visited January 29, 2008.

Margaret Weis Productions, Ltd. http://www.margaretweis.com. Weis's Web site. Last visited January 29, 2008.

If you like Margaret Weis

Weis' epic fantasies feature a familiar cast of elves, dwarves, dragons, and magic. The Dragonlance books, written with Tracy Hickman, have been especially popular and enduring.

Then you might like

David and Leigh Eddings

The Eddings' Belgariad series tells the story of young Garion as he slowly realizes his long prophesied destiny. They comprise *Pawn of Prophecy*, *Queen of Sorcery*, *Magician's Gambit*, *Castle of Wizardry*, and *Enchanters' End Game*.

Kate Elliott

Elliott's epic fantasies are based on a densely thought out alternate world reminiscent of European myth. Her interest in religious and political conflict is especially evident in her Crown of Stars series (*King's Dragon*, *Prince of Dogs*, *The Burning Stone*, *Child of Flame*, *The Gathering Storm*, *In the Ruins*, and *The Crown of Stars*).

Anne McCaffrey

Although McCaffrey's dragons are actually genetically altered life forms, they still inspire an almost religious reverence among the people of the planet

Pern. A good place to start is her Dragonriders of Pern series, including *Dragonflight*, *Dragonquest*, and *The White Dragon*.

Patricia McKillip

McKillip's Riddle Master of Hed trilogy follows Morgan, Prince of Hed, as he journeys far from his home and finds himself embroiled in war beyond his imaginings (*The Riddle-Master of Hed*, *Heir of Sea and Fire*, and *Harpist in the Wind*).

John Ronald Reuel Tolkien (J.R.R. Tolkien)

Tolkien's Middle Earth fantasies reflect his scholarly interests in languages and myth. Beginning with prequel *The Hobbit*, they continue with *The Fellowship of the Ring*, *The Two Towers*, and *The Return of the King*.

Martha Wells (1964–)

Biographical Sketch

A Texan native, Martha Wells did a BA in Anthropology from Texas A & M. Wells started writing as a young child and submitted her first short story when she was a college freshman. She has used her anthropology background to more fully develop the imagined worlds of her novels and is known for her detailed world building.

In addition to fantasy novels, Wells has also published a media tie-in novel for the "Stargate" television series. She currently lives in College Station, Texas.

> For fantasy novels, I usually don't outline at all, except for maybe two or three chapters in advance, when I'm setting up the ending. I usually just like to start out, and discover the book as I go along. This does mean I end up doing a lot of revision.—(Martha Wells, *Martha Wells*. http://marthawells.livejournal.com/94023.html. Last visited January 29, 2008)

Major Works

Novels

Fall of Ile-Rien series: *The Wizard Hunters* (2003), *The Ships of Air* (2004), *The Gate of Gods* (2005)
The Element of Fire (1993)
City of Bones (1995)
The Death of the Necromancer (1998)
Wheel of the Infinite (2000)

Short Stories

"The Potter's Daughter" In Steve Savile and Alethea Kontis, eds., *Elemental.* New York: Tor Books. May 2006.

Other Important Writings

"Basic Blogging on LiveJournal: A Primer." *The Broadsheet.* Broad Universe. April 2006. http://broaduniverse.org/broadsheet/archive/0604mw.html. Last visited January 29, 2008.

"Guerilla Marketing at the Conventions: Help the Booksellers Sell Your Books." *The Broadsheet.* May 25, 2005. http://broaduniverse.org/broadsheet/archive/0505mw.html. Last visited January 29, 2008.

"Neville Longbottom: The Hero with a Thousand Faces." In Mercedes Lackey, ed., *Mapping the World of Harry Potter.* Dallas, TX: BenBella Books, January 2006, pp. 101–109.

Research Sources

Encyclopedias and Handbooks: EF, HDF, SJGF

Biographies and Interviews

Merle, Chris. "Martha Wells Interview." *Conestoga 11.* http://www.sftulsa.org/conestoga/podcasts/conestoga_10_podcast_03_96k.mp3. Last visited January 29, 2008.

Todd, Elizabeth. "The Fantasy Life." *Insite Magazine* (June 1998). Available online at http://www.marthawells.com/insite.htm. Last visited January 29, 2008.

Criticism and Readers' Guides

Kelso, Sylvia. "'*Loces genii*': Urban Settings in the Fantasy of Peter Beagle, Martha Wells, and Barbara Hambly." *Journal of the Fantastic in the Arts* 13(1) (2002), pp. 13–32.

Web Sites

Martha Wells. http://marthawells.livejournal.com. Last visited January 29, 2008. Author's personal journal.

Martha Wells: Worlds of Fantasy http://www.marthawells.com. Last visited January 29, 2008. Author's Web site.

Gene Wolfe (1931–)

Biographical Sketch

Gene Wolfe was originally an industrial engineer. More precisely, he helped design the original Pringle's potato-chip machine. He also edited *Plant Engineering*, a technical journal, for some years. Wolfe began publishing his fiction after he had returned from the Korean War and finished college via the GI Bill. He and his young family needed money, and fiction was something he could do in his spare time. In 1984, he became a full-time writer.

Wolfe is known for writing three speculative genres—science fiction, fantasy, and horror. However, he tends to mix genres, so the distinctions aren't always clear. His best known "fantasy," in fact, the *Book of the New Sun* series mixes science fiction and fantasy. He has often been compared to Jack Vance as well as writers such as Nabokov and Borges.

> My whole life experience feeds into my writing. I think that must be true for every writer.—(Gene Wolfe, *Infinity Plus* interview, 2003. Available online at http://www.infinityplus.co.uk/nonfiction/intgw.htm. Last visited January 29, 2008)

Major Works

Novels

Book of the New Sun series: *The Shadow of the Torturer* (1980), *The Claw of the Conciliator* (1980), *The Sword of the Lictor* (1981), *The Citadel of the Autarch* (1982)
Soldier of the Mist series: *The Soldier of the Mist* (1986), *The Soldier of Arete* (1989), *Soldier of Sidon* (2006)
Wizard Knight series: *The Knight* (2004), *The Wizard* (2004)
The Devil in a Forest (1976)
Free Live Free (1984)
The Urth of the New Sun (1987)
Castleview (1990)
Pandora by Holly Hollander (1990)

Short Story Collections

The Island of Doctor Death and Other Stories (1980)
Gene Wolfe's Book of Days (1985)
Storeys from the Old Hotel (1988)
Castle of Days (1992)
Innocents Abroad: New Fantasy Stories (2004)

Other Important Writings

The Castle of the Otter (1982)
Letters Home (1991)
A Walking Tour of the Shambles (2002, with Neil Gaiman)
Shadows of the New Sun (2002)

Research Sources

Encyclopedias and Handbooks: EF, HDF, SJGF

Biographies and Interviews

"Gene Wolfe." *Fast Forward.* November 2006. http://www.fast-forward.tv/audio/audio195.m3u. Last visited January 29, 2008.

"Gene Wolfe: Moral Fabulist." *Locus* 26(6) (June 1991), pp. 4, 66.

Gevers, Nick Michael Andre-Driussi, and James Jordan. "Some Moments with the Magus: An Interview with Gene Wolfe." *Infinity Plus.* December 20, 2003. http://www.infinityplus.co.uk/nonfiction/intgw.htm. Last visited January 29, 2008.

McCaffrey, Larry. "On Encompassing the Entire Universe: An Interview with Gene Wolfe." *Science-Fiction Studies* 15(3) (1988), pp. 334–355. Available online at http://www.depauw.edu/sfs/interviews/wolfe46interview.htm. Last visited January 29, 2008.

"The Wolfe and Gaiman Show." *Locus* 49(3) (September 2002), pp. 6–7, 81–84.

Criticism and Readers' Guides

Andre-Driussi, Michael. "Languages of the Dying Sun." In Damien Broderick, ed., *Earth is But a Star: Excursions Through Science Fiction to the Far Future.* Crawley: University of Western Australia Press, 2001, pp. 217–236.

Andre-Driussi, Michael. "Posthistory 101." *Extrapolation* 37(2) (Summer 1996), pp. 127–138.

Borski, Robert. "Masks of the Father: Paternity in Gene Wolfe's Book of the New Sun." *New York Review of Science Fiction* 138 (February 2000), pp. 1, 8–16.

Borski, Robert. "Swimming with Undinees: Sex and Metamorphosis in Gene Wolfe's Book of the New Sun." *The Internet Review of Science Fiction* 1(1) (January 21, 2004). http://www.irosf.com/q/zine/article/10016. Last visited January 29, 2008.

Clareson, Thomas D. "'The Book of Gold': Gene Wolfe's 'Book of the New Sun'." *Extrapolation* 23 (1982), pp. 270–274.

French, Rod. "Gene Wolfe and the Tale of Wonder: The End of an Apprenticeship." *Science Fiction: A Review of Speculative Literature* 5(2) (June 1983), pp. 43–47.

Gerlach, John. "The Rhetoric of an Impossible Object: Gods, Chems, and Science Fantasy in Gene Wolfe's Book of the Long Sun." *Extrapolation* 40(2) (1999), pp. 153–161.

Gevers, Nick. "A Magus of Many Suns: An Interview With Gene Wolfe." *The SF Site.* January 2002. http://www.sfsite.com/03b/gw124.htm. Last visited January 29, 2008.

Gevers, Nick. "Master of the Universe: Could a Former Engineer Who Helped Invent Pringles be Our Greatest Living Writer?" *Washington Post.com.* April 7, 2002. P. BW05. Available online at http://www.washingtonpost.com/ac2/wp-dyn?pagename=article&node=&contentId=A62473-2002Apr4. Last visited January 29, 2008.

Heldreth, Lillian M. "The Mercy of the Torturer: The Paradox of Compassion in Gene Wolfe's World of the New Sun." In Robert A. Latham and Robert A. Collins, eds., *Modes of the Fantastic: Selected Essays from the Twelfth International Conference on the Fantastic in the Arts. Contributions to the Study of Science Fiction and Fantasy, 66*. London: Greenwood Press, 1995, pp. 186–194.

Malekin, Peter. "Remembering the Future: Gene Wolfe's The Book of the New Sun." In Donald E. Morse, ed., *The Fantastic in World Literature and the Arts*. Westport, CT: Greenwood, 1987, pp. 47–57.

Palumbo, Donald. "The Monomyth in Gene Wolfe's The Book of the New Sun." *Extrapolation* 46(2) (2005), pp. 189–234.

Wright, Peter. "Grasping the God-Games: Metafictional Keys to the Interpretation of Gene Wolfe's The Fictions of the New Sun." *Foundation* 66 (Spring 1996), pp. 39–58.

Web Sites

Gene Wolfe. http://members.bellatlantic.net/~vzc2tmhh/wolfe.html. Last visited January 29, 2008.

"Gene Wolfe." *Free Speculative Fiction Online*. http://www.freesfonline.de/authors/Gene_Wolfe.html. Last visited January 29, 2008. Online fiction by Gene Wolfe.

Ultan's Library. http://www.ultan.org.uk/index.html. Last visited January 29, 2008. "A journal for the study of Gene Wolfe."

Urth List. http://www.urth.net. Last visited January 29, 2008. Web site for an online discussion group on Wolfe's works. Includes archives of past postings.

Patricia Wrede (1953–)

Biographical Sketch

A prolific writer, Patricia Wrede wrote her first (and unpublished) novel in high school. She majored in Biology at Carleton College, and then did an MBA. She started writing full time after several years as an accountant because, as she explains in a recent interview, it was easier to combine accounting with writing than writing with accounting (*Mike Hodel's Hour 25*). She is known for her extensive, detailed world building, many of which are set in Regency England. Although she writes for herself, many of her works have been marketed for children and young adults.

> [Y]ou can make magic work however you want. Therefore it can mean whatever you want. For me magic is a metaphor for power. In real life, you'd have to look at political power, the power of money, or charisma and personality. But in fantasy I can distill all that and say, "Here's pure power, what do you do with it?"—(Patricia Wrede, "Between Planets," 2004. Available online at http://citypages.com/databank/25/1225/article12152.asp. Last visited January 29, 2008)

Major Works

Novels

Lyra series: *Shadow Magic* (1982), *Daughter of Witches* (1983), *The Harp of Imach Thyssel* (1985), *Caught in Crystal* (1987), *The Raven Ring* (1994)
Magician series: *Mairelon the Magician* (1991), *The Magician's Ward* (1997)
The Seven Towers (1984)
Shadow Magic (1988) with Walter Velez
Snow White and Rose Red (1989)

Children's/Young Adult Fiction

Cecelia and Kate series (with Caroline Stevermer): *Sorcery and Cecelia: or The Enchanted Chocolate Pot* (1988).
The Grand Tour: or The Purloined Coronation Regalia: Being a Revelation of Matters of High Confidentiality and Greatest Importance, Including Extracts from the Intimate Diary of a Noblewoman and the Sworn Testimony of a Lady of Quality (2004).
The Mislaid Magician: or Ten Years After (2006)
Chronicles of the Enchanted Forest: *Dealing with Dragons* (1990, also published as *Dragons Bane*), *Searching for Dragons* (1991, also published as *Dragon Search*), *Calling on Dragons* (1993), *Talking to Dragons* (1985)

Short Story Collections

Book of Enchantments (1996)

Other Important Writings

"Fantasy Worldbuilding Questions." 1996. http://www.sfwa.org/writing/worldbuilding1.htm. Last visited January 29, 2008.

Research Sources

Encyclopedias and Handbooks: EF, HDF, SJGF

Biographies and Interviews

James, Warren W. "Interview with Patricia Wrede." *Mike Hodel's Hour 25*. November 23, 2001. http://www.hour25online.com/hr25_2001–11-23_patricia-wrede_interview.m3u. Last visited January 29, 2008.
"Patricia Wrede." *Fast Forward*. February 2005. http://www.fast-forward.tv/audio/audio175.m3u. Last visited January 29, 2008.
"Patricia Wrede." *TV Bookshelf*. September 1, 2004. http://tvbookshelf.ws/Wrede.mov. Last visited January 30, 2008.
Sutton, Teri. "Between Planets." *City Pages*. May 26, 2004. http://citypages.com/databank/25/1225/article12152.asp. Last visited January 29, 2008.

Web Sites

Bernardi, Michael. *Patricia C. Wrede*. http://www.dendarii.co.uk/Wrede/index.html. Last visited January 29, 2008.

Lenander, David. *The Enchanted Chocolate Pot: A Page for Caroline Stevermer/C.J. Stevermer and for Patricia C. Wrede*. http://www.tc.umn.edu/~d-lena/Stevermer%20page.html. Last visited January 29, 2008.

"Patricia Wrede." *The Library of Congress Webcasts*. http://www.loc.gov/today/cyberlc/feature_wdesc.php?rec=3647. Last visited January 29, 2008. Video file of a reading and question and answer session that Patricia Wrede did at the 2004 National Book Festival.

Jane Yolen (1939–)

Biographical Sketch

An extremely prolific writer who has published over 280 books, Jane Yolen has worked in a number of genres including fantasy, children's and young adult books, and poetry. She is especially well known for her short prose including fairy tales. In edition to writing, Jane Yolen has also edited numerous books, most recently at Harcourt under her own imprint. Awards for her work include Nebula, World Fantasy, and the Mythopoeic Fantasy Award for Adult Literature.

> I believe that humans are storytelling animals and that even our so-called 'history' is really just storying about stuff that has happened. And it's wrong to think that those stories are any more 'accurate' than the magical or made-up stories we tell.—(Jane Yolen, *DownHomeBooks.com* interview, 2004. Available online at http://www.downhomebooks.com/yolen.htm. Last visited January 29, 2008)

Major Works

Novels

Books of the Great Alta: *Sister Light, Sister Dark* (1988), *White Jenna* (1989) *The One Armed Queen* (1998)

Briar Rose (1992)

Children's/Young Adult Fiction

The Wizard of Washington Square (1969)

The Magic Three of Solatia (1974)

The Transfigured Hart (1975)

The Mermaid's Three Wisdoms (1978)

Brothers of the Wind (1981)

Pit Dragons trilogy: *Dragon's Blood* (1982), *Heart's Blood* (1984), *A Sending of Dragons* (1987)
Cards of Grief (1984)
The Devil's Arithmetic (1988)
The Dragon's Boy (1990)
Wizard's Hall (1991)
The Wild Hunt (1995)
Young Merlin trilogy: *Passenger* (1996), *Hobby* (1996), *Merlin* (1997)
The Sea Man (1997)
Tartan Magic: *The Wizard's Map* (1999), *The Pictish Child* (1999), *The Bagpiper's Ghost* (2002)
Sword of the Rightful King: A Novel of King Arthur (2003)

Short Story Collections

The Girl Who Cried Flowers and Other Tales (1973)
The Moon Ribbon: And Other Tales (1976)
The Hundredth Dove: And Other Tales (1977)
Merlin's Booke (1982)
Tales of Wonder (1983)
Dragonfield and Other Stories (1985)
Sister Emily's Lightship: And Other Stories (1997)
Twelve Impossible Things Before Breakfast (1997)
The Fish Prince: And Other Stories (2001)

Other Important Writings

"'Oh God, Here Come the Elves!'." In Nicholas Ruddick, ed., *State of the Fantastic: Studies in the Theory and Practice of Fantastic Literature and Film: Selected Essays from the Eleventh International Conference on the Fantastic in the Arts, 1990*. Westport, CT: Greenwood, 1992, pp. 3–11.
Touch Magic: Fantasy, Faerie, and Folktale in the Literature of Childhood (1981)
Writing Books for Children (1973, 1983)
Guide to Writing for Children (1989)
The Radiation Sonnets (2003) poetry
Take Joy: A Book for Writers (2003)

Research Sources

Encyclopedias and Handbooks: EF, HDF, SJGF

Biographies and Interviews

"Jane Yolen." *DownHomeBooks.com*. January 2004. http://www.downhomebooks.com/yolen.htm. Last visited January 29, 2008.
"Jane Yolen: The Bardic Munchies." *Locus* 26(1) (January 1991), pp. 4, 78.

"Jane Yolen: Telling Tales." *Locus* 39(2) (August 1997), pp. 4–5, 72.

Schweitzer, Darrell. "An Interview with Jane Yolen." *Science Fiction Chronicle* 24(7) (July 2002), pp. 21–22.

Stone, RoseEtta. "A Book Review and a Discussion with Jane Yolen, Author." *The Purple Crayon*. Ed., Harold D. Underdown. 2001. http://www.underdown.org/yolen.htm. Last visited January 29, 2008.

Thompson, Raymond H. "Interview with Jane Yolen." *Interviews with Authors of Modern Arthurian Literature* (part of the University of Rochester's *Camelot Project*). 1988. http://www.lib.rochester.edu/Camelot/intrvws/yolen.htm. Last visited January 29, 2008.

White, Claire. "A Conversation with Jane Yolen." *Writers Write: The Internet Writing Journal*. June 2002. http://www.writerswrite.com/journal/jun02/yolen.htm. Last visited January 29, 2008.

Criticism and Readers' Guides

Baer, Elizabeth R. "A Postmodern Fairy Tale of the Holocaust: Jane Yolen's *Briar Rose*." *Studies in American Jewish Literature* 24 (2005), pp. 145–152.

Hanlon, Tina L. "'To sleep, Perchance to Dream': Sleeping Beauties and Wide-Awake Plain Janes in the Stories of Jane Yolen." *Children's Literature* 26 (1998), pp. 140–167.

May, Jill P. "Jane Yolen's Literary Fairy Tales: Legends, Folktales, and Myths Remade." *Journal of Children's Literature* 21(1) (Spring 1995), pp. 74–78.

Weil, Ellen R. "The Door to Lilith's Cave: Memory and Imagination in Jane Yolen's Holocaust Novels." *Journal of the Fantastic in the Arts* 5(2) (1992), pp. 90–104.

Web Sites

The Book of Jane Yolen. http://www.janeyolen.com. Last visited January 29, 2008. Includes Yolen's online journal "Jane Yolen: Bookfest 03."

The Library of Congress Webcasts. http://www.loc.gov/today/cyberlc/feature_wdesc.php?rec=3577. Last visited January 29, 2008.

Roger Zelazny (1937–1995)

Biographical Sketch

Part of the New Wave movement in the 1960s, Roger Zelazny published a number of novels, short stories, and poems, for which he won a number of awards including six Hugos and three Nebulas. Zelazny earned an MA in literature at Columbia University and was known for his literary allusions and experimentation with form. He wrote in both science fiction and fantasy, but is probably best known for his Chronicles of Amber.

> I see myself as a novelist, period. I mean, the material I work with is what is classified as science fiction and fantasy, and I really don't think about these things when I'm writing. I'm just thinking about telling a story and developing my characters.—(Roger Zelazny, *Science Fiction* interview, 1978. Available online at http://zelazny.corrupt.net/19780408int.html. Last visited January 29, 2008)

Major Works

Novels

First Chronicles of Amber: *Nine Princes in Amber* (1970), *The Guns of Avalon* (1972), *Sign of the Unicorn* (1975), *The Hand of Oberon* (1976), *The Courts of Chaos* (1978)

Second Chronicles of Amber: *Trumps of Doom* (1985), *Blood of Amber* (1986), *Sign of Chaos* (1987), *Knight of Shadows* (1989), *Prince of Chaos* (1991)

Short Story Collections

The Doors of His Face, the Lamps of His Mouth (1971)
The Last Defender of Camelot (1978)
Unicorn Variations (1983)

Other Important Writings

"Fantasy and Science Fiction: A Writer's View: Alternatives." In George E. Slusser and Eric S. Rabkin, eds., *Intersections: Fantasy and Science Fiction*. Carbondale: Southern Illinois University Press, 1987, pp. 55–60.
When Pussywillows Last in the Catyard Bloomed (1980)
To Spin is Miracle Cat (1981)
Roger Zelazny's Visual Guide to the Castle Amber (1988) with Neil Randall

Research Sources

Encyclopedias and Handbooks: EF, HDF, SJGF

Biographies and Interviews

Dowling, Terry and Curtis, Keith. "A Conversation with Roger Zelazny: 8th April, 1978." *Science Fiction: A Review of Speculative Literature* 1(2) (June 1978), pp. 11–23. Available online at http://zelazny.corrupt.net/19780408int.html. Last visited January 29, 2008.

Nizalowski, John. "An Interview with Roger Zelazny." *New York Review of Science Fiction* 18(7) (March 2006), pp. 1, 6–7.

"Roger Zelazny: Forever Amber." *Locus* 27(4) (October 1991), pp. 5, 68.

Criticism and Readers' Guides

Gardner, Lyn. "The Solitary Quest: The Hero's Search for Identity in Roger Zelazny's Amber." *Strange Horizons.* September 25, 2006. http://www.strangehorizons.com/2006/20060925/zelazny-a.shtml. Last visited January 29, 2008.

Krulik, Theodore. *The Complete Amber Sourcebook.* New York: Avonva, 1996.

Krulik, Theodore. "Roger Zelazny's Road to Amber." *Extrapolation* 43(1) (Spring 2002), pp. 80–88.

Levack, Daniel J.H. "Amber Dreams: A Roger Zelazny Bibliography." San Francisco, CA: Underwood/Miller, 1983.

Lindskold, Jane M. "All Roads Do Lead to Amber." *Extrapolation* 31(4) (Winter 1990), pp. 326–332.

Lindskold, Jane M. *Roger Zelazny* New York: Twayne Publishers, 1993.

Lingen, Marissa K. "The Suburbs of Amber" *Strange Horizons.* May 21, 2001. http://www.strangehorizons.com/2001/20010521/suburbs_of_amber.shtml. Last visited January 29, 2008.

Sanders, Joseph. "Roger Zelazny: A Primary and Secondary Bibliography." Boston, MA: G. K. Hall, 1980.

Web Sites

Roger Zelazny Page. http://zelazny.corrupt.net. Last visited January 29, 2008. Fan site. Includes pictures.

Zelanzy and Amber. http://www.roger-zelazny.com/index.html. Last visited January 29, 2008. Fan site Includes a "Which Prince of Amber Are You?" quiz.

"Zelazny Mss." *Lilly Library Manuscript Collections.* http://www.indiana.edu/~liblilly/lilly/mss/html/zelazny.html#xtocid291271. Last visited January 29, 2008. Brief description of materials held at the Lilly Library at Indiana University.

Lists of Authors by Type

We have identified various "types" of writers and included the type categories in the lists below. In addition to getting a quick sense of the sort of books that a given writer publishes, you can also use these lists to find other writers that you might enjoy (i.e., if you enjoy Terry Pratchett's satire, then you might also enjoy Esther Friesner's novels).

Early Writers

Highly influential on later writers, these early writers are considered key to the development of the fantasy genre.

Cabell, James Branch
Carter, Angela
Dunsany, Lord
Eddison, Eric Rucker (E.R. Eddison)
Gilman, Charlotte Perkins
Haggard, H. Rider (H. Rider Haggard)
Howard, Robert E.
MacDonald, George
Moore, Catherine Lucille (C.L. Moore)
Nesbit, Edith (E. Nesbit)
Norton, Andre
Peake, Mervyn
Tolkien, John Ronald Reuel (J.R.R. Tolkien)
Vance, Jack
Walton, Evangeline

Feminist

These writers, both male and female, have written works with feminist ideas and ideals.

Block, Francesca Lia
Bradley, Marion Zimmer
Bujold, Lois McMaster
Carter, Angela
Emshwiller, Carol
Gentle, Mary

Gilman, Charlotte Perkins
Hambly, Barbara
Hopkinson, Nalo
Johnson, Kij
Kirstein, Rosemary
Kushner, Ellen
Lee, Tanith
Le Guin, Ursula K.
McKinley, Robin
Medley, Linda
Moon, Elizabeth
Moore, Catherine Lucille (C.L. Moore)
Murphy, Pat
Norton, Andre
Pullman, Philip
Shwartz, Susan
Smith, Jeff
Springer, Nancy
Tepper, Sheri S.
Wells, Martha

Fairy Tales/Myth

These writers make use of myths and fairy tales in their works, some from a traditional perspective, and others from a more revisionist angle.

Alexander, Lloyd
Anderson, Poul and Karen Anderson
Beagle, Peter S.
Bradbury, Ray
Brust, Steven K.
Cooper, Susan
de Lint, Charles
Gaiman, Neil
Holdstock, Robert
Hopkinson, Nalo
Johnson, Kij
Keyes, J. Gregory
Lawhead, Stephen
Lee, Tanith
Le Guin, Ursula K.
MacDonald, George
Maguire, Gregory
McKillip, Patricia
McKinley, Robin
Medley, Linda
Moon, Elizabeth
Nesbit, Edith (E. Nesbit)
Paxson, Diana L.
Peake, Mervyn
Pratchett, Terry
Scarborough, Elizabeth Ann
Smith, Jeff
Snyder, Midori
Stewart, Mary
Tarr, Judith
Tepper, Sheri S.
Tolkien, John Ronald Reuel (J.R.R. Tolkien)
Walton, Evangeline
Yolen, Jane

High Fantasy/Sword & Sorcery

These writers write works in the "classic" high fantasy style, often involving magic and various heroics.

Alexander, Lloyd
Anderson, Poul and Karen Anderson
Anthony, Piers
Bradley, Marion Zimmer
Brooks, Terry
Brust, Steven K.
Cherryh, Carolyn Janice (C.J. Cherryh)
de Camp, L. Sprague and Catherine Crook
Dickson, Gordon R.
Eddings, David and Leigh
Elliott, Kate
Feist, Raymond E.
Foster, Alan Dean
Garrett, Randall and Vicki Ann Heydron
Goldstein, Lisa
Goodkind, Terry
Hickman, Tracy
Howard, Robert E.
Jordan, Robert
Kay, Guy Gavriel
Kerr, Katharine
Lackey, Mercedes
Lawhead, Stephen
Lee, Tanith
Le Guin, Ursula K.
Leiber, Fritz
Martin, George R.R.
McKillip, Patricia
McKinley, Robin
Medley, Linda
Moorcock, Michael

Norton, Andre
Paxson, Diana L.
Pratchett, Terry
Rowling, Joanne Kathleen (J.K. Rowling)
Saberhagen, Fred
Salvatore, Robert Anthony (R.A. Salvatore)
Scarborough, Elizabeth Ann
Shwartz, Susan
Silverberg, Robert
Smith, Jeff
Stevermer, Caroline
Stewart, Mary
Tepper, Sheri S.
Tolkien, John Ronald Reuel (J.R.R. Tolkien)
Vance, Jack
Walton, Evangeline
Weis, Margaret
Wells, Martha
Wolfe, Gene
Wrede, Patricia
Yolen, Jane
Zelazny, Roger

Humorous/Satirical

These writers are known for their use of humor and/or satire, which is often quirky and offbeat.

Alexander, Lloyd
Anthony, Piers
Asprin, Robert Lynn
Beagle, Peter S.
Brust, Steven K.
Dickson, Gordon R.
Dunsany, Lord
Foster, Alan Dean
Friesner, Esther
Gentle, Mary
Lackey, Mercedes
Leiber, Fritz
Maguire, Gregory
Medley, Linda
Moon, Elizabeth
Nesbit, Edith (E. Nesbit)
Pratchett, Terry
Scarborough, Elizabeth Ann
Smith, Jeff
Springer, Nancy

Non-European Themes and Motifs

These writers make use of non-European themes, motifs, and mythologies.

Alexander, Lloyd
Bradbury, Ray
Card, Orson Scott
de Lint, Charles
Ford, John M.
Gaiman, Neil
Haggard, Henry Rider (H. Rider Haggard)
Hopkinson, Nalo
Johnson, Kij
Le Guin, Ursula K.
Moon, Elizabeth
Murphy, Pat
Norton, Andre
Pini, Wendy and Richard Pini
Powers, Tim
Pullman, Philip
Shwartz, Susan
Snyder, Midori
Yolen, Jane

Shared Worlds

These writers created worlds and/or story arcs that they then invited other writers to contribute to.

Asprin, Robert Lynn
Bradley, Marion Zimmer
Brust, Steven K.
Ford, John M.
Gaiman, Neil
Hickman, Tracy
Pini, Richard and Wendy Pini
Weis, Margaret

Urban Fantasy

These writers set much of their fiction in an urban, often "modern" setting, often with a dark tinge.

Beagle, Peter S.
Blaylock, James P.
de Lint, Charles
Ford, John M.
Gaiman, Neil
Hopkinson, Nalo
Lee, Tanith
Maguire, Gregory
Miéville, China
Moon, Elizabeth
Moorcock, Michael
Powers, Tim
Pullman, Philip
Snyder, Midori

Young Adult/Children's

These writers have written a number of works intended for young adults and children. However, many adults enjoy these works as well.

Baum, L. Frank
Blaylock, James P.
Block, Francesca Lia
Cooper, Susan
Ford, John M.
Kerr, Katharine
Lackey, Mercedes
Lawhead, Stephen
MacDonald, George
McCaffrey, Anne
McKillip, Patricia
Miéville, China
Nesbit, Edith (E. Nesbit)
Nix, Garth
Pratchett, Terry
Pullman, Philip
Springer, Nancy
Stevermer, Caroline
Wrede, Patricia

Lists of Major Fantasy Awards

There are a number of awards given every year for the best fantasy novels, novellas, novelettes, short stories, and career achievement. Most are sponsored by organizations of writers and/or fans. Although many are listed as "science fiction" awards, they are also awarded to works of fantasy as well as works in other related speculative genres such as horror.

We have listed major awards given to writers featured in this volume. Because many of these writers write in science fiction or other speculative genres as well as in the fantasy genre, we have awards awarded for works that were out of scope for this volume.

The James Tiptree, Jr. Award

Created by Alice B. Sheldon, who wrote under the pseudonym James Tiptree, Jr., these awards are given every year for works of fantasy and science fiction that explore gender roles and the role of women (http://www.tiptree.org/. Last visited January 29, 2008).

1995 – Nancy Springer (*Larque on the Wing*)
1995 – Ursula K. Le Guin ("The Matter of Seggri")
1996 – Ursula K. Le Guin (Retrospective Tiptree for *The Left Hand of Darkness*)
1997 – Angela Carter (Special Award)
1997 – Ursula K. Le Guin ("Mountain Ways")

Hugo Awards

Named for Hugo Gernsback, who founded of *Amazing Stories* magazine, these awards are given every year by the World Science Fiction Society (http://www.worldcon.org/hugos.html. Last visited January 29, 2008).

Best Novel

1958 – Fritz Leiber (*The Big Time*)
1965 – Fritz Leiber (*The Wanderer*)
1966 – Roger Zelazny (*This Immortal*) tied with Frank Herbert's *Dune*
1968 – Roger Zelazny (*Lord of Light*)
1970 – Ursula K. Le Guin (*The Left Hand of Darkness*)
1975 – Ursula K. Le Guin (*The Dispossessed*)
1991 – Lois McMaster Bujold (*The Vor Game*)
1992 – Lois McMaster Bujold (*Barrayar*)
1995 – Lois McMaster Bujold (*Mirror Dance*)
2001 – Joanne Kathleen Rowling (J. K. Rowling) (*Harry Potter and the Goblet of Fire*)
2002 – Neil Gaiman (*American Gods*)
2004 – Lois McMaster Bujold (*Paladin of Souls*)
2005 – Susanna Clarke (*Jonathan Strange & Mr. Norrell*)

Best Novella

1968 – Anne McCaffrey ("Weyr Search") tied with Philip José Farmer's "Riders of the Purple Wage"
1969 – Robert Silverberg ("Nightwings")
1970 – Fritz Leiber ("Ship of Shadows")
1971 – Fritz Leiber ("Ill Met in Lankhmar")
1972 – Poul Anderson ("The Queen of Air and Darkness")
1973 – Ursula K. Le Guin ("The Word for World is Forest")
1975 – George R.R. Martin ("A Song for Lyra")
1976 – Roger Zelazny ("Home is the Hangman")
1981 – Gordon R. Dickson ("Lost Dorsai")
1982 – Poul Anderson ("The Saturn Game")
1986 – Roger Zelazny ("24 Views of Mt. Fuji, by Hokusai")
1990 – Lois McMaster Bujold ("The Mountains of Mourning")
1997 – George R.R. Martin ("Blood of the Dragon")
2003 – Neil Gaiman (*Coraline*)

Best Novelette

1967 – Jack Vance ("The Last Castle")
1968 – Fritz Leiber ("Gonna Roll the Bones")

1969 – Poul Anderson ("The Sharing of Flesh")
1973 – Poul Anderson ("Goat Song")
1979 – Poul Anderson ("Hunter's Moon")
1980 – George R.R. Martin ("Sandkings")
1981 – Gordon R. Dickson ("The Cloak and the Staff")
1982 – Roger Zelazny ("Unicorn Variations")
1987 – Roger Zelazny ("Permafrost")
1988 – Ursula K. Ke Guin ("Buffalo Gals, Won't You Come Out Tonight")
1990 – Robert Silverberg ("Enter a Soldier. Later: Enter Another")
2006 – Peter S. Beagle (*Two Hearts*)

Best Short Story

1961 – Poul Anderson ("The Longest Voyage")
1963 – Jack Vance ("The Dragon Masters")
1964 – Poul Anderson ("No Truce with Kings")
1965 – Gordon R. Dickson ("Solider, Ask Not")
1974 – Ursula K. Le Guin ("The Ones Who Walk Away from Omelas")
1976 – Fritz Leiber ("Catch that Zeppelin!")
1980 – George R.R. Martin ("The Way of Cross and Dragon")
2004 – Neil Gaiman ("A Study in Emerald")

Nebula Awards

These are awarded every year by the Science Fiction and Fantasy Writers of America (http://www.sfwa.org/awards/. Last visited January 29, 2008).

Best Novel

1970 – Lois McMaster Bujold (*Paladin of Souls*)
1972 – Robert Silverberg (*A Time of Changes*)
1975 – Ursula K. Le Guin (*The Dispossessed*)
1982 – Gene Wolfe (*The Claw of the Conciliator*)
1988 – Pat Murphy (*The Falling Woman*)
1989 – Lois McMaster Bujold (*Falling Free*)
1990 – Elizabeth Ann Scarborough (*The Healer's War*)
1991 – Ursula K. Le Guin (*Tehanu: The Last Book of Earthsea*)
2003 – Neil Gaiman (*American Gods*)
2004 – Elizabeth Moon (*The Speed of Dark*)
2005 – Lois McMaster Bujold (*Paladin of Souls*)

Best Novella

1966 – Roger Zelazny ("He Who Shapes") tied with Brian W. Aldiss' "The Saliva Tree"

1967 – Jack Vance ("The Last Castle")
1968 – Michael Moorcock ("Behold the Man")
1969 – Anne McCaffrey ("Dragonrider")
1971 – Fritz Lebier ("Ill Met in Lankhmar")
1974 – Gene Wolfe ("The Death of Doctor Island")
1975 – Robert Silverberg ("Born with the Dead")
1976 – Roger Zelazny ("Home Is the Hangman")
1982 – Poul Anderson ("The Saturn Game")
1986 – Robert Silverberg ("Sailing to Byzantium")
1990 – Lois McMaster Bujold ("The Mountains of Mourning")
2004 – Neil Gaiman (*Coraline*)

Best Novelette

1966 – Roger Zelazny (*The Doors of His Face, the Lamps of His Mouth*)
1967 – Gordon R. Dickson (*Call Him Lord*)
1968 – Fritz Leiber ("Gonna Roll the Bones")
1972 – Poul Anderson (*The Queen of Air and Darkness*)
1973 – Poul Anderson ("Goat Song")
1980 – George R.R. Martin ("Sandkings")
1986 – George R.R. Martin (*Portraits of His Children*)
1988 – Pat Murphy ("Rachel in Love")
1996 – Ursula K. Le Guin ("Solitude")
1999 – Jane Yolen ("Lost Girls")

Best Short Story

1970 – Robert Silverberg ("Passengers")
1972 – Robert Silverberg ("Good News from the Vatican")
1975 – Ursula K. Le Guin ("The Day Before the Revolution")
1976 – Fritz Leiber ("Catch That Zeppelin!")
1996 – Esther M. Friesner ("Death and the Librarian")
1997 – Esther M. Friesner ("A Birthday")
1998 – Jane Yolen ("Sister Emily's Lightship")

Damon Knight Memorial Grand Master (Career Achievement)

1979 – L. Sprague de Camp
1981 – Fritz Leiber
1984 – Andre Norton
1989 – Ray Bradbury
1997 – Jack Vance

1998 – Poul Anderson
2003 – Ursula K. Le Guin
2004 – Robert Silverberg
2005 – Anne McCaffrey

World Fantasy Awards

Associated with the World Fantasy Convention, these are awarded yearly (http://www.worldfantasy.org/awards/. Last visited January 29, 2008).

Life Achievement

1976 – Fritz Leiber
1977 – Ray Bradbury
1981 – Catherine Lucille Moore (C.L. Moore)
1984 – L. Sprague de Camp
1984 – Jack Vance
1989 – Evangeline Walton
1995 – Ursula K. Le Guin
1996 – Gene Wolfe
1998 – Andre Norton
2000 – Marion Zimmer Bradley
2000 – Michael Moorcock
2003 – Lloyd Alexander
2005 – Carol Emshwiller

Best Novel

1975 – Patricia A. McKillip (*The Forgotten Beasts of Eld*)
1978 – Fritz Leiber (*Our Lady of Darkness*)
1979 – Michael Moorcock (*Gloriana*)
1981 – Gene Wolfe (*The Shadow of the Torturer*)
1990 – Jack Vance (*Madouc*)
1991 – Ellen Kushner (*Thomas the Rhymer*) tied with James Morrow's *Only Begotten Daughter*
1993 – Tim Powers (*Last Call*)
2001 – Tim Powers (*Declare*) tied with Sean Stewart's *Galveston*
2002 – Ursula K. Le Guin (*The Other Wind*)
2003 – Patricia A. McKillip (*Ombria in Shadow*) tied with Graham Joyce's *The Facts of Life*
2005 – Susanna Clarke (*Jonathan Strange & Mr Norrell*)

Best Novella

1988 – Ursula K. Le Guin ("Buffalo Gals, Won't You Come Out Tonight")
1989 – George R.R. Martin ("The Skin Trade")
1991 – Pat Murphy ("Bones")

Best Short Fiction/Short Story

1976 – Fritz Leiber ("Belsen Express")
1983 – Tanith Lee ("The Gorgon")
1984 – Tanith Lee ("Elle Est Trois, (La Mort)")
1986 – James P. Blaylock ("Paper Dragons")
1991 – Neil Gaiman & Charles Vess ("A Midsummer Night's Dream")
1997 – James P. Blaylock ("Thirteen Phantasms")

Best Collection

1989 – Gene Wolfe (*Storeys from the Old Hotel*) tied with Harlan Ellison's *Angry Candy*
1991 – Carol Emshwiller (*The Start of the End of It All and Other Stories*)
2000 – Stephen R. Donaldson (*Reave the Just and Other Tales*)
2000 – Charles de Lint (*Moonlight and Vines*)
2002 – Nalo Hopkinson (*Skin Folk*)

Gandalf Grand Master Award

These were awarded yearly by the World Science Fiction Society from 1974 until 1980.

1974 – John Ronald Reuel Tolkien (J.R.R. Tolkien)
1975 – Fritz Leiber
1976 – Lyon Sprague de Camp (L. Sprague de Camp)
1977 – Andre Norton
1978 – Poul Anderson
1979 – Ursula K. Le Guin
1980 – Ray Bradbury

General Bibliography

This includes "frequently cited sources" from writer entries as well as more general sources on fantasy literature such as major academic journals and associations.

Encyclopedias and Handbooks

Clute, John and John Grant, ed. *The Encyclopedia of Fantasy*. New York: St. Martin's Press, 1997. Brief entries on authors, concepts, and genres.

Harris-Fain, Darren, ed. *British Fantasy and Science-Fiction Writers Before World War I (Dictionary of Literary Biography 178)*. Detroit, MI: Gale, 1997. Substantial articles on authors and selected works. Includes discussion of critical commentary.

———. *British Fantasy and Science-Fiction Writers, 1918–1960 (Dictionary of Literary Biography 255)*. Detroit, MI: Gale, 2002. Substantial articles on authors and selected works. Includes discussion of critical commentary.

———. *British Fantasy and Science-Fiction Writers Since 1960. (Dictionary of Literary Biography 261)*. Detroit, MI: Gale, 2002. Substantial articles on authors and selected works. Includes discussion of critical commentary.

Hunt, Caroline C., ed. *British Children's Writers Since 1960: First Series. (Dictionary of Literary Biography, 161)*. Detroit, MI: Gale, 1996. Substantial articles on authors and selected works. Includes discussion of critical commentary.

Literature Resource Center. Thomson Gale. http://www.gale.com/LitRC/. Last visited January 29, 2008. Incorporates materials from the Dictionary of Literary Biography series, as well as other printed reference series published by Gale. Available online by subscription; check your local library for availability.

Martin, Philip, ed. *The Writer's Guide to Fantasy Literature: From Dragons Lair to Hero Quest*. New York: Watson-Guptill Publications, 2002. Includes an overview of the genre as well as interviews and excerpts from leading writers.

Pringle, David, ed. *St. James Guide to Fantasy Writers*. New York: St. James Press, 1996. Entries include discussions of individual authors and their work, along with primary and secondary bibliographies.

Stableford, Brian. *Historical Dictionary of Fantasy Literature*. Lanham, MD: Scarecrow Press, 2005. Brief entries on significant authors, concepts, and genres.

Tixier, Diana., ed. *Fluent in Fantasy: A Guide to Reading Interests*. Englewood, CO: Libraries Unlimited, 1999.Reader's guide to fantasy novels and short stories. Groups authors and novels by "type" (i.e., "Historical Fantasy"). Also includes lists of various award winners.

Indexes and Databases

Annual Bibliography of English Language and Literature. Modern Humanities Research Association. http://collections.chadwyck.com/home/home_abell.jsp. Last visited January 29, 2008. Indexes scholarly articles on English language literature and film. Published in print and online. Available by subscription; check your local library for availability.

Modern Language Association International Bibliography. Modern Language Association. http://www.mla.org/bibliography. Last visited January 29, 2008. Indexes scholarly articles on English and non-English language literature, film, cultural studies, folklore, and linguistics. Published in print and online. Available by print and online by subscription; check your local library for availability.

Science Fiction and Fantasy Research Database. Compiled by Hal W. Hall. http://library.tamu.edu/cushing/sffrd/default.asp. Last visited January 29, 2008. "Online index to historical and critical items about science fiction, fantasy and horror." Encompasses and updates Hal W. Hall's classic *Science Fiction and Fantasy Reference Index* series. Freely available online. Sponsored by Texas A&M University.

Magazines and Scholarly Journals

Analog Science Fiction and Fact. http://www.analogsf.com/0707/issue_07.shtml. Last visited January 29, 2008. Original stories and novellas. Tends to run more to hard science fiction, but includes some fantasy.

Extrapolation: A Journal of Science Fiction and Fantasy. http://fp.dl.kent.edu/extrap/. Last visited January 29, 2008. "[T]he first [journal] to publish academic work on science fiction and fantasy and continues to be a leader in that specialized genre in the literature of popular culture."

January Magazine. http://januarymagazine.com/. Last visited January 29, 2008. Includes reviews, author interviews. Coverage extends to science fiction, fantasy, mystery, mainstream, children's books, and nonfiction.

LOCUS. http://www.locusmag.com/. Last visited January 29, 2008. Includes author interviews, book reviews, and news about the fantasy, science fiction, and horror publishing industry. Web site includes a variety of resources, including excerpts of published interviews and listings for major awards in science fiction, fantasy, and horror.

The Magazine of Fantasy and Science Fiction. http://www.sfsite.com/fsf/. Last visited January 29, 2008. Original stories and novellas, including both fantasy and science fiction.

Mythlore. http://www.mythsoc.org/publications/mythlore/. Last visited January 29, 2008. "[A] peer-reviewed journal that focuses on the works of J.R.R. Tolkien, C. S. Lewis, Charles Williams, and the genres of myth and fantasy."

New York Review of Science Fiction and Fantasy. http://ebbs.english.vt.edu/olp/nyrsf/nyrsf.html. Last visited January 29, 2008. Includes author interviews, reviews, and critical articles on fantasy, science fiction, and horror.

Science Fiction Studies. http://www.depauw.edu/sfs/. Last visited January 29, 2008. Publishes scholarly articles on science fiction and fantasy literature as well as some author interviews. The Web site includes free online full text from issues that were published at least one year ago.

Strange Horizons. http://www.strangehorizons.com/. Last visited January 29, 2008. Online magazine that publishes original speculative fiction and poetry, author interviews, and articles.

Annual Short Story Collections

Cramer, Kathryn and David G. Hartwell, eds. *Year's Best Fantasy*. http://www.tachyonpublications.com/book/YcarsBcst6.html?Session_ID = new&Reference_Page=/books.html. Last visited, January 29, 2008. Compiles stories published in magazines and anthologies during the preceding year.

Datlow, Ellen, Kelly Link, and Gavin J. Grant, eds. *Year's Best Fantasy and Horror*. http://www.lcrw.net/yearsbest/. Last visited January 29, 2008. Compiles stories published in magazines and anthologies during the preceding year.

Fantasy Organizations and Conventions

Science Fiction and Fantasy Writers of America, Inc. http://www.sfwa.org/. Last visited January 29, 2008. The Science Fiction and Fantasy Writers of America sponsors the yearly Nebula Awards. Its Web site includes a variety of resources for writers, as well as readers.

Science Fiction Research Association. http://www.sfra.org/. Last visited January 29, 2008 "the oldest professional organization for the study of science fiction and fantasy literature and film."

World Fantasy Convention. http://www.worldfantasy.org/. Last visited January 29, 2008. World Fantasy Conventions are held yearly around the world. The yearly World Fantasy Awards are associated with it.

World Science Fiction Society/World Science Fiction Convention http://www.worldcon.org/. Last visited January 29, 2008. The World Science Fiction Society sponsors the yearly Hugo Awards, as well as the yearly World Science Fiction Convention.

Web Sites

Fantastic Fiction. 2003. http://www.fantasticfiction.co.uk/. Last visited January 29, 2008. Includes bibliographies for over 4000 British and Americans including speculative genre writers. Some entries include portraits and biographical statements. Bibliographies include titles and images of book jackets of selected primary works (books and stories written by the author). Generally reliable, but has occasional glitches (for instance, in many cases, short story collections are listed as "novels").

Fast Forward. http://www.fast-forward.tv/. Last visited January 29, 2008. Online archives for "Fast Forward," an interview program featuring fantasy and science fiction authors. Includes video files.

Infinity Plus. http://www.infinityplus.co.uk/. Last visited January 29, 2008. British Web site featuring articles, author interviews, and some original fiction from science fiction and fantasy authors.

The Library of Congress Webcasts. http://www.loc.gov/today/cyberlc/. Last visited January 29, 2008. Includes media files for talks by authors given at Library of Congress events, including fantasy authors.

LOCUS.online. http://www.locusmag.com/. Last visited January 29, 2008. Web site for *Locus Magazine*. Includes a variety of resources, including excerpts of published interviews, convention listings, and listings for major awards in science fiction, fantasy, and horror.

Mike Hodel's Hour 25. http://www.hour25online.com/. Last visited January 29, 2008. Online archives for a science fiction/fantasy radio interview show. Includes audio files.

Sci Fi Channel. http://www.scifi.com/. Last visited January 29, 2008. Includes author interviews, reviews, and articles about fantasy and science fiction literature and media.

Science Fiction and Fantasy News. http://sffworld.com/. Last visited January 29, 2008. Includes author interviews, articles about science fiction and fantasy literature, and reviews.

SF Site. http://www.sfsite.com/. Last visited January 29, 2008. Includes science fiction and fantasy author interviews, articles, and reviews.

TV Bookshelf. http://www.tvbookshelf.ws/. Last visited January 29, 2008. "A public access cable TV program about science fiction, fantasy, and mystery books." Includes online audio archives of author interviews.

Wired for Books. Last accessed December 22, 2003. http://wiredforbooks.org. Last visited January 29, 2008. A production of the Ohio University Telecommunications Center, *Wired for Books* is a radio program that features interviews with authors. The *Wired for Books* Web site includes audio files of those interviews.

Online Full Text

Free Speculative Fiction Online. http://www.freesfonline.de/index.html. Last visted January 29, 2008. Includes free full text fiction from writers such as Gene Wolfe.

The Online Books Page. http://onlinebooks.library.upenn.edu/. Last visited January 29, 2008. Sponsored by Penn State University, this site indexes and/or provides access to over 25000 free online books. Tends to be better for early writers.

Project Gutenberg. http://www.gutenberg.net/index.shtml. Last visited January 29, 2008. Project Gutenberg is one the largest digital collections of uncopyrighted works. The site includes a search interface for locating the text of a specific author or title. Tends to be better for early writers.

Index

About the Authors

JEN STEVENS is the Humanities Liaison Librarian at George Mason University. She holds an MA in English and an MLIS. She previously published *The Undergraduate's Companion to Children's Writers and Their Web Sites* (Libraries Unlimited, 2004).

DOROTHEA SALO is Digital Repository Librarian for the University of Wisconsin System's MINDS@UW institutional repository (http://minds.wisconsin.edu). She holds one master's in Spanish and another in Library and Information Studies from the University of Wisconsin at Madison, and began her career in librarianship at George Mason University.